Augustyn · Reader, who are you now?

Studien zur Multikulturalität

Herausgegeben von Ljubov Bugaeva (Sankt-Peterburg),
Alfred Gall (Mainz), Arkadiusz Lewicki (Wrocław),
Petr Szczepanik (Praha), Izabela Surynt (Wrocław)
und Marek Zybura (Wrocław)

Band 12

2025
Harrassowitz Verlag · Wiesbaden

Kamila Augustyn

Reader, who are you now?

Understanding changes in reading engagement
under different circumstances

2025
Harrassowitz Verlag · Wiesbaden

Cover illustrations (left to right top to bottom):
Martin Rørbye, *Young Clergyman Reading*, 1836, The Art Institute of Chicago
Gerard Dou, *Old Woman Reading*, c. 1631–1632, Rijksmuseum
Frédéric Bazille, *Edmond Maître*, 1869, Courtesy National Gallery of Art, Washington
William McGregor Paxton, *The House Maid*, 1910, Courtesy National Gallery of Art, Washington
Nicolaes Maes, *An Old Woman Dozing over a Book*, c. 1655, Courtesy National Gallery of Art, Washington

Academic Reviewers:
Prof. dr. Gerhard Lauer, Johannes Gutenberg-Universität Mainz
Prof. dr. Mihael Kovač, University of Ljubljana

Book proofreading and translation of included interview excerpts by Eric Hilton

Research funding: "Excellence Initiative – Research University" (IDUB)
– Task No. 7 "Competitive funding for preliminary research"

The publication of this book was supported by an "Excellence Initiative – Research University" grant of the University of Wrocław and the research and commercialisation fund at the disposal of the Vice-Rector for Research at the University of Wrocław.

Bibliografische Information der Deutschen Nationalbibliothek
Die Deutsche Nationalbibliothek verzeichnet diese Publikation in der Deutschen Nationalbibliografie; detaillierte bibliografische Daten sind im Internet über https://dnb.dnb.de abrufbar.

Bibliographic information published by the Deutsche Nationalbibliothek
The Deutsche Nationalbibliothek lists this publication in the Deutsche Nationalbibliografie; detailed bibliographic data are available on the internet at https://dnb.dnb.de.

Informationen zum Verlagsprogramm finden Sie unter
https://www.harrassowitz-verlag.de
© Otto Harrassowitz GmbH & Co. KG, Wiesbaden 2025
Kreuzberger Ring 7c–d, 65205 Wiesbaden, produktsicherheit.verlag@harrassowitz.de
Das Werk einschließlich aller seiner Teile ist urheberrechtlich geschützt.
Jede Verwertung außerhalb der engen Grenzen des Urheberrechtsgesetzes ist ohne Zustimmung des Verlages unzulässig und strafbar. Das gilt insbesondere für Vervielfältigungen jeder Art, Übersetzungen, Mikroverfilmungen und für die Einspeicherung in elektronische Systeme.
Gedruckt auf alterungsbeständigem Papier.
Druck und Verarbeitung: docupoint, Magdeburg
Printed in Germany

ISSN 2749-7879
eISSN 2749-7887

ISBN 978-3-447-12379-2
eISBN 978-3-447-39679-0

Contents

Introduction	1
Methodology	3
Choosing the method	3
Recruiting	7
Interviewing	9
Coding	9
Reviewing the literature	11
Findings	19
Before reading	19
Choosing what to read: 19 – Becoming autonomous: 25 – Changing one's habits: 29	
During reading	43
Being immersed in the story world: 43 – Creating conditions for flow: 43 – (Re)constructing narratives: 51	
Identifying with the character and finding oneself	55
Getting to know the protagonist: 55 – Self-expanding through encountering with others: 60	
Dealing with negative emotions	69
Feeling pain or being in pain: 69 – Facing our fears: 73	
After reading	79
Looking for compensation: 79	
A tale of two systems	83
Defining the situation: 83 – Liking and judging: 85 – Satisfying needs: 89	
Further studies	95
Getting to know the reader	97
Acknowledgements	101
References	103
Appendix	119
Index	137

Introduction

In Raymond Carver's short story *What We Talk About When We Talk About Love* four friends discuss the nature of love over a bottle of gin. However, the scenes from the characters' personal lives do not provide a direct view into their emotions. Rather, they show how "ill-equipped are we all to envision one another's interior workings and invisible aims", as Philip Roth wrote in *American Pastoral* (2016, p. 35). As we read, we need to fill in some gaps in the text by asking ourselves: What is X thinking in this scene? How did X feel when Y said this? Why did X do this or that? What do we feel about X and Y when we read this and what does it mean? No less important is the question of what makes us think we know what the fictional character feels? Whether we use our cognitive abilities to understand the thoughts, feelings and intentions of others and interpret their behaviour, or whether we experience an emotional correspondence with the character's state that we feel thanks to the activity of our mirror neurons, which help us to mimic another person's reaction? There is also the question of the extent to which the author's mastery of creating a believable story and highlighting its features help to focus our attention, evoke episodic memories and transport us in the world of the story? The sense of being disengaged from one's life, detached from reality and transported to another world, where one wants to spend some time taking part in someone else's life or even becoming someone else for a while, is an experience that many readers are familiar with, but do not get with every book they read. It depends on the interaction between the readers' traits, the type of text, its features, and the circumstances in which the book is read. All of these are involved in the affective-cognitive response to a stimulus that we call emotion, or rather "emotion episodes"[1] to capture the processing nature of the emotional response. Readers may react differently in intensity or type of emotion under similar circumstances (Bortolussi & Dixon, 2003, p. 13). Although we may attempt to explain various emotional reactions dispositionally, this approach is limited because a reader's responses may change as they learn about the world and gain life experience. Therefore, the reactions to narrative events and the meanings attached to books, even beloved ones, may not remain affectively constant. The evaluation of objects and events may change during reading, due to the "temporal" nature of reading (Scherer, 2005, p. 698). The investigation of reading experiences is undoubtedly impeded by this. However, as Marisa Bortolussi and Peter Dixon suggest, "literary processing is not entirely idiosyncratic", allowing for empirical research into readers' responses (2003, p. 43). In

---

1 James A. Russell and Lisa Feldman Barrett define a "prototypical emotional episode" as including: core affect, behaviour, attention to an object, its evaluation based on its attributions, "an experience of oneself as having a specific emotion", and neural, chemical, and bodily events (1999, p. 806).

order to understand how readers engage with a book, it is essential to find out what determines their emotional responses and evaluations, and how these may change while reading and over time. Therefore, research should start by giving individual readers a voice, rather than referring to them as a group and ignoring the element of possible differences in how they respond (Bortolussi & Dixon, 2003, p. 9).

This monograph presents findings from an exploratory study[2] of adult Polish readers of different ages and occupations, shedding light on their motivations for reading and the circumstances that can influence the reading experience. From May to September 2022, I conducted 30 unstructured interviews with Polish avid readers. I was interested in studying the reading of books, whether for leisure, as required reading, or for professional or academic purposes, in order to get a comprehensive picture rather than focussing on a particular aspect or type of reading. However, during the course of the discussion with the interviewees, it became evident that the focus was predominantly on leisure reading. Nevertheless, this did not result in a narrower scope.

The research adopts Kathy Charmaz's approach based on the grounded theory developed by Anselm Strauss and Barney Glaser (Charmaz et al., 2013, Charmaz, 2014; Charmaz et al., 2019). To avoid projecting preconceptions and prior knowledge onto our findings, grounded theory researchers do not pose hypotheses before collecting data. In the constructivist reinterpretation, knowledge is not discovered but created. As a result, theories do not emerge from data. They are the result of interpretation. Therefore, the study does not reveal objective reality, but rather how people construct narratives about themselves. Both researchers and participants construct empirical data. Grounded theory emphasises the importance of simultaneous data collection and analysis (coding, note taking, comparison). By not separating these stages, preliminary conclusions from interviews can be used in subsequent interviews with research participants. After the initial coding phase, which includes open coding, axial coding, and then theoretical coding, the researcher compares the findings with relevant literature on the topic. It is at this point that grounded theory differs significantly from other approaches.

In order to provide a comprehensive understanding of the cognitive and emotional processes involved in reading, the analysis of readers' statements is supported by findings from a variety of disciplines, including book studies, literary studies, psychonarratology, psychology of fiction and psychology of emotion, and cognitive science.

---

2 The original title of the research project was *What We Talk About When We Talk About Books: An Analysis of Readers' Experiences*. However, it came to my attention that a book with almost the same title was published in 2019 by Leah Price.

Methodology

Choosing the method

It is challenging to comprehend the multifaceted experiences of readers from diverse backgrounds when relying solely on quantitative data. Reports on readership can offer insights into trends and changes in overall reading habits. Data on reading pace or passages marked as favourites, collected through digital devices, mainly for business purposes, usually remain inaccessible to scholars.[1] What this data does not show, however, is the relationship with the book – only the way in which it is consumed. We do not know what readers think or feel or what memories of the past they recall as they read. We can only infer some patterns of behaviour (when and for how long they read[2], whether they read regularly or only on certain days, whether they return to unfinished books, how many books remain unopened, how many pages are turned, what is underlined, etc.). Another source of knowledge on the reception of books is online forums and the social networking and cataloguing platforms devoted to them, such as Goodreads, Library Thing or Lubimy czytać (Góralska, 2021ab; Kuijpers et al., 2023; Murray, 2018, 2021). Obtaining a large set of data, including reviews and opinions, requires consent to use the website users' reviews, as well as a large financial outlay to establish an interdisciplinary research team to process, tag and analyse the data (Murray, 2018, p. 378). Even if all this is supported, the insight into readers' feelings, emotional states and reactions through reviews on social media platforms is rather limited due to the lack of wider context and personal references, as well as the anonymity of the samples collected. In addition, book reviews are usually about the quality of the author's work or craftsmanship, not necessarily about the reader's feelings or personal beliefs. Finally, some reviews are driven by the marketing agendas of the publishing industry (Murray, 2018, p. 379; 2021, p. 978). Rich empirical material from a large, diverse and well-defined group of people can be obtained through questionnaires and structured interviews. Despite this, the reader's experience still remains elusive for us. The content, order of questions, and options for responses may distort an answer, forcing a particular way of thinking about the subject. Open-ended questions can result in incomplete responses, filled in blindly, and often rushed, with generic and similar-sounding words and phrases. The researcher does not

---

1 One of the exceptions is *Reading Audio Readers: Book Consumption in the Streaming Age* by Karl Berglund, published in 2024.
2 The time spent reading has been identified by scholars specialising in the field of book studies as a salient factor that should be incorporated into questionnaires in surveys across European countries, with a view to enhancing the comparability of data on reading habits (Reinke & Bläsi, 2023). Examples of how much media we consume on a daily basis can be found, for example, in Gottschall, 2021, p. 21.

have the chance to correct some inadequate questions or to clarify concepts which may be understood differently by the participants, and which are not in line with the researcher's intention. Moreover, this approach is driven more by the beliefs and intuitions of the researcher or the paradigm in which they are embedded, so the interaction with the readers is one-sided. The hypothesis has to be verified in order to achieve a specific goal that the researcher has in mind in accordance with their agenda. It is therefore not about exploring, but about verifying, which is fine at a certain stage of the research process but seems too rigid to begin with. Understanding the reader's attitude is also difficult, as is in the case of online forum reviews, because of lack of personal references and a broader context.

A research technique that is mainly used in exploratory qualitative research and that fosters in-depth reflection and learning about readers' experiences in the context of their lives is an unstructured interview. Unlike its standardised type, it does not allow for the hypotheses to be verified. Moreover, the active attitude of the researcher interacting with the respondent during the interview strongly influences the results. As with any kind of self-reporting, we also need also to bear in mind that what we hear about people's habits, feelings and opinions is driven by what they think is right, or what fits with their self-concept and what they want to believe about themselves, and how they manage the impression they make when interacting with others (Hogan, 2019, pp. xiv–xv). We know, therefore, that what people say about themselves is not necessarily the same as what they actually do. We should "never trust a storyteller," says literary scholar Jonathan Gottschall (2021, p. 7). However, in grounded theory studies, how people perceive themselves, how they assess their abilities and needs and how they think they should behave or even feel in a given situation can be a valuable source of knowledge. As readers are aware that they are part of a testing process, it may have a significant impact on what they decide to tell the researcher. As the interview progresses, they may also forget about the recording and enter the zone. By using such a data collection technique, researchers gain access to a great deal of information about readers' motivations, subjective feelings, evaluations and, to some extent, physiological arousal. This data is integrated into cause-and-effect sequences by the readers themselves. They construct a narrative through a synthesis of memories, feelings and actions. This book explores some of the situational antecedents of readers' experiences and evaluations. Appraisal theory, which is employed here, is based on the assumption that "emotions result from an individual's meaning analysis of the implications of his/her circumstances for personal well-being" (Smith & Kirby, 2009, p. 1352). Collecting information on the experiences of book readers, investigating their motivations, reconstructing hidden meanings, and then creating a narrative does not reveal the objective reality, but the systems of social and psychological mechanisms behind its construction.

Given the qualitative and exploratory nature of this study, it was not my objective to develop a typology of readers based on demographic characteristics or personal attributes. I deemed the idea of creating personas to be inadequate for the intended research purpose, as I did not want to reduce complex individuals to artificial, biased, more or less static and deeply decontextualised types (Pawley, 2002, p. 149). Instead, I adopted a descriptive approach, providing a detailed account of how readers describe their reading practices and how different factors change them over time. My interest was in examining the reading practices of the participants, as well as gaining insight into affective-cognitive processes and exploring the ways in which actual readers process the texts they read (Bortolussi & Dixon, 2003, p. 24). This entailed investigating how they relate to their personal history while reading, how they sympathise or empathise with characters and how they try to understand their motivations. In a way, it is also an attempt to answer the question posed by Richard Altick: "How do texts change the minds and lives of common readers?" (Rose, 1992, p. 48). Examining how "textual experiences" are remembered[3] and under what circumstances they emerge is crucial to explaining how literary reading affects readers' wellbeing helping them to experience transformative change and to maintain a coherent self-identity in everyday life (Andersen & Hakemulder, 2024; Hogan, 2019).

Obviously, researchers may know only some of the factors that determine a reader's response to specific stimuli. It is difficult to have a complete picture of the life story that might explain a particular reader's response and to predict how they will react in a given situation. Individual emotional reaction is shaped by inborn tendencies, formative experiences, episodic memories, and an aesthetic response may be influenced by sensitivity to certain object properties, the degree of the pattern recognition, the degree of avoidance of aversion to disorientation, differences in the timing of pattern recognition, and the degree of lingering aversive emotional responses that can inhibit the experience of pleasure (Hogan, 2015, pp. 112, 116). Furthermore, it is only within a controlled setting that researchers can isolate the phenomenon under study from the "biocultural dynamic", and only to a certain extent. As Rob Boddice and Mark Smith have pointed out, "Experience is fluid. Discrete things in the world that 'happen' are experienced as such by the brain through a constructive process that includes the prior experience of the individual and the social relations (including different kinds of perceptions of the self), and the cultural conceptual web in which the individual is caught" (2020, pp. 49–51). As a result, access to the real experience may be limited by not knowing the place, time, situational context, linguistic or cultural meaning, or physiological or behavioural response (2020, p. 32).

In the interviews, the readers talked about their current and past reading practices, and how these had been influenced by different factors or changed by circumstances. This was not an account of different points in time, but only of one, in the present. By comparing the statements of thirty adult avid readers, one can infer certain regularities in shifting reading attitudes from one period to the next. What remains elusive, though, are the impressions one experiences while reading. Time, gaps in memory and inter-

---

3 Tine Riss Andersen and Frank Hakemulder refer to memories about reading experiences as "echoes". They also mention the term "reverberations", used by Charlotte Christiansen and Anne Line Dalsgård to describe the lingering nature of some reading experiences, "moments of a different temporality, the significance of which is still open and undefined", which can encourage readers to change their lives (2021, p. 302).

acting with the researcher distort reconstructing experiences (Csíkszentmihályi, 2014, p. 22). In addition, emotions are to some extent culturally conditioned and not always expressed directly. Communication about emotions occurs thanks to words, but also "in between words." Shaped in interaction with an individual object or an interlocutor, they are affected by the situation, place, time, and circumstances of the communication. That is why it is not only difficult to systematically observe and measure how readers actually read, think and feel, but also to elicit some episodic memories and recall certain states during the interview. Questions that are too straightforward rarely prove effective, and some reminiscences are difficult to retrieve from memory without making associations. When the interview is unstructured and the conversation is free flowing, what course the conversation takes depends on the interaction between the researcher and the reader (Charmaz et al., 2019, p. 25). Text materials such as short stories, poems and excerpts of novels can also be used to access reading experiences (Andersen & Hakemulder, 2024, p. 5). However, this exploratory study is based solely on interviews with participants and does not include organised reading sessions or additional materials. The study is also limited by its relatively small sample size (thirty participants), and non-probability sampling method (voluntary, convenience and snowball sampling). Unstructured interviews make it more difficult to compare participants' responses. Free-flowing discussion leads a researcher down different paths of reading experiences. Some readers may easily recall memories from their childhood, while others may reflect on more recent experiences and discuss their current habits, such as how digital technologies affect their reading. Nevertheless, it should be acknowledged that such an approach also facilitates the acquisition of insight into the diverse experiences of individual participants. This, in turn, enables the construction of a measuring scale or instrument for more systematic, quantitative studies.

The empirical material collected from Polish readers may be culturally distinct from that obtained from readers in other countries, because the extracted data is "embedded in historically and spatially located print cultures", as Christine Pawley notes (2002, p. 157; Fuller & Rehberg Sedo, 2013, p. 28; Murray, 2018, p. 375). The system of cultural references conveyed by the language may be different, but this would require a separate linguistic study. The main objections raised by linguists, psycholinguists and translators concern naming emotions (Scherer, 2005, pp. 697–698). Anna Wierzbicka and Donald Klopf have drawn attention to differences in the way emotions are conceptualised. Wierzbicka argues for using descriptive definitions (as used in the natural semantic meta-language she has created) rather than single-word definitions of emotions (Łukaszewicz, 2022, p. 62). When discussing this topic, it is also important to explain the relationship between feelings and emotions. Wierzbicka notes that those who seek to quantify emotional states tend to prefer the term "emotion" to "feeling" because the former is perceived to have a biological basis, making it a more suitable analytical tool. Keith Oatley states that "emotion" is a term of literary and scientific origin, more recent than "passions, sentiments, feelings, affections", and in use for approximately two centuries (2004, p. 13). Richard Lazarus defines an emotion as a complex state involving the appraisal of subjective affect, physiological change and a tendency to act (1991, p. 824).

The notion of "emotion" or "feeling" is to some extent shaped by one's native language. "The English word emotion combines in its meaning a reference to 'feeling', a reference to 'thinking', and a reference to a person's body", so feelings may be related to both physiology and thought/cognition. This is evidenced by the fact that we may describe in English a feeling of "hunger" as well as a feeling of "loneliness", as Wierzbicka says. However, in some languages (e. g. Russian or German) the plural form of a feeling ("Gefühl/e" or "čuvstvo"/"čustva") refers only to mental feelings, not as a single form that makes no distinction between mental and physical feelings. Another example is French, where the word "sentiment" refers only to mental feelings, not physical ones. After examining a number of examples from different languages, Wierzbicka asserts that "the concept of 'feeling' is universal [and intuitive even for children] and can be safely used in the investigation of human experience and human nature" (1999, pp. 1–4) and to scaffold the meaning of such "complex and language-specific notions" as "emotion". This leads to the conclusion that the concept of "emotion", as opposed to "feeling", is not worth further maintaining, because the use of "emotion", especially without a cultural context, is too vague, even if for analytical purposes we have to use more abstract, jargon-laden, reductive concepts in order to avoid becoming entangled in the vernacular and the individual. Wierzbicka says that the "emotional process" or "emotional state" is triggered by feeling something. Sociologist Eva Illouz describes it in much the same way. Drawing on readings from Martha Nussbaum's *Upheavals of Thought. The Intelligence of Emotions* and Michelle Z. Rosaldo's *Toward an Anthropology of Self and Feeling*, Illouz explains that a "feeling" is a kind of intrinsic energy that drives us to act in certain ways. This "energy" is a combination of the ability to feel, to perceive and to evaluate. It involves both the mind and the body (2010, p. 8). In other words, instead of thinking of "emotion" and "feeling" as opposites that refer to different domains (mind/body or objective science / subjective life experience), we should assume that an "emotional process" is a composite of what someone feels, knows, thinks, believes and does.

Recruiting

In order to assemble a group of participants (adult avid readers), a variety of recruitment methods were employed. Seven participants (23 %) responded to Facebook posts (published at different times on my own profile and the profiles of one bookshop, two libraries, and Institute of Information and Media Studies at University of Wrocław); most of the responses came from the bookshop's post. The interviews were mainly conducted remotely within a week of the recruitment announcement being published. Twelve participants were recruited from friends or acquaintances who were interested in taking part in the project after hearing about it (one of them in response to the Facebook posts). I decided that by including them in the sample, I would be able to draw interesting conclusions on both the subject and the method of the study, since conversations with friends may differ from those with strangers. When readers are asked to talk about their reading experiences for research, trust in the researcher is essential, stemming from either a recommendation or direct acquaintance. In this regard, people I know played an invaluable role in the recruitment process. Although I did not ask them to disseminate information about the research, they were eager to share this experience with other and encouraged another twelve individuals (40%) to take part in the study. Some of the respondents had familial or romantic ties, including a father and son, husband and wife, boyfriend and girlfriend, and three women who were sisters-in-law. The interviews were conducted remotely (via Microsoft Teams) and in-person, depending on the preferences of the participant. Only the audio was processed. Each participant was given a book voucher worth PLN 50 (the average price of a trade book) for the local bookshop as compensation for their time. A total of 19 women (63%) and 11 men (37%) participated in the study. Most of the women (74%) and half of the men (46%) were unknown to me. Sixty per cent of the interviews were conducted remotely using Teams. A greater number of friends participated in the in-person interviews (9 out of 12). Two interviews were conducted at the participants' homes. On the registration form, 24 participants (80%) indicated their profession (see Table 2). The people interviewed were professionals and non-professionals readers. Six out of 30 participants were academics. Tables 1–2 in the Appendix show the dates and types of interviews (remote/in-person), the gender of the participant, their stated occupation and the method of recruitment (a Facebook post, other research participant, personal acquaintance).

The participants were informed of the aims of the study and how it would be conducted (open, unstructured interview), the voluntary nature of their participation and the option of taking part in person or remotely. I explained what data would be collected using which methods and tools and asked for permission to use the textual data (after transcription) for research purposes, including the publication of quotes derived from the interviews. Participants were also reassured that the data would be anonymised and that they had the right to withdraw from the study at any time and to revoke their consent to use the data, which would result in their data being removed. Excerpts from the interviews are presented in two languages – Polish (original) and English translation. They are randomly numbered. This avoids the risk of deanonymisation due to the order of the interviews. In the case of particularly sensitive quotations, I decided to use letters (Reader "A" see RA) rather than numbers in order to avoid links to other quotes from the same participants. Quotes disclosing gender, occupation or age are marked with the appropriate label. Original quotations in Polish have been modified by using [x] to mask the gender of the interviewee.

All participants gave their informed consent by clicking "yes, I agree" in all appropriate fields on the registration form. The design of the data processing form was discussed with and approved by the Data Protection Officer of the University of Wrocław. This research project has been approved and funded by the Excellence Initiative – Research University (IDUB) under Task No. 7, "Competitive funding for preliminary research". The participants in this study were invited to review the text of this book and provide comments.

Interviewing

All interviews were conducted in 2022, with the majority (22 out of 30) taking place over three months, in July (8), August (7) and September (7) (Table 1). The in-person interviews were recorded using a Zoom H4 audio recorder, whereas the remote interviews were recorded and transcribed automatically through the Teams platform. The process of editing and proofreading took less time than manual transcription (roughly 2–3 hours for text cleaning, re-listening and proofreading). I found that transcribing the in-person interviews using the Teams app was more effective and faster than writing them down. Occasionally, I had to repeat sentences aloud if they were indistinctly pronounced.

According to the lexical analysis, my statements accounted for 30% of the words and 31% of the characters, which is why I filtered them out. When the participants were unknown to me, my participation increased by approximately 10%. In general, interviews with known participants lasted 11 minutes longer than interviews with strangers. There was a greater tendency for in-person interviews than remote interviews to last longer than the median 72 minutes. The shortest interview lasted 48 minutes and the longest 151 minutes.

The participants were informed about the study, its duration, purpose and how the data would be used. They were encouraged to articulate their experiences and feelings in relation to the books and to share the subjective meanings they ascribed to them. Questions that evoked autobiographical (episodic) memories helped to start the conversation smoothly, familiarized the reader with the situation, and gave the narrative momentum, making the story more dynamic (Hogan, 2022, p. 153; Oatley, 2012, p. 15). With known participants, I usually began the interview by referring to situations in their lives that I was already familiar with. This approach was designed to make them forget that the interview was being recorded. Putting things in context, giving examples and comparing experiences of reading with those of other media, starting with questions such as "Do you sometimes experience…" or "Do you ever…" or "What do you feel then?" elicited a range of rich responses.

Coding

Given that perception in our culture is primarily driven by object rather than process thinking, it is somewhat challenging to label and compare what readers say using gerunds than tagging their statements with themes. However, Charmaz recommends this method for two reasons: labels in the form of gerunds keep the researcher close to the data and provide an opportunity to explore certain mechanisms (processes) that govern reading selection and content reception. Coding line-by-line, as I have done, reduces the risk of oversimplification, projecting of one's own experience and over-interpretation. I avoided theoretical coding in the first stage to keep my open coding as close to the data as possible. Categories for coding the data were developed at the time of analysis. In some cases, I used the *in vivo* codes instead of my own labels. I then reduced the meaning of the coded statements (several sentences, a whole sentence or a segment) to gerunds indicating the same or similar things. These "child items" were grouped under the following core codes, which I refer to as "parent categories":

Actions/practices – 3380 codes ("What do you do?" or "What do you usually do?). The first "parent category" describes some action towards books, a typical routine, such as reading crime novels, reading at home or on the way to work, buying or borrowing books. The coded utterances of the participants were grouped together as answers to certain categories of questions, such as the following:

- What do you read or listen to, or what books do you not read? (authors, titles, genres, types and themes, tropes).
- What format do you read? (printed books, e-books, audiobooks?)
- Do you use any reading apps?
- How do you get the books? (buy and/or borrow, search on the internet or follow recommendations).
- How do you read? How intense? How much? (one book at a time, from beginning to end, "one-off reading", rereading or skipping descriptions).
- Where do you read? (at home, in the kitchen, at work, while commuting, in a café, sitting down, lying down, walking or while cleaning or shopping)
- When do you read? (mornings, evenings, at night, on holiday, during breaks, now, in childhood, at school/university).
- What do you do with books other than just read them? (collect, arrange, throw away, pass on, get rid of, write about books)?
- Do you talk about books with others?

Opinions, beliefs, judgments – 3332 codes ("What do you know?", "How do you judge?"). The second "parent category" describes opinions about books or their specific elements, based on knowledge of the subject matter (factual basis) and/or the reader's tastes and beliefs formed through socialisation and emotional development (i. e. moral or aesthetic judgments). The research participants made judgments about the following: book/s (specific titles, genres, types of literature, elements of books or the function of books/reading), plot, language, characters, creators and contributors (authors, translators, readers or voice narrators), other readers, institutions (bookstores, publishing houses, libraries or schools), activities (reading and listening to books, as well as writing them), book market (prices, promotion or literary events), digital technologies.

Experiences[4], *emotions, sensations, needs* – 2685 codes ("How do you perceive? How do you imagine it?", "What do you feel?", "What do you want?"). The third category encompasses a comprehensive range of phenomena, including experiences, sensations,

---

4 Mihály Csíkszentmihályi follows William James' definition of *experience*, who said: "Millions of items in the outward order are present to my sense which never properly enter into my experience. Why? Because they have no interest for me. My experience is what I agree to attend to", linking consciousness and attention (2014, pp. 3, 5). Alberto Manguel suggests that reading experiences have the potential to evoke a sense of *déjà vu*. He describes how, on occasion, he feels that he has previously encountered a particular experience, only to realise that it was, in fact, an experience derived from a literary work (2023, p. 24).

emotions, feelings, bodily reactions, and all perceived affective-cognitive and physical events that occur during or after reading. I grouped the codes of the third category by answering the following questions:

- What do you want/need? (motivations)
- How do you feel while reading? (feelings and emotions)
- What do you experience when you read (imagining, mentalising, or identifying)
- How do you react while reading? (bodily responses, e.g. crying or laughing)
- How do you process information during or after reading (learning to read, focusing attention, recognising, reasoning, associating, interpreting, understanding, finding meaning, predicting, remembering or recalling memories).

A total of 10,161 codes (of which 764 codes with varia label) were assigned to the interviews. The next step was to look closely at the coding tree to see which concepts seemed related and how they might be related. To do this, I made use of notes about the characteristics and experiences of each reader, some frequency lists[5] showing the words or concepts (e.g. identification), and the matrices generated using MAXQDA software, which shows the intensity of certain codes associated with particular readers. Throughout the process of generating theoretical concepts, I drew a number of diagrams to help me understand "what is going on here". The full open coding scheme is included in the supplementary material. The research conducted and described here was an exploratory pilot study. The coding was done by myself, which can be seen as a significant limitation. As the study uses constructivist grounded theory, the sample is limited in number of participants and the research technique is an unstructured interview, the findings should not be perceived through a quantitative lens. When I use some generalities such as "reader/s say/s that…", I mean "some readers" or "there are readers who have said this". While this could be taken as anecdotal evidence, in the approach adopted it serves more as a representation of different reading practices, opinions, reactions and experiences found under various circumstances. Following Jonathan Gottschall's observation, I do not want to observe the crowd, but rather "zoom in on a sequence of individuals" (2021, p. 2). As some practices, approaches or experiences were more closely associated, as evidenced by the quoted excerpts from the interviews, I have chosen to highlight them as core processes that could be explored further with a larger and more carefully selected sample, more precise measures and designed tools (see *Further studies*).

Reviewing the literature

The field of *reader response studies* is based on the assumption that we should consider *a relationship*, *an interaction* or *a transaction* between the text and the reader, rather than subordinating the reader to the text (Holland, 2009; Murray, 2018, p. 374; Pawley, 2002, p. 143; Rosenblatt, 1985). Such an approach includes the "context" by taking into account the reader's knowledge, past experiences, feelings, thoughts, expectations and

---

5 Frequency lists were generated after filtering out my utterances.

motivation to read.⁶ Instead of focusing solely on the structure of the literary work and its stylistic form and features, on the basis of which literary critics establish its aesthetic value, we are encouraged to recognise that the act of reading is an inherently performative one, as the *actual reader*⁷ engages with a literary work and brings it to life through their own interpretation, meaning-making processes and embodiment. We should also bear in mind that the reader's response to the text/book may change over time, in different circumstances and with further readings.

"How do people read?" remains a subject of ongoing empirical study in a wide range of disciplinary fields, including but not limited to, literary studies and linguistics (Gottschall, 2012, 2021⁸; Procter & Benwell, 2015; Rosenblatt, 1985), and cognitive poetics (Holland, 1976, 2009; Stockwell, 2019), and psychonarratology (Bortolussi & Dixon, 2003, 2015; Hogan, 2011; Van Peer & Pander Maat, 1996); book history, book studies, media and communication studies and sociology of literature (Bartsch et al., 2014; Bálint & Tan, 2019; Cupchik et al. 1998; Fischer, 2003; Fuller & Rehberg Sedo, 2013, 2023; Góralska, 2018, 2021ab; Knobloch et al., 2004; Knobloch-Westerwick & Keplinger, 2006; Kovač & van der Weel, 2020; Mangen, 2009; Mangen & van der Weel, 2016; Murray, 2018, 2021; Norrick-Rühl, 2019; Oliver, 2003; Oliver et al., 2018; Pawley, 2002; Price, 2019; Rehberg Sedo, 2011; Reinke & Bläsi, 2023; Rose, 1992; Schwabe et al., 2021, 2023; Thumala Olave, 2022; van de Ven et al., 2023; van der Weel, 2011; Vorderer, 2003; Wirth et al., 2012; Wojciechowski, 1991, 2000; Zasacka, 2023); different subfields of psychology (Keen, 2007) – cognitive psychology (Gerrig, 2018; Gerrig & Bernardo, 1994; Gerrig & Jacovina, 2009; Djikic et al., 2009ab; Djikic et al., 2013; Green, 2004; Green & Brock, 2000), psychology of fiction and media psychology (Cupchik, 1995, 2011; Cupchik et al., 1998; Miall, 2006, 2015; Miall & Kuiken, 1994, 1995, 1999, 2002; Kuijpers et al., 2014, 2023; Kuiken et al., 2004; Oatley, 2004, 2011, 2012), psychology of emotion (Csíkszentmihályi, 2014, 2022; Hakemulder, 2004, 2020; Hakemulder & Koopman, 2010, 2015; Hogan, 2003, 2022; Koopman, 2011, 2014, 2015, 2016ab), psychology of aesthetics (Hogan, 2015), personality psychology with a particular emphasis on self-changes (Djikic, 2009ab), behavioural psychology (Bandura, 1977; Nowak, et al. 2013), and cognitive science, particularly cognitive neuroscience (Damasio, 2022; de

---

6 See Louise Rosenblatt's (1985) "reader response theory" and Norman Holland's (2009) "psychological theory of reader response". The latter draws upon on psychoanalysis and highlights the "identity theme" as a key factor influencing the reading experience. According to Holland, each reader recreates and reaffirms their identity while reading by using a specific modality, "(D) avoiding anxiety (F) gratifying unconscious wishes, (E) absorbing the event as part a sequence of events, and (T) shaping it with that sequence into meaningful totality" (1976, p. 342).

7 Not a hypothetical, "ideal" or "implied reader", as suggested by Jonathan Culler and Wolfgang Iser (Fuller & Rehberg Sedo, 2013, p. 39).

8 Acknowledging that "humans are storytelling animals…using story as a [mental] tool", Jonathan Gottschall calls for a more critical approach to "storytelling", focusing on how deeply narratives can influence other people's minds and, consequently, affect how others think and behave (2021, pp. 4, 11; Van Laer et al., 2014, p. 798).

Vignemont & Singer, 2006; Decety, 2005, 2007; Decety & Batson, 2009; Dvash & Shamay-Tsoory, 2014; Hsu et al., 2014; Ruby & Decety, 2004; Wolf, 2019).

The history of reading or reading response draws on a wide variety of sources, including personal documents, marginalia, correspondence, memoirs, etc., as well as library borrowing records, sales records, publishers' catalogues, reviews, blogs, questionnaires, structured or unstructured interviews, focus groups and observations of reading communities such as book clubs or "issue-oriented groups" (Christiansen, & Dalsgård, 2021; Hartley & Turvey, 2001; Howie, 2011; Koryś, 2018; Michalak, 2018; Murray, 2018, p. 375; Pawley, 2002; Rehberg Sedo, 2011). All these materials are used by book historians and media scholars to investigate *who could read, what people read* in a given period ("old book history"), *how they read* ("new book history studies", Rose, 1992, p. 48) and *how their reading practices change* over time, influenced by socio-cultural, political, technological and economic factors (Fischer, 2003; Góralska, 2018, 2021ab; Norrick-Rühl, 2019; Pawley, 2002; Price, 2019; Rose, 1992; van der Weel, 2011).

One of the aspects of reading that is of particular interest to researchers who study readers' responses experimentally is the ability to process and understand written text, known as reading *comprehension*. This is relevant to the issues I consider here in terms of strategies such as: visualising the objects and events of the text, self-monitoring, recalling background knowledge, integrating it with new information, making personal connections, predicting and drawing conclusions (Brewer & Treyens, 1981; Carpenter & Just, 2013; Delgado et al., 2018; Goldman & Varma, 1995; Just & Carpenter, 1992; Kendeou et al., 2011; Kintsch, 1988; Kneepkens & Zwann, 1995; Mangen, 2023; Perfetti & Stafura, 2014; Sosnoski, 1999; van de Ven et al., 2023; van Dijk & Kintsch, 1983; Williamson et al., 2012; Woolley, 2011). Comprehension is analysed using frameworks and theories such as *scripts* or *schemata, the text–knowledge interaction model, the landscape model, the structure-building theory* and *the event-existing model*, to name a few (for a comprehensive review see e. g. Perfetti & Stafura, 2014, p. 23).

Researchers study medium's influence on *attention*. They draw inferences regarding the experiences of reading paper books in comparison to using media devices[9], reading interactive digital books, text-based narratives or social reading on digital storytelling platforms such as Wattpad (Baron, 2015, 2021; Fuller & Rehberg Sedo, 2023; Kovač & van der Weel, 2020; Loi et al., 2023b; Mangen, 2009; Murray, 2018, 2021; Pianzola et al., 2020; van de Ven et al., 2023).

There is a large body of research on *reading practices and behaviours* (defined as all reading activities). They have mostly been studied in relation to demographic characteristics such as the age of the reader, social context, level of education, occupation/profession, socio-cultural background and prior knowledge. The study of behaviour may encompass the collection of data on various parameters, including but not limited to: reading frequency, reading choices, environmental reading settings, and the duration of reading activities. Practices such as purchasing or borrowing books, reading a single book at a

---

9 See the "medium matters hypothesis" in Hakemulder & Mangen, 2024, p. 70; Mathiesen et al., 2024, p. 680).

time, or rereading may also be considered (Chelsea & Joseph, 2022; Fernandez-Blanco et al., 2015; Guthrie et al., 1986; Kirsch et al., 1984; Soederberg et al., 2008; Smith, 1990; Smith & Stahl, 1999; Stine-Morrow, 2004). It may also include more affective-cognitive measures of reading motivation, enjoyment and cognitive skills. As some researchers have suggested, it would be beneficial to go beyond the concept of frequency when defining habits (Schmidt & Retelsdorf, 2016; Verplanken, 2006).

Another area of ongoing research is that of *absorption*. This phenomenon can be defined as an affective-cognitive process that involves grabbing readers' attention, imagining the fictional world, becoming fully immersed in the story, and engaging with fictional characters in a way that elicits emotional responses (Bal & Veltkamp, 2013; Bilandzic et al., 2019; Csíkszentmihályi, 2014, pp. 3–19; Gerrig, 2018; Green, 2004; Green & Brock, 2000; Kuijpers et al., 2014, 2023; Lu et al., 2024; Mathiesen et al., 2024; McQuillan & Conde, 1996; Riggs & Knobloch-Westerwick, 2023; Thissen et al., 2018; Towey, 2000; Van Laer et al., 2014). A variety of methodologies are employed to investigate the phenomenon of absorption. Scholars more closely aligned with literary studies examine the influence of foregrounding features (Hakemulder, 2004, 2020; Kidd & Castano, 2013; Koopman, 2016; Miall & Kuiken, 1994), comparing the reader's responses in fiction (narrative texts) and non-fiction (expository texts) or written narrative fiction and audiovisual screen narrative.

A substantial body of current research is also dedicated to determining the influence of readers' personal characteristics, self-concept assessment, and attachment style (Djikic et al., 2009a; Wojciehowski & Gallese, 2022, pp. 61, 63). There are many empirical studies attempting to determine whether reading fiction affects *empathy* and describing different types of empathic responses, more emotional (to feel with the protagonist) and affective-cognitive (to understand the motivations behind their actions) (Aue et al., 2021; Bal & Veltkamp, 2013; Coplan, 2004; Davis, 1983; Djikic et al., 2013; Dvash & Shamay-Tsoory, 2014; Johnson, 2012; Keen, 2007; Koopman, 2016; Mar et al., 2009; Singer & Klimecki, 2014). Researchers analyse the influence of various factors (e.g., warmth, competence perceptions, social identification or situational valence) and use various self-esteem scales (Green, 2004; Knobloch-Westerwick & Keplinger, 2006). They also seek to elucidate the role of emotions in transporting and identifying with characters, the nature of such para-social interaction, and the process of *experience-* or *perspective-taking* by the reader (Bálint & Tan, 2019; Gerrig & Jacovina, 2009; Hakemulder & Koopman, 2010; Hartung et al., 2016, 2017; Jacovina & Gerrig, 2010; Kaufman & Libby, 2012; Oatley, 2012; Zillmann & Cantor, 1977).

Some researchers focus on specific emotions such as "sadness" (Koopman, 2013) or states such as "being moved" (Bartsch et al., 2014; Djikic et al., 2009b; Schindler et al., 2022) or feeling "elevated" (Oliver et al., 2012) or "tender", to explain why some readers are drawn to tragic narratives (need for deep insight, for catharsis, see more in Koopman, 2011) and to predict attraction to such stories; others try to explain the global mechanisms such as "excitation transfer" using psychological or physiological theories of emotion (Bryant & Miron, 2003; Zillmann & Cantor, 1977).

Data on the behavioural, cognitive and emotional processes involved in reading[10] are obtained through observation of participants' physiological responses (stimulus-response tests or neuroimaging), surveys, self-report measures (in real time or post-exposure) in the form of daily activity diaries (bibliomemoirs) (Andersen & Hakemulder, 2024) or using experience sampling method (ESM – Csíkszentmihályi, 2014, p. 21–34), in-depth interviews (Bálint & Tan, 2019; Christiansen & Dalsgård, 2021; Howie, 2011; Zhang et al., 2021), and experiments. Participants are often asked to:

- answer a series of questions after reading a text;
- rate how much they liked a story (evaluative feelings);
- rate their affect (from no feeling to strong feeling) or strikingness (Miall & Kuiken, 1994);
- label parts of the text with the letter "E" when they are experiencing a particular emotional state (fresh memories), the letter "M" when they are recalling a past memory experience and "T" when they are thinking about something (Cupchik et al., 1998; Oatley, 2011, pp. 63–65; 2012, p. 32);
- think aloud after reading each section of the story in order to analyse what kind of comments they make while reading (character explanation, association, anticipation, world knowledge, quotation, style, imagery, question, reader emotion and thematisation) (Miall & Kuiken, 1999, p. 132; 2002);
- indicate how much they were transported into the world of the story (Kuijpers et al., 2023);
- recall emotionally moving situations (Schindler et al., 2022) and those they have recently experienced;
- mark passages that they consider to be "foregrounding"[11] (see Mukařovský's "aktualisace"; Miall & Kuiken, 1994 following Hunt & Vipond, 1985; Van Peer, 1986);
- read a text from a different culture to see how the participants remember and process it, and whether they transform some of the elements into more familiar forms that correspond to the schemas that are valid and socialised in their own culture (Bartlett, 1995 [first published in 1932].

The texts used in the experiments are original literary (narrative) fiction, such as a literary short story, and its non-fiction (expository) counterpart, mainly versions based on the literary original after eliminating the foregrounding features (Djikic et al., 2013). Some researchers use the "self-probed retrospection" method to compare the memories that readers have while reading literary and non-literary (expository) texts in order to determine which perspective (actor or observer) is characteristic of the text type (Hakemulder & Koopman, 2010; Seilman & Larsen, 1989). They also investigate what aspects of read-

---

10 It has been suggested by Jaka Gerčar and Adriaan van der Weel that the development of a Reading Health Index could be beneficial (2023).
11 These would be stylistic features/devices such as metaphor, irony, inversion, alliteration, etc., which grab the reader's attention ("strike them", "catch their eye" desautomate (defamiliarise) reading [Shklovsky] and evoke affect, which "guides "refamiliarizing" interpretive efforts" and prolongs the reading time required for cognitive and emotional processing (Scapin et al., 2023, pp. 274–275).

ing literary texts trigger affective-cognitive responses (feelings, emotions and thoughts) during reading and afterwards (Djikic et al., 2009ab, 2013; Hakemulder & Koopman, 2010; Koopman, 2016; Scapin et al., 2023). Of great importance are changes in readers' emotions and personality traits (personal transformation through a work of art), which are assessed using a standard personality inventory (personality tests, questionnaires or a checklists of emotions and self-reports before and after reading), as well as aesthetic appreciation (Hakemulder, 2004), reading time (Reinke & Bläsi, 2023; Miall & Kuiken, 1994) and ability to mentalise (De Mulder et al., 2022; Djikic et al., 2013; Oliver et al., 2012). Some of the measuring questionnaires and scales used in empirical research of reader responses are the following:

- Private Self-Consciousness Scale (Fenigstein et al., 1975);
- Interpersonal Reactivity Index (IRI-PT) with subscales perspective-taking fantasy, empathic concern and personal distress (Davis, 1983);
- SCS-R (Scheier & Carver, 1985);
- Positive and Negative Affect Scale (PANAS; Watson et al., 1988);
- The Author Recognition Test (ART, Stanovich & West, 1989);
- Demographics Questionnaire, the Big-Five Inventory (Donahue & Kentle, 1991);
- Literary Response Questionnaire (Miall & Kuiken, 1995) – it can be used to measure individual differences in reading reception, taking into account aspects such as insight, empathy, vividness of imagery, leisure escape, concern for the author, story-driven reading and rejection of literary values;
- Green and Brock's Transportation Scale (2000);
- Cohen's Identification Measure (2001);
- Neef for Affect Questionnaire (Maio & Esses, 2001);
- Reading the Mind in the Eyes Task (RMET, Baron-Cohen et al., 2001);
- Children's Motivations for Reading Scale (CMRS, Baker & Scher, 2002);
- Epistemological Beliefs Survey (EBS) (Wood & Kardash, 2002);
- Empathy Quotient (Baron-Cohen & Wheelwright, 2004);
- Suspense and Mystery Questionnaire (Knobloch et al., 2004);
- Busselle and Bilandzic's Narrative Engagement Scale (2009);
- Multidimensional measure of eudaimonic entertainment (Wirth et al., 2012);
- Aesthetic Emotions Scale (Schindler et al., 2017, 2022);
- RFSS – Reading Flow Short Scale (Thissen et al., 2018);
- The Narrative Engageability Scale (Bilandzic et al., 2019);
- SWAS – The Story World Absorption Scale (Kuijpers et al., 2014, 2023).

This book examines the ways in which different situations and circumstances, as well as motivations deemed significant by the reader, may influence reading experiences (see also Andersen & Hakemulder, 2024; Tangerås, 2020). It also reviews the findings of previous studies on related topics in the fields of literary and book studies, the psychology of fiction, media entertainment and cognitive science. The results of research in related fields may help to interpret the actions and attitudes described by the readers interviewed. The research methodology employed in this study, namely constructivist grounded theory, has expanded my book studies into a cross-disciplinary area involving the psychology of fiction and cognitive science (Carnahan & Jacobs, 2012; Charmaz, 2014; Charmaz et al., 2019; Howie, 2011; Jørgensen et al., 2024; Silvestri & Wang, 2018). As I present my analysis through the lens of a literary and media scholar, I acknowledge that my findings might appear elementary to professionals working in the field of cognitive science. Nevertheless, my aim was to understand the complexity of the mechanisms involved in reading, so it seems necessary to delve into related fields in order to fully present this phenomenon that is reading. More in-depth research is needed to fully elucidate these intersections with the help of an interdisciplinary research team.

Findings

The findings presented here are divided into sections representing the stages of the reading process. These include *pre-reading*, *reading*, and *post-reading*. The present approach may be considered congruent with the conceptual framework developed by Anne Mangen and Adriaan van der Weel for interdisciplinary empirical research on the digitisation of text reading, which includes "preparation" (*text*: substrate affordances, genre, complexity, length, text design, interface; *reader*: profile, purpose and motivation; *environment*: infrastructure, assessing text, choosing a location), "the act of reading itself" (*embodied interaction*, *mental interaction*: mental resources, comprehension level, immersion level; *environmental factors*: aloud vs. silent reading, location) and "the effects of reading" (*personal:* evaluation, learning, modification, retention, pleasure and *social:* information, education, cohesion, manipulation) (2016, pp. 120–122). What is outlined in the following subsections should be seen as a preliminary attempt to describe a dynamic process of reading that involves *actions/practices* (searching, selecting, changing what to read, buying, borrowing and collecting), *evaluations* (forming opinions about books, authors, characters, other readers and oneself, talking about books and encouraging reading) and *experiences* (imagining, immersing, associating, remembering, identifying, role-playing, dealing with emotions, having sensations and meeting needs).

Unlike most scientific studies of literature, which are based on statistically processed empirical data, this book provides only a description and interpretation of reading practices and affective-cognitive states. What readers read or what their current preferences are has been less important than how they engage with texts, read, interpret and respond to different types of texts, as well as why they read, what their expectations are and have been. The aim was not to develop a typology of readers, which seems to be in line with what Jacek Wojciechowski recommends as good librarian practice, arguing that reading choices change over time, and that these new readings result from unexpected circumstances or a problem that forces the reader to look for a solution (1991, pp. 98, 104–105).

Before reading

Choosing what to read

Unlike the value of utilitarian goods, the value of reading depends on the subjective meaning that the reader ascribes to it, not on how the book is made or how well it fulfils its basic function of being suitable for reading. One of the interviewees puts it in the following way:

> There are different kinds of books, the point is not that one reads a book, but that one has decided to read a book… when someone bought me a book because they knew that I like reading, but they didn't care to find out what I like to read and what it actually does for me, I know that they meant well, but the book is not necessarily for me [R92].
>
> Są książki i książki, to nie chodzi o to, że się czyta książkę, tylko jednak się czyta z wyboru jakąś książkę… ktoś kupił mi książkę, bo wiedział, że ja lubię czytać, ale w ogóle się nie zainteresował tym, co lubię czytać i co tak naprawdę mi daje, wiedział[x]m, że chce dobrze, ale to niekoniecznie jest dla mnie.

The choice of a particular book can be seen as a conscious act of the reader's agency, influenced to some extent by affect and mood (Mar et al., 2011, p. 818), to satisfy their needs, which may not be recognised or understood by others. If someone else chooses or recommends a book, it will not always suit the reader's background knowledge of the world, personal experience and current needs, and will probably not be read:

> Wrong style, wrong language, wrong plot. I mean, I don't take it to mean that, oh God, how much someone must not understand me, or not know me… the thing with books is that it's very easy for us to start believing that we know someone else's taste, while that special spark in a book is a unique mix of things so two books can be 99 percent similar and one will speak to you and the other won't [R21].
>
> Nie ten smak, nie ten język, nie ta fabuła. Natomiast nie odbieram tego, że, o Boże, jak ktoś bardzo musi mnie nie rozumieć, albo nie znać… z książkami jest tak, że bardzo łatwo nam się zaprzyjaźnić z myślą, że znamy czyjś gust, a w książce żre tak unikatowa mieszanka rzeczy, że książki mogą być podobne w 99 procentach i jedna zażre, a druga nie.
>
> It seemed to me that it would appeal to him, but he started reading it and says it's extremely boring [R34].
>
> Tak mi się przynajmniej wydawało, że jemu to podpasuje, on zaczął to czytać i mówi, że to jest tak ekstremalnie nudne.

As a result, the "usefulness" of the book given as a gift may be significantly limited. In the light of this, we might ask, are we able to properly assess the value of the book before reading it? As long as we do not think of it in a financial or material sense, the answer is "No". The quality of the reading experience is determined by the individual's choice rather than inscribed in the text (Csíkszentmihályi, 2014, p. 7; Purchase, 2019, pp. 2, 11). Involuntary focus can cause aversive experiences and inhibit or prevent the *flow* state:

> Obligation takes the fun out of reading. I separate this very clearly in my mind, which doesn't mean that I've never, for example, read a mandatory book with pleasure, it happened to me very often, but I also just feel the difference [R49].

> Przymus obdziera lekturę z przyjemności. Ja to w swojej świadomości bardzo wyraźnie rozdzielam, co nie oznacza, że nigdy na przykład nie przeczytał[x]m książki obowiązkowej z przyjemnością, bardzo często mi się to zdarzało, ale też po prostu czuję tę różnicę.

Whether a reading experience turns out to be immersive therefore depends not only on the book, but also on the reader, their willingness or ability to focus their attention, to immerse themselves in the fictional world and to use their skills in order to meet the challenge posed by the book. It seems to be a certain disposition, difficult to measure or describe, which is formed on the basis of previous experiences and background knowledge, reading habits and life situation. It uses a *self-concept* (a *self-image* or *self-schema*), which is "what people currently believe to be true about themselves" (Baumeister, "Ideal Self" 209 as cited in Hogan, 2019, p. xiv), what they define as their own, their values, feelings, attributes, characteristics, and what tends to be stable or slowly changing, as opposed to *the self*, which can be seen as a continuous process of experiencing and developing (Charmaz et al., 2019, pp. 34–35; Hogan, 2019, p. 8; Kristjánsson, 2010, p. 25). The reason why *self-concept* seems to be so important in this matter is that, as Patrick Hogan puts it, "we may act in a certain way because we think we are inclined to act in a certain way" (2019, p. xiii):

> I don't think that we should read only highbrow literature, but I have the impression that there is pressure on us to participate a certain way in culture… or maybe I put such pressure on myself [Profession].
>
> Nie uważam, że powinniśmy czytać wyłącznie literaturę wysoką, ale mam wrażenie, że to jednak jest taka presja na nas pewnego bycia w kulturze… sam/a chyba na siebie nałożył[x]m taką presję.

Readers are challenged from an early age to adapt their self-concept to social and cultural demands. Our categorical identity (*social identity*) is part of our *self-concept*, and the sense of belonging to a particular group or groups underpins the norms we use in real life and guides our behaviour and judgments (*ought-own self*).[1] During interviews, study participants often talked about the need to conform to certain standards. They also constantly monitored their competence and skills and compared themselves to others, which may indicate a need to feel unique and to distinguish themselves from others (Sinykin, 2023, 25):

> I never learned to read fast, but I seem to read fast compared to others [R25].
>
> Nigdy się nie uczył[x]m szybko czytać, natomiast wydaje mi się, że szybko czytam na tle innych.

---

1 See for example Młynarczyk, 2006, p. 190 or Waters et al., 2004.

> I felt that I had very discerning tastes and that I was light-years ahead of my peers in terms of reading. To this day I gloat with pride that I read "1984" in the sixth grade... To this day it actually surprises me why I actually read such things? [R21].
>
> Miał[x]m wrażenie, że mam bardzo wyrobiony gust i że jestem lata świetlne niż moi rówieśnicy w lekturach. Do dzisiaj napawam się dumą, że „Rok 1984" przeczytał[x]m w szóstej klasie podstawówki... i do dzisiaj mnie w zasadzie zaskakuje, dlaczego właściwie czytał[x]m takie rzeczy?

What they thought of themselves was in some cases repeated several times at different points in the interviews. This suggests a desire to control how they might be perceived by the researcher (Charmaz et al. 2019, pp. 5, 53).

This dynamic process of "determin[ing] desired end-point [behaviour, attitude or emotional state] and then taking action to move toward it", can be called *self-regulation* (Inzlicht et al., 2021, p. 2). Depending on the approach adopted, this encompasses various elements, including *standards, monitoring, strength/willpower* and *motivation* (Baumeister & Vohs, 2007, pp. 116–117).[2] All these components seem to be important in interpreting what readers say about their attitudes to reading. In everyday life, we find ourselves acting in a variety of social roles and expressing our *practical identity* through our actions, preferences and values. However, everything we do seems to be congruent with our sense of identity, which can also have an impact on what and how we read. Sharing personal stories helps us to organise what we have experienced and to maintain a sense of self (Gottschall, 2021, p. 26). Since the interviewed readers contextualized their experiences chronologically, it was possible to observe how they reported changing over time. Respondents' utterances were full of adverbials of time, the most common of which emphasised the time of reading, indicating the age and level of education at which readers encountered a particular book or genre, and the context in which they read it, whether they read *before* or *after* watching a film adaptation, *before* or *after* a life change such as the birth of a child, *before, during* or *after* a global event (war, pandemic), or finally, in a particular state (when ill or stressed).

Readers easily recall who encouraged them to read and what happened as a result. Family, friends, partners, peers, neighbours and, less frequently, teachers were external motivators for some readers, influencing reading practices (Charmaz et al., 2019, p. 62; Fish, 1980; Murray, 2018, p. 376):

> My reading taste was basically shaped by my grandfather and my father, who would give me books to read. Since my dad didn't live to have a son... he suggested literature that mainly boys read [Gender].

---

2 It may also be "learning, self-monitoring / self-management agency / self-determination / locus of control / helplessness, self-control, social behaviour, self-monitoring" (Burman et al., 2015, p. 1519).

Mój gust czytelniczy to tak naprawdę kształtował mój dziadek i mój tato, podsuwając mi książki. Ponieważ mój tato nie doczekał się syna... to podsuwał literaturę taką, którą czytają głównie chłopcy.

I hated reading, but somewhere around the sixth grade I came across some two or three cool books, surprisingly they were school readings... and that's where it started... my parents both love to read and we had a huge library at home, so my mother, who was a teacher, began to suggest some books that might fascinate me [R56].

Nienawidził[x]m czytania, no ale gdzieś od szóstej klasy trafił[x]m wtedy na jakieś dwie, trzy fajne książki, o dziwo lektury... no i od tego się zaczęło... moi rodzice oboje kochają czytać i mieliśmy w domu ogromną biblioteczkę, to mama też jako nauczyciel zaczęła mi podsyłać coś takiego, co by mogło mnie zaintrygować.

Reading choices have also been heavily influenced by pop culture, particularly the film industry, which is a useful framework for analysing the generational experiences of particular groups of readers:

I just started reading Tolkien's books, I think that's when "The Lord of the Rings" was in the movie theaters [R81].

Zacz[x]ł[x]m czytać właśnie książki Tolkiena, chyba wtedy nawet „Władca Pierścieni" wchodził do kin.

I used to read fantasy books by the dozen in my college days, I don't know if I was influenced by something, in any case, everyone was reading Tolkien then, I was also a big fan of Ursula Le Guin, and then after college I lost interest, which doesn't mean that I dismiss fantasy, but for example, I'm more interested in things that are more real [R99].

Fantasy czytał[x]m masowo w czasach studenckich, nie wiem, czy pod wpływem czegoś, w każdym razie wtedy się czytało Tolkiena, ja też był[x]m fanem/fanką Ursuli Le Guin, a potem mi jakoś tak po studiach przeszło, co nie znaczy, że odrzucam, ale na przykład bardziej mnie interesują rzeczy, które są bardziej realne.

My generation didn't get into it so much [Tomek Wilmowski Series]... if someone wasn't into social issues, they were really into, for example, Tolkien, or were generally fans of Sapkowski or Harry Potter. Our generation just didn't get into that [R1].

Moje pokolenie tak szeroko akurat w to nie weszło [cykl powieści o Tomku Wilmowskim autorstwa Alfreda Szklarskiego]... jak ktoś nie wchodził w tematykę społeczną, to się mocno interesował na przykład Tolkienem albo w ogóle Sapkowskiego łykał albo Harry'ego Pottera, po prostu generacyjnie na to nie trafiliśmy.

Despite changing perceptions of what constitutes a "quality reading experience", reading both so-called highbrow literature and popular books can be regarded as a cultural obligation for many readers. Some of them cave in to peer pressure, and pick up books that are popular enough to be talked about. The need for acceptance and common topics of conversation may be greater in a group of people from the same profession or a national, ethnic or racial minority in a country/region, although this would require more systematic research.

As well as the presence of readers in the immediate environment, the availability of books can also be a stimulus to reading and the development of reading practices. If this availability is limited in some way, books are out of sight or are destroyed by children (e.g. younger siblings), it may be more difficult to maintain motivation to read. In such circumstances, reading may change, as reported by a reader who returned to reading up to retirement age.

Some readers have told me that at some point they have been buying books instead of borrowing them from libraries. This may be due to the limitations of the library's catalogue, or because they like to own books or have them available at all times. Collecting books is associated with a need to own. However, the types of books collected depended on at least three things: firstly, their availability (via the library or e-book apps); secondly, their price; and thirdly, the subjective perceived usefulness of the book. Some readers, not just academics, purchase mainly reference or popular science books, others only literary fiction.

Although the nature of the research was qualitative and the interviews unstructured, some interesting conclusions can be drawn from the authors and book titles mentioned in the interviews. However, it should be emphasised that no specific questions were asked about book titles and authors in order to collect a list of the most important books at any stage of the readers' stories. Sometimes readers mentioned their favourite titles or childhood favourites; on other occasions it was recently read books or books they disliked. Some readers did not remember the title or the author, but rather a general feeling associated with a book. 42% of the authors mentioned were Polish (Table 3). Authors from English-speaking countries (United States, United Kingdom, Ireland, Canada, Australia, New Zealand and Jamaica) represented 30%, followed by French (6%), German and Russian (3%), then Swedish, Czech, Spanish and Austrian (2%) writers. Among both Polish and foreign authors the share of female authors did not exceed 30% (28% for the former and 22% for the latter). Of the 205 titles mentioned in the interviews, only 37% were in Polish and 24% were written by women (Table 4). What seems to be more important, however, is not which titles or authors readers indicated, but how what readers read changes over time. Reading paths can be explored through the choices readers make at different stages of their lives, such as starting with Polish authors and then reading only foreign fiction, reading fantasy novels in high school, discovering fantasy after a "crime novel hangover", or reading literary fiction after being diagnosed with cancer. Interesting directions, not only for the study of adolescent reading, are also literary tropes or themes. Rather than naming titles or genres of books they have read, adult readers often name what they like or dislike to read – books about other countries,

World War II, great people, health – to name a few. There are many aspects of this subject that could be explored. For instance, it would be interesting to see how readers who reject certain types or genres of books that do not suit their current preferences (e.g. non-fiction, fantasy, science fiction, romance) react when they are required to read a book without knowing its genre.

Becoming autonomous

While readers may not remember the authors or titles of books they have read, or the endings of those books (which some of them confess to being ashamed of), they can usually tell when their attitudes towards books of a particular type or genre and their reading habits have changed. They often compare the types of literature they consume and the pace at which they read with what they read at different stages of their lives. Many respondents said they read more as children or teenagers than now, even late at night, forgetting the whole world. They were driven by curiosity and enthusiasm, hungry and eager to read, and they really enjoyed reading:

> Back then I would read two, three, four books a week, today if I read so many books a month, it's a miracle [R81].

> Wtedy to się czytało po dwie, trzy, cztery książki tygodniowo, dzisiaj jak przeczytam tyle książek miesięcznie, to jest cud.

> I remember those moments when I would walk home from the library with those books under my arm, with so much anticipation that I would soon sit down and read them, and I terribly regret losing that feeling, and I have been missing it for a long time, because I also remember that moment when I stopped reading novels [R88].

> Pamiętam takie momenty, kiedy idę z biblioteki z tymi książkami pod pachą do domu, z takim oczekiwaniem, że zaraz usiądę i będę czytać i strasznie mi szkoda tego uczucia, a szkoda mi już od dawna, bo pamiętam też taki moment, kiedy przestał[x]m czytać powieści.

At that time, they were exploring different genres (jumping from one to the other) in order to find out what they liked. Some books were just for the moment and readers never returned to them ('one-off reading'), especially if the motivation for reading was mainly external. Others were seen as a form of reader's training in voluntarily confronting something that is not easily accessible and digestible:

> I read "Doctor Faustus" by Thomas Mann; it was terribly boring literature, ... but I would always read whole books for myself from beginning to end, and it never happened that I didn't finish a book ... then I just harped on the idea that maybe there will be something interesting later, today I know that if the beginning is weak, the rest will also be weak ... there would be a good review somewhere, in general the book belonged to what we generally call the canon and so I

stubbornly decided that I need to know it… I was like a coach for myself telling myself that I have to read it [R81].

„Doktora Faustusa" Tomasza Manna się czytało, to też była strasznie nudna literatura,… ale człowiek czytał sobie całe książki od początku do końca i nie zdarzyło mi się nigdy książki nie dokończyć… wtedy po prostu się uparł[x]m, że może będzie później coś ciekawego, dzisiaj wiem, że jak początek jest słaby, to później też będzie słabe… gdzieś tam jakaś fajna recenzja była, w ogóle należało do czegoś, co ogólnie nazywamy kanonem i tak się uparł[x]m, że trzeba to znać… sam/a był[x]m dla siebie takim coachem, że masz to przeczytać.

The eminent literary critic, Harold Bloom recognises the value of pursuing such "difficult pleasure" by confronting oneself and engaging in an interpretive process. Although he does not advocate reading the Western canon as a means of forming one's moral, social or political values, he sees such reading as helping to evoke a profound memorable experience and facilitating personal growth, enabling an individual to embrace a change of the self (2019a, pp. 20, 22; 2019b, pp. 41–42). As can be seen, books that are considered more difficult do not automatically have to be rejected. They are read in stages, rather than while traveling or on holiday. They require some dedication from the reader. Reading them is motivated by the need for value and testing one's abilities, which helps overcome the barrier of emotional rejection (rewarding motivation). "The emotion with the greater motivational force wins" says Hogan (2015, p. 125; 2022, p. 157):

I accept that it will be a little more difficult for me to read it, it may bore me at times, but I know that it is an important book in world literature and will have some value beyond the story itself [R76].

Godzę się na to, że będzie mi troszeczkę trudniej, żeby ją przeczytać, momentami może mnie przynudzić, ale wiem, że to jest istotna pozycja dla literatury światowej i będzie miała jakąś tam wartość większą ponad samą historię.

Sometimes I also enjoy reading a book that requires more concentration, it is perhaps a little more difficult, but it is meant to be read in stages, it is obvious that you do not read such books in one breath [R39].

Czasami lubię też poczytać książkę, która wymaga większego skupienia, jest może trochę trudniejsza, ale to na takie etapy, wiadomo, że nie czyta się ich jednym tchem.

I did not start reading it yet, but I had already decided that it probably would not be for me exactly, but I struggled with those emotions until halfway through the book, and I decided that no, I guess every book is for me… I'll just read it, I'll look up the words that I may not understand, and I'll commit to it… for me it's always a learning experience even if something is difficult for me… if I am able to understand a passage, analyse it, it brings me satisfaction that I took the time, opened one book, another book to understand the subject [R48].

> Ja jeszcze jej nie zaczął[x]m czytać, ale już stwierdził[x]m, że ona chyba nie do końca będzie dla mnie, ale zmagał[x]m się z tymi moimi emocjami gdzieś do połowy książki i stwierdził[x]m, że no nie, no chyba każda książka jest dla mnie… ja przeczytam, ja sobie jeszcze posprawdzam wyrazy, których ewentualnie nie rozumiem i się poświęcę… dla mnie to jest zawsze taka nauka, że nawet jeśli coś mi sprawia trudność… jeśli jestem w stanie zrozumieć jakiś fragment, przeanalizować go, to daje mi to satysfakcję, że poświęcił[x]m swój czas, otworzył[x]m jedną książkę, drugą książkę po to, żeby zrozumieć temat.

Such utterances also illustrate what Jonathan Rose has pointed out in relation to the comprehension skills of the "common reader", namely "readers ignorant of the appropriate literary conventions sometimes read difficult works anyway, and thereby manage to puzzle out those conventions" (1992, p. 67).

Reading "on one's own terms" begins with the stage of exploration. It is characterised by more reading, more intense reading and more varied reading without a clear aim:

> I read the weirdest things in high school… I don't know why I read this stuff [R34].
>
> Najwięcej i najdziwniejszych rzeczy naczytał[x]m się w liceum… Ja nie wiem, po co ja to czytał[x]m.

It is in high school or college that readers gain the most independence in deciding what to read and how to read it:

> I was 14–15 years old when I had a new realization that, wow, literature is fun, you can learn cool things [R81].
>
> Miał[x]m 14–15 lat i akurat mi się zmieniło, że, wow, ta literatura to jest fajna zabawa, można się fajnych rzeczy dowiedzieć.
>
> When positivist novels like "The Doll" were read at school, I got hooked, and by the third year I thought to myself that I would read what I wanted. I started going to bookstores more often. I started reading a little bit on my own terms by then, and well, that's what I still do today [R53].
>
> Jak się pojawiły powieści pozytywistyczne typu „Lalka", to już mnie wciągało, a na trzecim roku pomyślał[x]m sobie, że czytam to, co chcę. Zacz[x]ł[x]m częściej chodzić do księgarń… czytać już trochę tak własnym tropem, no i robię to do dzisiaj.

For some of the interviewees this happened at a different stage in life, especially if their reading opportunities were limited in childhood. [With the] "liberation from school, which was very limiting… [because it] interpreted [literature] from one single angle and reduced it to "it's supposed to be like this" [R45] readers gradually get rid of the shame and fear of misreading a book, and thus reinforce their self-esteem and the purpose of reading, which is to satisfy their needs:

> I sometimes stay away from official interpretations because I'd rather rely on my own opinion and I want to have one, and it's important to me at that moment because I know it increases my satisfaction from reading [R49].
>
> Zdarza mi się unikać wykładni, bo raczej opieram się na własnej opinii i chcę ją mieć i ona jest dla mnie w tym momencie ważna, bo wiem, że przyczynia się do mojej większej satysfakcji z czytania.

Regaining autonomy in reading comes with the realisation that satisfying the *ought-own self* ("how [readers] feel they ought to be") or *ought-other self* ("how others wish reader ought to be")[3] does not bring satisfaction, but at best relief. Shaping one's self-concept does not have to take place in subordination or contradiction to the world and others, but in interaction with them in a continuous process of voluntarily testing one's limits and broadening ones perspective. Even if we perceive reading as a solitary practice, it is also a social one, and as such, individuals must first acquire the skills necessary to navigate social and institutional norms in order to locate themselves within the relevant context (Fuller & Rehberg Sedo, 2013, pp. 26, 28). Part of that involves fitting in (Hogan, 2019, p. 4), but it should not only be seen as a constraint:

> – I also read "Harry Potter" as a child, but mainly because a lot of people around me were reading it, too.
> – Did you feel any pressure?
> – I mean, a little bit, yes, to have shared topics of conversation, to be accepted in a group, although when I got older later, in high school, I discovered my own path and my own interests, and I also no longer felt such pressure to think that if I read something else and/or was interested in something else, then let's say I was inferior or something like that. In high school, I also met different people who didn't have typical interests, and this also motivated me to search for my own path… it was a feeling of liberation for me and finally joy that I could read what I wanted, and I will also say this change worked out for the better, because by actually reading and being interested in what I wanted, I was accepted by a broader group [R80].
>
> – W dzieciństwie też czytał[x]m „Harry'ego Pottera", ale to było też bardziej uwarunkowane tym, że dużo osób wokół mnie czytało.
> – Czuł/a Pan/i presję?
> – To znaczy, troszkę tak, żeby mieć wspólne tematy do rozmów, być akceptowanym w danej grupie, aczkolwiek jak później zrobił[x]m się starsz[x], tak w liceum, to odkrył[x]m własną drogę i własne zainteresowania i też już nie czuł[x]m takiej presji, że jak czytam coś innego i/lub interesuję się czymś

---

3   See in Waters et al., 2004, p. 251–252.

innym, to załóżmy jestem gorsz[x] czy coś takiego. W liceum poznał[x]m też różnych ludzi, którzy nie mieli takich typowych zainteresowań i też mnie to tak zmotywowało do poszukiwania własnej ścieżki… to było dla mnie takie uczucie wyzwolenia i wreszcie radości, że czytam to, co chcę i powiem też, że ta zmiana wyszła na lepsze, bo dzięki temu, że rzeczywiście czytał[x]m i interesował[x]m się tym, co chcę, był[x]m przez szersze grono akceptowan[x].

Active self-exploration, through a variety of different books and approaches to identify the main needs that the reader is trying to satisfy, results in more independence in deciding what to read and changes the approach to reading ("choice gives agency" – Charmaz et al., 2019, pp. 21, 53)[4], which can lead to development of self (self-expansion). Marie-Laure Ryan et. al. describe such an approach as "eudaimonic" and explain that it involves "(1) pursuing intrinsic goals and values for their own sake, including personal growth, relationships, community, and health, rather than extrinsic goals and values, such as wealth, fame, image, and power; (2) behaving in autonomous, volitional, or consensual ways, rather than heteronomous or controlled ways; (3) being mindful and acting with a sense of awareness; and (4) behaving in ways that satisfy basic psychological needs for competence, relatedness, and autonomy" (2006, p. 139). However, the need for status, social recognition or validation can be a significant obstacle to the pursuit of eudaimonia (Ryan et al., 2006, p. 145).

Changing one's habits

Studying reading experience means taking into account the fact that it is an ongoing process (Andersen & Hakemulder, 2024, p. 16). The perception of changes in reader's practices may be different. Some of them may feel that they have experienced transformative moments, while others may be convinced that their experiences or attitudes to reading have been changing gradually rather than radically (Hogan, 2019, p. 8). The changes experienced by readers whose reading habits are relatively constant, and who reach for other types of books occasionally, are not easily discernible: "they were not revolutionary, but evolutionary, I'm certainly a different reader today than I was in my childhood or youth, while I don't notice big milestones" [57] – says one of the study participants. Becoming pickier seems to be a symptom of age-related change (Nick Hornby…, 2024). As readers gain experience, their reading choices become more deliberate:

> Before I sit down and pick up a book, I take the time to read a good deal about what it's about, to read the reviews and so on, so the books I choose are rarely flops [R56].
>
> Ja zanim siądę, wezmę się za książkę, to zdążę dobrze przeczytać, o czym ona jest, poczytać opinie i tak dalej, więc rzadko kiedy mam wtopę.

---

4 For more on the "self-determination theory", which emphasises the value of intrinsic rather than extrinsic goals see Ryan et al., 2006, pp. 146, 163; Šileris, 2023, p. 42; Wirth et al., 2012, pp. 408, 411–412.

> I'm more choosy... I wouldn't pick up just anything anymore, whatever someone has on the shelf, but look up the author myself... possibly read one or two reviews, whether it's worth it [R57].

> Jestem bardziej wybredn[x]... że już bym po byle co nie sięgn[x]ł/a, co tam ktoś ma na półce, tylko wyszukał[x] sobie autora... ewentualnie jedną, dwie recenzje, czy warto.

> I don't dip into books that would disappoint me a lot... some non-fiction books put me off, like, I read about the topic and think about it for a while, and then I figure out that basically I either don't want to read about it, or I read an excerpt and find out that the book only covers the subject, but there's no quality there, and I don't waste my time on it [R76].

> Nie pakuję się w rzeczy, które by mnie bardzo rozczarowywały... z literatury faktu niektóre rzeczy mnie odrzucają, jak przeczytał[x]m temat i się chwilę zastanawiam, a potem stwierdzam, że w gruncie rzeczy albo nie chcę o tym czytać, albo przeczytam fragment i stwierdzam, że to jest zrobiony tylko temat, ale nie ma tam jakby jakości, i nie tracę na to czasu.

Early on, in the exploration phase, readers were more spontaneous in picking up different types of books and their reading was more extensive:

> I would go to the library and just pick something out, it didn't matter if it was a title I found interesting, sometimes I would even choose something because I liked the cover. I would grab it and say, let's give it a try, and read it, I would take three to five books at a time and read them one by one, something I don't get a chance to do now [R34].

> Szedłem/szłam do biblioteki i po prostu wybierał[x]m sobie coś, nieważne, czy to był tytuł, który mnie interesuje, niekiedy nawet po okładce, że mi się spodobała, brał[x]m i mówię, spróbujemy, i czytał[x]m, brał[x]m po trzy do pięciu książek i czytał[x]m je po kolei, coś, na co teraz nie ma szans.

At some point, readers reach a stage where they can identify their needs and preferences:

> I'm already at a stage where I already more or less know what I like... which themes I prefer, which I will probably like more, of course it's not that one excludes the other... I'm more likely to read fantasy than science fiction books... I'm more likely to read a book about a vampire than about a werewolf. I don't know why, but that's how it works with me [R74].

> Jestem już na takim etapie, że już mniej więcej wiem, co lubię... które motywy wolę, które zapewne mi się spodobają bardziej. Oczywiście to nie jest tak, że to wyklucza innych... chętniej sięgnę po fantasy niż po science fiction... chętniej

sięgnę po wampira niż po wilkołaka. Nie wiem czemu, ale coś takiego we mnie działa.

They can also admit what they are trying to avoid, what they do not particularly like or what they are not (yet) ready for, and what makes it difficult for them to be transported to the world of the story (the foreignness or strangeness of the world, the number of volumes, the genre, the language, or the subject matter):

> Maybe if she hadn't told me, it was fantasy, I would have started reading… once I hear that it's fantasy, then well, ….. I react the same way as to some light-hearted novel [R92].

> Może gdyby mi nie powiedziała, że to jest fantastyka, to bym zacz[x]ł[x] czytać… tylko usłyszę, że to jest fantastyka, to noo… tak samo teraz reaguję na to, że jest jakaś powieść obyczajowa, lekka.

> These fantasy books require wrapping your head around some new universe, some reality, one that is usually very elaborate, in which everything is different, different language, different places, different rules… and these are usually books that come in thick volumes… to really know something about it and delve into world, you have to spend a very long time on these stories [R62].

> Te książki fantastyczne wymagają ogarnięcia jakiegoś nowego uniwersum, jakiejś rzeczywistości, takiej z reguły bardzo rozbudowanej, w której wszystko jest inne, inny język, inne miejsca, inne reguły… i to najczęściej są książki, które gdzieś tam przyrastają tomami… żeby rzeczywiście coś z tego wiedzieć i w coś tam wejść, to trzeba bardzo dużo czasu w tych historiach spędzić.

> I haven't been able to get into fantasy because it just has a lot of sentences that are badly written. This is probably the main problem, while there are books with every sentence well written from beginning to end [R76].

> W fantastykę nie był[x]m w stanie wejść, bo ona ma po prostu mnóstwo zdań, które są źle napisane. To jest chyba podstawowy problem, a są książki, które mają od początku do końca każde zdanie dobrze napisane.

They also become more aware of their limitations:

> Unfortunately, I'm not a lover of history and never will be, so I avoid such books… I'm definitely more into magic and strange powers, ghosts, miracles and such. It's definitely so different that it really allows me to completely mentally detach from what's going on here [R56].

> No ja niestety nie jestem miłośnikiem historii i nigdy nie będę, więc unikam takich książek… zdecydowanie lepiej czuję się w takim klimacie jakiejś magii i dziwnych mocy, duchów, cudów i innych takich. To zdecydowanie jest tak

> inne, że rzeczywiście pozwala mi się całkowicie myślowo oderwać od tego, co mamy tutaj.

Some respondents have their favourite titles and return to them regularly, even ritually, in order to experience the same feelings again. Beloved books give them a sense or even a guarantee of fulfilment of needs:

> On average, once every five years there is a point where it's a week to read "Harry Potter" [R21].
>
> Średnio raz na pięć lat jest taki moment, gdzie jest tydzień na czytanie „Harry'ego Pottera".

> It doesn't matter how many books you read, when you've already found, fortunately, the one and only titles, and sometimes it's better to reach for the same book again, which will give you the experiences you expect, rather than constantly go on a journey into the unknown in the hope that it will live up to your expectations... I had this ritual for literally probably five years, that every year I would read "The Witcher" during the summer, and every year I simply enjoyed it [R49].
>
> Nie ma znaczenia, ile się tych książek czyta, bo już znalazło się na szczęście takie tytuły, które rzeczywiście są tymi jedynymi tytułami i czasami lepiej sięgnąć jeszcze raz do tej samej książki, która dostarczy tych przeżyć oczekiwanych, niż ciągle udawać się w podróż w nieznane w nadziei, że one spełnią oczekiwania... Miał[x]m taki rytuał przez dosłownie chyba z pięć lat, że co roku czytał[x]m w wakacje „Wiedźmina" i co roku po prostu było mi z tym dobrze.

Rereading allows the reader to discover what they missed the first time, to identify overlooked details, and to focus on aspects that may not have seemed as important when their attention was focused on the plot. It can also prepare readers for the next book in the series. Finally, rereading may be a way of postponing that pleasure, thereby increasing the enjoyment of reading the new instalment:

> If the book is interesting, then I will definitely come back to it in a year, two, three, then I already know how it will end, and I can focus on all the extra stuff... I read the end of the previous volume, and, for example, I prefer to read the first or second once again a year later and only then move on to the latest one, as a sort of warm-up before the next one [R57].
>
> Jeżeli książka jest interesująca, to do niej za rok, dwa, trzy na pewno wrócę. Wtedy już wiem, jak się skończy i mogę się skupić na całej tej otoczce... czytam sobie końcówkę poprzedniego tomu i na przykład wolę sobie po tym roku jeszcze raz ten pierwszy czy drugi przeczytać i dopiero wtedy przejść do tego najnowszego, taka rozgrzewka przed tym dodatkowym.

Sometimes, by chance or out of cultural guilt, readers return years later to books they once failed to read or understand. Being free of pressure and having more experience, they are then able to discover previously inaccessible meanings:

> As I was 12 years old at the time, I didn't look at it that way at all... I wasn't fully aware of the significance of it all and at 20 years old, when I read it, it struck me and made that kind of impression on me [R1] [about "Antek" by Bolesław Prus].

> Jak miał[x]m 12 lat, to w ogóle nie patrzył[x]m na to w ten sposób... nie do końca był[x]m świadomy wagi tego wszystkiego, a mając 20 lat, jak to przeczytał[x]m, to tak trafiło do mnie i takie wrażenie to na mnie zrobiło [o "Antku" Bolesława Prusa].

Another reading practice worth mentioning is that of reading books from beginning to end. Some readers stopped doing this at some point when they realized that they could do so without consequences or harm to themselves. Their reading needs have become more important than their obligations:

> In our group of friends, people hate not finishing books, but also, we're old, to be blunt, and we found that at our age we can get away with it [Age].

> Mamy towarzystwo takie, które nienawidzi nie kończyć książek, no, ale też jesteśmy już starzy, za przeproszeniem, i stwierdziliśmy, że już w tym wieku możemy sobie na to pozwolić.

However, there are also those who feel obliged to finish every book they start:

> I very rarely leave books unfinished, I read them longer, but I always try to get to the end of every book [R74].

> Bardzo rzadko zostawiam książki niedokończone, czytam je dłużej, ale staram się zawsze z każdą książką dojść do końca.

> It's hard to say whether this is related to books as such, or just in general to some feature of my character, that if I make up my mind, I have to finish, whether it makes sense or not. At some point, I decided that I've put so much work in, that if I don't finish, all that work is pointless, so that's the way I approach many things, not just books [R62].

> Trudno powiedzieć, czy to jest związane z książkami jako książkami, czy tak w ogóle z jakimś takim rysem mojego charakteru, że jak się zaprę, to muszę skończyć, czy ma sens, czy nie ma. W którymś momencie stwierdzam, że tyle włożył[x]m pracy, że jak nie dokończę, to cała ta praca jest bez sensu. W taki sposób podchodzę do wielu rzeczy, nie tylko do książek.

> I like, if I start something, I like to finish it, even if I'm tired, even if I don't understand something sometimes, because I am annoyed by the behaviour of certain characters, but I try to finish, I don't like to leave things unfinished like that, because if I am to be discontented, I want to be discontented to the end, proven that I was right [R48].
>
> Lubię, jeżeli coś zacznę, to skończyć, może jestem i umęczon[x], może czasami czegoś tam nie rozumiem, bo denerwuje mnie zachowanie pewnych bohaterów, ale staram się kończyć, nie lubię tak zostawić czegoś niedokończonego, bo jak mam być niezadowolon[x], to chcę być niezadowolon[x] do końca, że miał[x]m rację.

This practice can have many interpretations, for example as a need for confirmation of the reader's reading. A need for closure may arise if the reading material is unappealing or challenging. In the latter case, it may also be a self-test for the reader to see if they can meet the challenge. For those readers who like to think of themselves as people who judge things fairly, this might be a way of giving a book or an author a chance. Without finishing a book, the time spent reading may seem poorly invested, which can affect self-efficacy and lead to a sense of loss.[5] Reading to the end may satisfy the need to confirm that time has not been wasted and that reading has resulted in a well-formed opinion about the book (Mar et al., 2011, p. 822; Webster & Kruglanski, 1994, p. 1049). Some readers even admitted that after reading, they sometimes check the opinions of other readers on forums and book recommendation services for some kind of validation. This leads us to conclude that reading can also be seen as a specific *task to be done* or *investment of time* (Gerrig, 2018; Martínez, 2014; Stockwell, 2019).

Further research should also take into account that some readers read only one book at a time and start another after finishing it, while others read several books in the same period, sometimes not finishing any of them. They also change books or their forms according to the setting or daily activities. In such cases, it may be important to investigate how this affects transportation into the story world.

When readers' needs are not satisfied, when they see no place for further exploration of a subject because they find nothing surprising or new in the kinds of books they usually read, they turn to another genre, sometimes after a crisis that could be called a "reading hangover". Only when a reader steps beyond their previous interests can they rediscover the joy of reading, often by overcoming their earlier reluctance to pick up a particular type of book:

> Then I logged on to some fantasy lovers' forums, where I started looking for someone to recommend something that would not be overwhelming for a beginner fantasy reader, and yet be gripping, but would not be boring either… for the past five years I have been reading only fantasy [R56].

---

5   See the "loss aversion" effect and taking "role choice" in "identity theory", Charmaz et al., 2019, p. 7.

Potem się po prostu pologował[x]m na jakieś fora miłośników fantasy, gdzie zaczął[x]m szukać, żeby ktoś polecił coś, co dla takiego początkującego czytelnika fantasy nie będzie przytłaczające, a zarazem pozwoli mi się gdzieś tam wciągnąć, no i też nie będzie nudne… od pięciu lat czytam tylko i wyłącznie fantastykę.

As Craig Smith and Leslie Kirby elucidate, the arousal of interest is contingent upon the novelty and complexity of the stimulus, or the likelihood that the individual will comprehend it (2009, p. 1356).

I had the feeling that I was reading about the same thing over and over again, that nothing would surprise me anymore, that I wouldn't get any more out of it [R92].

Miał[x]m wrażenie, że ciągle czytam o tym samym, że już mnie nic mnie nie zaskoczy, że już więcej z tego nie wyciągnę.

As one's interests broaden over time, changes in the type or genre of books read can also occur more seamlessly:

My interests simply tend to change so I start to be fascinated by other currents in literature. I started with mainstream literature, for example, Polish books, and read books only in this trend. Then for a very, very long time I was fascinated by fantasy, mainly Polish writers, and now, for example, I read a lot of memoirs, biographies, and I am drawn in that direction [R71].

Tak po prostu mi się zmienia, że gdzieś tam inne nurty w literaturze mnie interesują. Zaczynał[x]m od literatury powszechnej, na przykład polskiej, i czytał[x]m gdzieś tam tylko w tym nurcie książki. Potem bardzo, bardzo długo mnie fascynowało fantasy, głównie polscy pisarze, a teraz na przykład czytam bardzo dużo dzienników, jakichś takich biografii i w tym kierunku mnie gdzieś tam ciągnie.

Literary prizes can also encourage people to push boundaries and reach out for books that are far from their interests, but whose quality is recognised by others:

I read this particular book with great pleasure, it was also a completely different experience for me, because it was a bit of a fantasy book, and I was not really interested in fantasy, I never tried to break this taboo of mine… I watched the award ceremony and somehow it made me want to read it [R48].

Akurat tę książkę przeczytał[x]m z wielką przyjemnością. Było to też zupełnie inne doświadczenie dla mnie, ponieważ to była książka taka trochę fantastyczna, a mnie fantastyka troszeczkę jakby tak mało interesowała, nigdy nie próbował[x]m przełamać tego mojego tabu… oglądał[x]m rozdanie nagród i tak jakoś mnie to zmobilizowało, że chciał[x]m to przeczytać.

Moreover, a book from the literary canon or with bestseller status may also help to transport into the world of the story (Green & Brock, 2000, p. 708). The social group, be it literary critics, influencers or our friends and family members, can be an important moderator in narrative transport by providing a quality endorsement (Van Laer et al., 2014, p. 811).

Significant breakthroughs in what readers read, for what reasons and how can occur when readers are faced with challenges that require them to define their current situation and consider their future, which may be in jeopardy. This is particularly relevant in the context of life-threatening diseases. Two participants admitted that their attitude towards books and reading changed significantly after being diagnosed with cancer. The first participant recalls the experience as follows:

> In the past, I got leukemia and was lying in the hospital and at that time I was quite narrow-minded about the world and that's when I started to read more, because I was able to escape a little bit into this book… My illness was a turning point in my life, because my values completely changed. Books didn't interest me that much, I didn't have the will, desire, or time for something like that at all, and it was only later that I started to pick up any books at all, that was in middle school… it used to be just fairly straightforward books that just whisked me away from reality. It was only later that I moved to the kind of books that pull me back into reality… I saw that books really have a positive effect on how I cope with my illness, and so I began to turn to slightly more ambitious titles, including philosophical books [e.g. works of philosophical fiction written by Nietzsche], so that I could cope with my illness on some deeper level [RA].
>
> Kiedyś zachorował[x]m na białaczkę i leżał[x]m w szpitalu i w tamtym momencie miał[x]m dosyć zamknięte horyzonty na świat i wtedy właśnie zacz[x]ł[x]m więcej czytać, bo mogł[x]m trochę uciec w tę książkę… Moja choroba to był taki punkt zwrotny w moim życiu, bo kompletnie mi się wartości zmieniły. Kiedyś książki mnie aż tak nie interesowały, no nie miał[x]m chęci, w ogóle czasu na coś takiego i dopiero potem zaczął[x]m sięgać po jakiekolwiek książki, to było w gimnazjum… kiedyś to były tylko takie dosyć proste książki, które właśnie mnie wyrywały z rzeczywistości. Potem się przeniosł[x]m dopiero do takich, które mnie do tej rzeczywistości z powrotem wciągają… zobaczył[x]m, że książki naprawdę działają pozytywnie na to, jak sobie radzę z chorobą i tak dalej zaczął[x]m sięgać po nieco ambitniejsze pozycje, w tym książki filozoficzne, tak, żeby już poradzić sobie na jakimś głębszym poziomie z tą moją chorobą.

This example illustrates how the book becomes *an instrument of change*. The reader gradually moves from escaping problems to dealing with them. The second study participant decides from the outset to confront, understand and tame the experience by turning to non-fiction, which allows such direct comparison. In the second step, the reader begins to seek out some literary fiction to elevate the feelings and gain a broader understanding of the human condition:

— I read books that were about the experiences of people with cancer, because I also went through such an illness myself, and I wanted to get, I don't know, in some way close to it, to learn something about what one feels, whether what I feel is normal, so to speak... these were rather diaries, books written by therapists, I read probably most of the books, if not all of them, Irvin Yalom's books, "Exercises in Loss" by Agata Tuszyńska. I was also reading in those days, I remember, and it stuck with me for a long time, Wiesław Myśliwski's "Treatise on Shelling Beans". All in all, it was probably the best book I read at that time and that I remembered, it somehow got through to me, even though it didn't talk about the disease, but about life in general, about the meaning of life, and maybe that's when I think I was trying to find the answer to what the meaning of life is... then I started reading prose similar to Myśliwski's. Books that talk about people. Not just describe this sort of fantasy world, I've moved away from fantasy... just books that talk about the human condition, about what we are like, that can give answers to the questions of what direction we are heading. I don't know, more philosophical books, I guess, you could say.
— And did you find answers to these questions?
— Just more questions, but I find these books enjoyable, I don't think I could go back to reading horror stories, detective stories [RB].

— Czytał[x]m książki, które mówiły może bardziej o doświadczeniach ludzi z chorobą nowotworową, bo sam/a też taką chorobę przeszedłem/przeszłam i chciał[x]m w jakiś sposób do tego zbliżyć, dowiedzieć czegoś o tym, co się czuje, czy to, co ja czuję, jest normalne, że tak powiem... raczej to były dzienniki, to były książki pisane przez terapeutów, przeczytał[x]m chyba większość książek, jeśli nie wszystkie, Irvina Yaloma, „Ćwiczenia z utraty" Agaty Tuszyńskiej. Czytał[x]m też wtedy, pamiętam, i to mocno mi utkwiła lektura „Traktatu o łuskaniu fasoli" Wiesława Myśliwskiego. To w sumie chyba była najlepsza książka, którą w tamtym czasie przeczytał[x]m i którą zapamiętał[x]m, która jakoś do mnie trafiła, mimo że ona nie mówiła o chorobie, ale no o całym życiu, o sensie życia, a może właśnie wtedy chyba starał[x]m się znaleźć odpowiedź na to, co jest sensem życia... wtedy zaczął[x]m czytać prozę podobną do Myśliwskiego. Książki, które mówią o człowieku. Nie tylko opisują ten jakiś taki fantastyczny świat, odszedłem/odeszłam bardziej od tych fantastycznych... tylko takie właśnie, które mówią o kondycji człowieka, o tym, jacy jesteśmy, które mogą udzielić odpowiedzi na pytania, w jakim kierunku zmierzamy? No nie wiem, takie bardziej chyba filozoficzne można powiedzieć.
— Znalazł/a pan/i odpowiedzi na te pytania?
— Tylko więcej pytań, ale te książki sprawiają mi przyjemność, nie potrafił[x] bym chyba już wrócić do czytania horrorów, kryminałów.

As can be seen, moments of medical treatment force us to slow down and encourage us to reflect deeply, to reassess the life we are living. The second interviewee gained a deeper understanding of themselves, and not just of their current situation, by reading artistic prose, and the first by reading philosophical works. In their search for meaning and understanding, both readers eventually turned to books, which brought a new quality to their lives and helped them to reconstruct their sense of self, rather than simply escaping reality. The initial approach and subsequent coping with a problem, cognitively and/or emotionally, may differ depending on various factors (see *Dealing with negative emotions*). What is common is that "we [all] need narratives during challenging times", as they help with self-change and healing (Andersen & Hakemulder, 2024, p. 2).

A change in the way readers read and talk about a book, often as *a tool* or *instrument*, can be an indicator of a significant process taking place in their lives. The verb *to use* [korzystać], which in Polish means "to profit from something" but also "to use something as a tool", emphasises the importance of the form of the book serving the needs of a particular reader. The usability of the book is best reflected in its role as required or professional reading. The reader's occupation (i.e. type of job, intensity and stress level) can significantly influence their approach to books, affecting both the type of content and the pace of reading:

> In this business of doing science, you simply read whatever fits in with your line of work and your interests [Profession].
>
> W tej branży, jaką jest robienie nauki, po prostu czytasz to, co jest po drodze, i co gdzieś tam się mieści w twoim kręgu zainteresowań.
>
> For me, reading, I mean, reading for pleasure, devouring books ended around the 2nd year of university. Then there was a gap, 4–5 years, where I basically hardly read for pleasure at all, and only after that did I kind of force myself to read a bit [R21].
>
> Moje czytanie, takie dla przyjemności, takie pochłanianie książek, skończyło się mniej więcej z drugim rokiem studiów. Potem była taka luka, cztery-pięć lat, gdzie w zasadzie prawie w ogóle nie czytał[x]m dla przyjemności i dopiero potem tak trochę się zmuszał[x]m.

In the case of academics or any professional reader, the most obvious changes are in language and scope. The former expands, while the latter narrows over the years. The term *publication* is often used instead of *book* or *novel*. Technical terms for genres or types of books are commonly used by professional readers, and may even indicate the reader's field of specialisation. Self-reporting by non-professional readers is subject to a high margin of error for at least two reasons: first, they may not be familiar with the terminology or may not be able to distinguish one genre or type from another, or may not be sure of its classification; second, the boundaries between genres are sometimes too loose to identify accurately.

One's reading habits can also be significantly altered by the birth of a child. Some readers I spoke with admitted that when their children were young, there was less leisure reading in their life. They didn't have the time or strength to read or found it difficult to fully immerse themselves in books. However, there were also mothers who switched from printed books to e-books or audiobooks in order to continue reading. They were then able to read while feeding their children and taking them out for walks, or even while putting them to sleep. Some were even more engaged in reading than before. So not only did the readers not have to give up reading, but they discovered a completely different dimension to it with this new medium.

The assertion that the medium shapes the user's experience, as postulated by Marshall McLuhan, leads us to conclude that the format of the book can have a significant impact on the reader's engagement. A few of those interviewed have strongly confirmed this, saying:

> I have noticed that I am more drawn into an audiobook than a printed book [R76].
>
> Zauważyłem, że bardziej wciąga mnie audiobook niż czytana książka.

> I like to use paper books… but listening to audiobooks is more attractive to me… I'm sort of always with the book… You can be in the bathroom, you can be on your way to the store, you can be lying in bed, you can be doing anything, and the book is constantly with you [R43].
>
> Lubię korzystać z papierowych książek… ale jednak to słuchanie dla mnie jest bardziej atrakcyjne… ja jakby ciągle jestem z tą książką… Możesz sobie być w toalecie, możesz sobie iść do sklepu, możesz sobie leżeć, możesz cokolwiek robić i ona ciągle, ta książka, jest z tobą.

When listening to a book, it is not just the text that matters, but also features of the audiobook such as the narrator's tone, modulation, speed, etc., so these should also be taken into account when comparing listening with reading:

> Because if the voice talent is not good and doesn't suit me, there's no option for me to listen to the book to the end, because some readers can put you to sleep… they can't really do this well and discourage you from listening [R43].
>
> Jeżeli lektor jest zły i nie podpasuje mi, nie ma opcji, żebym ja tę książkę przesłuchał/a do końca, bo niektórzy lektorzy są strasznie usypiający… nie potrafią naprawdę czytać i bardziej zniechęcają do słuchania.

We should also consider the role of potential distractions from applications installed on digital devices used for reading and, most importantly, the reader's previous experience and attitude towards audiobooks. For some readers, a digital book does not have the same function as a print book (it is not a substitute), so they may agree with Max Bruinsma's statement that "screens are for watching, paper is for reading" (*Typotheque…*

2004). This is also confirmed by Martha Pennington and Robert Waxler, who claim that, "screen trains people to watch and wait for something to happen, reading requires a person to do something to a text to make it come alive". Some readers who participated in the study would also agree with this statement:

> I have never read a book on an e-reader, and I have other distractions on my cell phone, funny cats, whatever's on Facebook and so many more distractors and this fiddling with these apps, just like on the computer, I'm reading a book, and I could be playing a video game, after all, that's not what it's for [R81].
>
> Nigdy nie czytał[x]m na czytniku, a na komórce to człowiek ma inne rozrywki, śmieszne koty, co tam na Facebooku i tyle jeszcze rozpraszaczy i to skakanie z tymi aplikacjami, podobnie jak na komputerze, czytam książkę, a mógłbym/mogłabym grać w grę, przecież to nie temu służy.

The question of how reading from a screen differs from reading a printed page has been the subject of numerous studies. There is some evidence that printed books may be more beneficial for reading literary fiction, leading to better comprehension, "following the sequence of the plot" and "remembering what happened when and where", as Anne Mangen suggests (Wolf & Gottwald, 2016, p. 148; Baron, 2021, pp. 83–84). A meta-analysis by Pablo Delgado et al., which looked at reading comprehension research conducted between 2000 and 2017, has provided evidence of the advantage of paper reading over digital reading. "People adopt a shallower processing style in digital environments," the researchers conclude. This is why the advantage of reading on paper is particularly evident when reading more complex informational texts, rather than narrative texts. Paper reading is also preferred for better comprehension of texts under time pressure (2018, pp. 34–35). Miha Kovač and Adriaan van der Weel point out that a number of factors, including life experience and lifestyle, can influence comprehension. For example, when comparing print and screen reading, the state of the reader – whether they are fresh or tired when they read – emerges as a significant factor alongside age and education level. However, a major limitation to conducting such research in a controlled environment is the length of the reading material, which limits the use of longer fictional texts. Researchers also highlight the lack of a universally accepted standard measure of text length and complexity, a factor that makes it difficult to draw general conclusions (2020, p. 9).

This research shows that readers' practices can evolve over time. Therefore, their stated preferences only reflect their current habits and specific ways of reading (linear, close and deep or hyper-reading) or types of text preferred (narrative, fictional or informative, expository), as well as attitudes such as the idealisation of print (see Baron, 2021, p. 13).

> I do not listen to audiobooks, which does not mean that I contest this form of transmission of texts… it is a matter of some kind of habit, I am used to reading something that is in paper form [R99].

> Ja nie słucham audiobooków, co nie znaczy, że kwestionuję taką formę przekazywania tekstów jakichkolwiek… to jest kwestia jakiegoś przyzwyczajenia, ja jestem przyzwyczajon[x] do czytania czegoś, co jest w formie papierowej.

Listening to a book requires some extra motivation to change one's habits. It could be triggered by a specific life situation, a change in the reader's commute, doing work that does not require mental effort or much attention, a stimulus in the form of a free trial of a book app, etc. Readers gradually learn that with the right training they can also "read with their ears", to use Naomi Baron's phrase (2021, pp. 1, 15). Starting with something the reader has already read and knows the ending of helps. Then the reader can listen to the same book in a foreign language they are learning, as one of the interviewees recommends.

The inability to fully engage with a book, whether in print or digital format, can be attributed to a lack of focus on the part of the reader. This may stem from a number of factors, including a lack of familiarity with the genre or format of the book or inconvenience in using it due to its design (e.g. font, layout, paper colour or binding, and voice narrator):

> I have to bend this book… sometimes I cover something with my finger, because the margins are too small… it's not such a smooth process that I just focus on reading and following the plot, I have to do some additional activities besides turning the pages [R57].

> Muszę tę książkę jakoś tak odginać… tutaj coś za chwilę znowu tym palcem sobie zasłaniam, bo są za krótkie marginesy… to nie jest taki płynny proces, że skupiam się tylko na lekturze i gonię za fabułą, tylko muszę robić jakieś dodatkowe czynności oprócz przewracania stron.

A stressful situation or job, as well as fatigue, can also affect the reader and make it more difficult to immerse oneself:

> There was a period in my life when I realized that I basically stopped reading, I couldn't focus on one article, I was constantly in a rush… even when I had some free time, I was too tired, or had something else to deal with and didn't have time for such leisure pursuits, it's such an unpleasant experience… it is associated with a busy job and stress at work so I was able to sit down with a book and read the same page ten times, then put it down, still not understanding what I'm reading, I'm here, I want to read, I want to switch off, and my head is still full of other thoughts, well there were such moments that not even a book would do it anymore [R31].

> Był taki okres, kiedy sobie uświadomił[x]m, że ja w zasadzie przestał[x]m czytać, ja nie mogę się skupić na jednym artykule. Człowiek tak goni, goni… nawet jak ma ten czas wolny, to jest zbyt zmęczony, albo ma jeszcze coś innego do ogarnięcia i nie ma czasu na te swoje przyjemności, to takie przykre doświadczenie… wiąże się z taką napiętą pracą zawodową i stresem w pracy, że potrafił[x]m usiąść

> nad książką i czytać dziesięć razy tę samą stronę, po czym ją odkładać, ja dalej nie rozumiem, co ja czytam, że niby jestem tu, chcę poczytać, chcę się wyłączyć, a ta głowa ciągle po swojemu. No były takie właśnie momenty, że tutaj to nawet już książka nie dała rady.

Although changes in reading practices should be studied over the long term, across countries and with participants of different ages, genders and backgrounds in order to statistically confirm certain trends, some everyday observations can be used as premises to conclude that we are now facing a transition from linear reading to *hyper-reading*. This is reflected in the scanning or skimming of multiple documents "to get the gist", as Baron aptly puts it, rather than the more reflective or analytical, in-depth reading of a text through to the end (Baron, 2021, pp. 10–13; Sosnoski, 1999; van de Ven et al., 2023, p. 69). *Hyper-reading* seems to offer a potential advantage in that it involves more "extensive reading" – i.e. engaging with a wide range of content – but the main disadvantage of it may be that it prevents the reader from achieving a *flow* state (Wolf & Gottwald, 2016, p. 5):

> Lately I've been having trouble really plunging into a book or into games, I don't know why this is, whether it's because I spend a lot of time online and because I'm actually browsing rather than reading, looking for keywords. I have to get to the resolution and it's a bit scary and it bothers me, I feel like it used to be easy for me to immerse myself, maybe it was because I had fewer worries, more free time, I was able to read more carelessly [R74].

> Ostatnio mam kłopot z takim naprawdę zagłębieniem się w książkę czy w gry. Nie wiem, z czego to wynika. Czy to wynika z dużej ilości czasu spędzonego w sieci i tego, że już rzeczywiście przeglądam, a nie czytam, szukam słów kluczowych. Muszę dojść do pointy i to jest trochę przerażające i to mnie martwi. Mam wrażenie, że kiedyś było mi łatwo zanurzyć się, może to wynikało z tego że miał[x]m mniej zmartwień, więcej wolnego czasu, mógł[x]m bardziej sobie beztrosko czytać.

Since the advent of television, we have faced the challenge of evolving audiovisual media taking time away from the pleasure reading. As Leah Price puts it: "When we mourn the book, we're really mourning the death of those in-between moments (waiting in line, riding, a bus) that nineteenth-century changes in lighting and transportation made hospitable to light reading, and that twenty-first communications infrastructures made available to paid labor". (2019, p. 8). It seems that digital technologies, the third innovation to make books more accessible and affordable – following the movable printing press in the fifteenth century and the paperback revolution in the 1940s – have solved distribution problems by removing the limitations imposed by the materiality of the book, allowing people to buy or rent digital copies on demand and to consume much like fast food (Pennington & Waxler, 2018, p. 99) vast amounts of streaming content (in "all you can read" mode), in some cases even for a monthly flat fee for access to an entire platform rather than paying for a specific item (Augustyn et al. 2024). At the same time, however, growing problems for many consumers are the dilemma "of what to choose" (Góralska, 2021a) and the shrinking time and/or ability to consume the long form of any cultural content. This decreasing attention span results in watching 10-minute chunks, speeding up a video or listening to an audiobook at double speed to eliminate distractions and the anxiety caused by a lack of stimulation (Ellis, 2020). Content creators respond by breaking up their work into a series of episodes and building an audience around the series, which ultimately lasts much longer than a film, but has the potential to hold the viewers' attention more successfully and engage them more deeply. Compared to a video game, which somehow forces and supports attention by engaging players in a decision-making process, long-form reading may seem unengaging to some people, at least at certain stages of their lives:

> A game is closer to a complete transportation into another world. I think that a game is able to do a little more than a book, if it is good, because it is more engaging than a book. Because our generation and the younger generation has too many stimuli, and sometimes it's just hard to get that attention… Our ability to concentrate on one thing just through games can adapt more to this law [Age].
>
> Grze bliżej do takiego właśnie kompletnego przeniesienia się w ten inny świat. Uważam, że gra byłaby w stanie zrobić trochę więcej, jeśli jest dobra, od takiej książki, no bo ona jest bardziej angażująca niż książka. Bo jednak to moje pokolenie i młodsze ma zbyt wiele bodźców i czasami właśnie ciężko o ten „atenszyn"… Nasza umiejętność skupienia się na jednej rzeczy właśnie poprzez gry może bardziej się dostosować do tego prawa.

– notes one of the youngest participants in the study, and two others, much older, share his/her sentiments. Thus, it is not just the current generation of 20-somethings who are experiencing what is called *hyperattention* (Hayles, 2010). Although there is a hypothesis that attention span improves with age (van de Ven et al., 2023, p. 80), the habits of many media consumers and a lack of cognitive patience may ultimately reduce their ability to engage with reading long forms (Wolf, 2019, pp. 46, 72–72). In contemporary society of accelerated technological development, slowing down often means falling behind. However, the inability to focus and find our own voice in a cacophony of noise can become a real problem, and contribute to feeling distressed.

During reading

Being immersed in the story world

Creating conditions for flow
While reading a book, the reader tries to enter a state of mental activity that can be safely experienced. According to Mihály Csíkszentmihályi, when the challenges we face are in balance with our skills, we can experience *flow* (*an optimal experience, an autotelic*

experience, a peak experience) (2014, pp. XX, 273). An optimal experience should be seen as an affective-cognitive state (Duman & Aghajanian, 2012; Etkin et al., 2011; see "dual-process models of entertainment", e.g. in Bartsch et al., 2014, p. 136; Hogan, 2022; Stanovich et al., 2021, p. 793). In the context of reading, it may be defined as a state of voluntary focus on a book ("attentional focus"), resulting in complete involvement in reading. This phenomenon occurs when an individual's awareness is narrowed and their concentration is high, thereby creating a state in which everyday concerns and reflections on the ego are set aside[6] and the reader is fully engaged (emotionally, cognitively, behaviourally) in the activity under their control thanks to appropriate skills to the challenge: "In such a state person feels fully alive and in control, because he or she can direct the flow of reciprocal information that unites person and environment in an interactive system. I know that I am alive, that I am somebody, that I matter…" (Csíkszentmihályi, 2008, p. 8).

Flow is an autotelic, "intrinsically rewarding experience", resulting in the reader achieving a sense of satisfaction and self-efficacy. It allows one to "turn adversity into an enjoyable challenge". This state is preceded by a struggle with overwhelming information and destressing (known as "triggering release"), which comes from constantly comparing oneself to others. As a result of the aroused engagement, motivation becomes more intrinsic. The temporary deactivation of the dorsolateral prefrontal cortex frees one from the inner critic's disapproval of one's self-esteem and allows one to give full attention to the task at hand. The reader also seems to act effortlessly. Once the *flow* state has ended, the final phase involves returning to normal (recovery or prioritising recovery) and restoring emotional balance (Csíkszentmihályi, 2022, pp. 91–117).

There are types of books, stories or passages that do not require a deep dive, because they are designed to "assimilate" sequences of events and to primarily arouse curiosity and a hunger to read, while others invite slower and more careful reading, evoke emotional memories in the reader and present a challenge to cross the boundaries of their self-concept:

> If it's the kind of story that's light, easy and pleasant, where he loves her, she doesn't love him or he killed her, I can read it on a tram or on the beach… and if it's something that requires more attention, that I know I'd like to think about more… then I'll have this feeling that it's a pity… that I read it too fast… that maybe I could have gotten more out of it… so it's not a matter of someone watching… it's more about how I can focus in the circumstances and what kind of focus this particular book requires [R62].

> Jeśli to jest właśnie taka historia lekka, łatwa i przyjemna, gdzie on kocha ją, ona nie kocha go albo on ją zabił, no to ja to mogę przeczytać w tramwaju czy na plaży… a jak to jest coś takiego, co wymaga większej uwagi, co wiem, że

---

6 Some studies have shown, that too much accessibility of the self-concept (self-focus) during reading can reduce experience-taking and flow and inhibit the process of projection (inclusion of the self in the other) or introjection (inclusion of the other in the self) (Kaufman & Libby, 2012, pp. 5, 15).

chciał[x]bym sobie bardziej też przemyśleć… to będę miał/a takie poczucie, że mi szkoda tej książki… że za szybko ją przeczytał[x]m… że może mogł[x] m więcej z tego wynieść… więc to nie chodzi o to, że ktoś patrzy… tylko bardziej o to, jak ja się mogę w tych okolicznościach skupić i jakiego skupienia wymaga ta konkretna książka.

Without sufficient attention and "accommodation" in terms of time, place or circumstances, as well as knowledge and skills, the reader may miss meaning or be deprived of the satisfaction of reading, or feel that the product is wasted or at least not fully used. Furthermore, when they are not able to meet a challenge posed by the book (the skills do not meet the requirements or are insufficient), they may experience anxiety.

The ability to mentally isolate oneself from one's environment enables one to enter the state of *flow* (Bilandzic et al., 2019, p. 806; Oatley, 1994, p. 59). Some readers declare that they have no problem ignoring their surroundings[7], as long as the book seems engrossing enough:

> I can surprisingly switch off and really focus on the plot, even if there is some commotion and something going on around me [R31].

> Potrafię się o dziwo wyłączyć i naprawdę skupić na akcji, nawet jak tam naokoło jest jakiś ruch i coś się dzieje.

There are also those who, in order to immerse themselves deeply, have to cut themselves off from outside stimuli or even experience a kind of sensory deprivation (Holland, 2009, pp. 45, 47). It might be helpful to put the phone away while reading, perhaps in another room, to help you focus on what you are reading. For some readers, night-time reading in bed is a deeply immersive experience. It creates a special feeling of intimacy and of experiencing something that seems forbidden because it happens out of sight of others (Manguel, 2023, p. 221):

> It's not that I'm not able to read at all, let's say when something is going on… I don't dive deep… if we're talking about perfect conditions for reading, I'll always strive to create them for myself, that is, an isolated bubble not only mentally, but also tangibly, that is, in the evening, when it's really quiet, in general the atmosphere of night reading… then words have more power… it creates such conditions a bit like in a vacuum chamber, that then this content gets to you even more [R49].

> To nie jest tak, że ja w ogóle nie jestem w stanie czytać, powiedzmy w momencie, kiedy coś się dzieje… nie wchodzę głęboko… jeżeli mówimy o takich idealnych

---

7 "Ease of being engaged despite adverse surroundings" is considered as one of the dimensions of narrative engageability developed by Helena Bilandzic et al. Others include: propensity for presence (related to story world), emotional engageability (related to character), propensity for suspense/curiosity (related to plot), and ease of accepting unrealism (2019, p. 806).

> warunkach do lektury, to ja zawsze będę dążył/a do tego, żeby je sobie stworzyć, czyli po prostu nie dość, że mentalnie taka wyizolowana bańka, to jeszcze właśnie wręcz namacalnie, czyli taka pora wieczorna, kiedy rzeczywiście jest cicho, w ogóle ta atmosfera tego czytania nocnego… te słowa działają ze zdwojoną mocą… to stwarza takie warunki trochę jak w komorze próżniowej, że wtedy ta treść w jeszcze większym stopniu do ciebie dociera.

Although it is impossible to predict which book will meet which reader's needs, even if they have read it before, it is much easier to indicate what reactions it is likely to provoke when the reader is in a state of *flow*; it should hold the reader's attention from the beginning, to involve them in the events, to make them experience what they imagine, and to stimulate them intellectually:

> It's something that hooks you from the first page and it's hard to tear yourself away from this book, really hard, and even when I think I'll put the book down after this chapter, it ends in such a way that I want to find out what happens next and I keep reading, because there is just such a suspense what will happen next… when a book is well written, I don't know until the end who is hiding what and who is the villain [R31].

> To jest też coś takiego właśnie, że wciąga od pierwszej strony i ciężko się od tej książki oderwać, no naprawdę ciężko i nawet jak myślę, że dobrze, to na tym rozdziale skończę, to jednak on się kończy tak, że mam ochotę dowiedzieć się, co dalej i jednak dalej czytam, bo właśnie jest to takie napięcie, że co będzie dalej… jak jest dobrze napisana książka, to do końca nie wiem, kto tu co ukrywa i kto jest tym winowajcą.

> The first chapter is decisive really, sometimes the second chapter, if it's so dense that it's hard to get through, I feel that it isn't getting me hooked, that I'm distracted by everything around me, I can't get into the book, it discourages me, as if it gives me a feeling that the book doesn't show promise… that I won't be able to tear myself away from the book, and I don't like things to be that way [R71].

> Decydujący jest pierwszy rozdział tak naprawdę, czasami drugi, jeżeli jest taki ciężki, że trudno przez niego przebrnąć, gdzieś tam czuję, że mnie nie wciąga, że rozprasza mnie wszystko dookoła, nie umiem się gdzieś tam zagłębić w tą książkę, no to mnie zniechęca, jakby daje mi przeczucie, że książka się nie zapowiada… że nie będę się mógł/mogła oderwać od tej książki, a ja tak nie lubię.

Reading is intense from the start. It is usually difficult to put a book down and not think about "what happens next". The compelling book has the potential to draw the reader in so thoroughly that they may find themselves completely immersed in the story:

It's a book that I really can't tear myself away from, it's hard for me to leave the house and put it down [R82].

To książka, od której naprawdę nie mogę się oderwać, aż mi ciężko po prostu wyjść z domu i ją zostawić.

When a book pulled me in, I was able to read almost non-stop, all day long, over the holidays, without any problem, on trams, buses, at home [R74].

Potrafił[x]m czytać, jak książka mnie wciągnęła, niemalże bez przerwy, całymi dniami, przez święta, bez żadnego problemu, w tramwajach, autobusach, w domu.

If something grabs me, I can read a book, depending on how thick it is, in one day, in a few hours, if it is captivating, I just lose myself in it and read [R71].

Jeśli mnie coś tu interesuje, potrafię książkę przeczytać, w zależności od grubości, w jeden dzień, w kilka godzin, jeżeli jest wciągająca, to gdzieś tam zatracam się po prostu i czytam.

I read something and I get so caught up in the reading that I think to myself "two more pages" and the two pages turn into 50… it feels like a shame to stop reading even though it's, for example, 2 a.m. [R1].

Czytam coś i tak bardzo się wkręcam w to czytanie, że myślę sobie, a to jeszcze dwie strony i z tych dwóch stron się robi 50… szkoda mi przerwać lektury pomimo tego, że jest na przykład druga w nocy.

Readers gradually lose track of time, and their reactions to what is going on outside (nightfall or discomfort) become lessened (Kuijpers, 2023, p. 3). Instead, they actually feel what is happening in the world of the narrative into which they have been transported:

> I remember when I was a child and I was reading James Oliver Curwood… a trilogy and one time I lost track of time while reading, I was sitting in my room in the attic, and it got dark. I simply didn't notice it because I was so engrossed in the story and I could no longer see the letters because it went dark and then I realized it was dark, for 15 minutes I couldn't get out of my chair, I was so afraid that I was just about to die a horrible death, that that tribe was lurking outside the door. It was such an irrational experience that I remember it to this day, that's why I was so frightened, because the book just totally sucked me in… it was winter there, they were following the trail of some wolves and I had the feeling that I had frost in my hair [R53].
>
> Pamiętam z dzieciństwa, jak czytał[x]m Jamesa Olivera Curwooda… taką trylogię i kiedyś się zaczytał[x]m, siedział[x]m na strychu w moim pokoju na poddaszu i zrobiło się ciemno. Ja po prostu nie zauważył[x]m tego, bo tak mnie to wciągnę-

> ło i przestał[x]m widzieć litery, bo się zrobiło ciemno i wtedy się zorientował[x]m, że jest ciemno, przez 15 minut nie mogł[x]m się ruszyć z fotela, tak się bał[x]m, że po prostu zaraz zginę marnie, że tamto plemię to już się czai za drzwiami. To było tak irracjonalne w ogóle doświadczenie, że pamiętam to do dzisiaj, dlatego się tego tak bał[x]m, bo po prostu to mnie totalnie wciągnęło... zima tam była, oni szli tropem jakichś wilków i miał[x]m wrażenie, że mam szron na włosach.

As can be seen, the return to reality in the psychological sense is not immediate. After a reader finishes reading, they remain "under the spell" of what they have experienced for some time. The moment of transportation itself is difficult to grasp. It is something that, as Gottschall puts it, "is done to us, not by us" (2021, p. 36).[8] The reader surrenders to the book, which "draws them in". Reading can strongly influence their imagination ("I could almost smell the scents"):

> She was wearing a blue dress and had beautiful buttoned gloves, and I am already imagining what kind of gloves she has, and thinking to myself that I have always wanted to have such gloves [Gender].
>
> Była w błękitnej sukni i miała przepiękne rękawiczki na guziczki zapinane i ja sobie już wyobrażam, jakie ona ma te rękawiczki i myślę sobie, że ja takie rękawiczki zawsze chciałam mieć.

The ability to form "personal images" (seeing the plot)[9] while reading, and not remembering the physicality of reading (reading without conscious effort), can indicate whether the reader is enough engaged (Wolf & Gottwald, 2016, p. 113; 2019, p. 41):

> – I am lucky that when I read a book, I do not put sentences together, I instantly see the plot in my head, I imagine it... when I am engrossed in reading, I do not remember the physicality of reading after the first two pages. I just project a movie in my mind.
> – And this happens with every book? I mean the images.
> – The ones that give me joy. If books don't get me to that stage, then they don't interest me [R21].
>
> – Ja mam to szczęście, że jak czytam książkę, to ja nie składam zdania, od razu widzę fabułę w głowie, ja sobie wyobrażam to... jak mnie lektura wciągnie, to ja po pierwszych dwóch stronach nie pamiętam fizyczności czytania. Po prostu wyświetlam sobie film.
> – A z każdą książką tak Pan/i ma? Chodzi mi o te obrazy.

---

8 Some studies suggest that there may be a gender difference in the ability to transport (particularly on the emotional subscale) and that women may transport more (Gottschall, 2021, p. 61; Green & Brock, 2000, pp. 703, 711; Van Laer et al., 2014, p. 803).

9 Imagining something as vividly as if it were real is called "hyperphantasia". The absence of images is called "aphantasia" (Wojciehowski & Gallese, 2022, p. 68).

> — Te, które sprawiają mi radość. Książki, w których nie przejdę na taki etap, to one mnie nie ciekawią.

But not all readers are capable of mental imagery, as Laura Otis argues on the basis of Ellen Esrock's research.[10] However, some responses, such as a change in breathing rhythm, may be physiological indicators of being in a different state (2022, p. 22). Moreover, as Melanie Green and Timothy Brock have shown that when readers are fully immersed in the world of the story, their beliefs are more "story-consistent" and their evaluations of the protagonist more favourable (2000, p. 701–702). It should be noted that regardless of the valence of the story (negative or positive), there may be an interest in reading it and the reader may be transported into the world of the story (Oliver & Bartsch, 2010, p. 501). Even stories that may seem uncomfortable or unpleasant to the reader can captivate them (Mar et al., 2011, p. 820). Also, knowing that the story is fictional may not affect the level of absorption (Bilandzic et al., 2019, p. 806; Hartung et al., 2017, p. 12; Thompson et al., 2023, p. 9). This is because reading suspenseful stories requires more cognitive effort to check their veracity. As a result, the reader may adopt a less critical approach (Bilandzic et al., 2019, p. 265; Gottschall, 2021, p. 31; Green & Brock, 2000, p. 703; Thissen et al., 2021, p. 2):

> I think that if a book grabs me, that is, it is interesting from the very beginning, I do not subject it to any analysis, because I just lose myself, zone out and read until I finish reading [R71].
>
> Myślę, że jak książka jest taka, że wciąga, czyli jest interesująca od samego początku, to chyba nie poddaję jakiejś takiej analizie, bo po prostu się zatracam, odpływami i czytam, aż nie skończę czytać.

It should be noted, that the perception of the narrative world as logical and believable may be a prerequisite for some readers with higher cognitive needs to experience transportation into the world of the story (Green & Brock, 2000, p. 711). Such readers may find it necessary to check facts. It can help them to orient themselves and navigate through the novel, thereby fostering a more comprehensive understanding of the text and enabling more accurate prediction of the plot, but more research is needed to confirm when this happens, during or after reading.[11]

> This has always fascinated me, no matter what I've been reading, how you can see things on a map, this is an old habit of mine, as in the 1970s–1980s I was reading this series of Simenon's Commissioner Maigret a lot. It took place in Paris,

---

10 "An emotional response can be embodied without using a person's own sensory experiences to reproduce what characters are doing. Alternatively, readers might react through their "somatic-viscero-motor system (SVM)" (Esrock, p. 79–80 – see in Otis, 2022, p. 22).

11 For more on the influence of self-efficacy on narrative transportation, see e.g. Van Laer, 2014, p. 811. The difference between *transportation* and *cognitive elaboration*, as highlighted by Green and Brock, should also be taken into account (2000, p. 718–719).

> I hadn't been to Paris at that time, I wanted to see how it looks on a map, where the streets are… how this commissioner in charge of the investigation moves around and actually the topography in Simenon was very accurate, although he was living in Brussels and writing about Paris [Age].
>
> To mnie zawsze fascynowało, niezależnie od tego, co czytał[x]m, jak to można zobaczyć na mapie. To jest moja stara przypadłość, jak w latach 70.-80. czytał[x]m masowo ten cykl o komisarzu Maigrecie Simenona, to się działo w Paryżu, nigdy nie był[x]m w Paryżu, chciał[x]m zobaczyć, jak to wygląda na mapie, gdzie są te ulice… jak ten prowadzący śledztwo komisarz się przemieszcza i rzeczywiście ta topografia u Simenona była bardzo dokładna, chociaż a on siedział w Brukseli i pisał o Paryżu.

What takes the reader from the real world to the story world is also its alternativity (the distance it establishes from reality). The quotes about losing oneself in a book and wanting to escape reflect this desire:

> We can get transferred to this entirely different world. And it's very interesting to see the vision of people who look through a kind of kaleidoscope at our world and create a completely different picture, and that's great, that's the element that transports me from our real world to this fantasy world [R84].
>
> Możemy się właśnie bardziej przenieść w ten zupełnie inny świat. I to jest takie bardzo ciekawe zobaczyć wizję ludzi, którzy patrzą przez jakiś taki kalejdoskop na ten nasz świat i tworzą zupełnie inny obraz i to jest wspaniałe właśnie, to jest ten element, który mnie przenosi z naszego rzeczywistego świata do tego świata fantastyki.

Apparently, the aesthetic distance created by the novel allows the reader to see themselves differently, and perhaps even to recognise what is happening in their lives by putting it into perspective. According to Roman Ingarden "aesthetic experience begins with a "preliminary emotion" that "interrupt[s] … the 'normal' course of our lives [such that we] begin to occupy ourselves with something which, while not appertaining, seemingly, to our lives, enriches it, at the same time, and confers upon it a new sense" (Kuiken et al., 2004, pp. 172–173). One of the four dimensions of absorption, beyond deep concentration, transportation[12] and mental imagery, is emotional involvement (Kuijpers et al., 2014, 2023). "Feeling" is the vehicle exile from daily routines, according to Mikel Dufrenne (Kuiken et al., 2004, p. 173). It builds up and stimulates engagement in both a suspenseful (action or plot-driven) story and a character-driven story:

> There are feelings… impressions connected with what is happening in the book, in my case it is usually tension, if I pick up a book that really pulls me in [R49].

---

[12] Cognitive and emotional engagement and mental imagery can also be seen as processes of experiencing transportation (Riggs & Knobloch-Westerwick, 2023, pp. 2–3).

> Pojawiają się odczucia… wrażenia związane z tym, co się dzieje w tej książce, u mnie jest to najczęściej napięcie, jeśli złapię taki tekst, który rzeczywiście mnie wciągnie.

A suspenseful plot encourages the reader to engage with the narrative. Greater investment in the protagonist evokes emotions that help to make the reader aware of the significance of certain events, to anticipate[13] what might happen next and how they should react to it. It also fosters a deeper understanding of a character's perspective and the intricacies of the plot (Brewer & Lichtenstein, 1982; Kuiken, 2004; Miall & Kuiken, 2002, p. 227; van Peer & Pander Maat, 1996).

(Re)constructing narratives

When we read, we combine what we have learnt in the process of socialisation and what we know well from the real world with what we learn from a story depicted in a book. The content is actively processed by the reader relating it to their own experiences. In order to construct meaning, the reader, on the basis of pre-existing knowledge (e.g., genre schemas and stereotypes), activates different mental models: *the story-world model* (including place, time period, and story-world logic), *the character model*, and *the situation model* (Busselle & Bilandzic, 2009, pp. 257–260; Bortolussi & Dixon, 2003, p. 16; Oatley, 2012, pp. 18–19). Richard Gerrig describes the script as „a memory structure that specifies a stereotypical sequence of actions that people carry out in familiar situations" (2018, p. 32). Similarly, David Miall characterises scripts as frames or schemata – "those stereotyped processes of behaviour by which we orient ourselves and know what to expect" (2006, p. 17).

Readers' expectations, attitudes and evaluations of the book and its individual elements are to some extent shaped by their familiarity with genre conventions and the culture in which the book was written, which gets honed as they learn more about the world and read more books. The quality of the representation depends on the reader's prior knowledge (Bortolussi & Dixon, 2003, pp. 16–17).[14] As Helena Bilandzic and Rick W. Busselle have shown, readers' familiarity with a particular genre helps them to enter the world of the story (2008, p. 523). Tom Van Laer et al. consider familiarity with a genre (defined as prior knowledge or experience) as one of the "story receiver antecedents" of narrative transportation, along with "transportability" (which is related to empathy and "mental imagery") and "demographic antecedents" such as age, gender or education. "Storyteller antecedents" include "identifiable characters", "verisimilitude" and "imaginable plot" (2014, p. 802–804).

To navigate an unfamiliar world, the reader needs to find some physical or mental landmarks to tame the space and make the book more accessible and cognitively and

---

13 The right prefrontal cortex is responsible for analysing the text and making predictions in order to evaluate the hypothesis (Wolf, 2019, p. 61).
14 Less-skilled readers may find it difficult to immerse themselves (Gerrig, 2018, p. 19 as cited in Nell, 1988).

emotionally appealing (Kuiken et al., 2004, p. 175). While more fantastical worlds can certainly arouse curiosity and a desire to explore, and encourage a search for analogies in the human condition portrayed, or activate predictions about the future, they can also potentially arouse a reluctance to change one's way of thinking through the extra processing required to enter a completely different universe, or a fear of getting too deeply involved in a multi-volume, time-consuming reading. Story worlds that are familiar or even close to the reader (family hometown, familiar place) can evoke some nostalgic memories:

> For example, when I read Sapkowski's "Hussite Trilogy", there are references to the city where I live, it's also fun to read about historical events in the place where you are at the moment. This adds to the appeal of the book. It's like home [Place].
>
> Na przykład jak czytał[x]m trylogię Sapkowskiego husycką, no to nawiązania do miasta, w którym mieszkam, to też się fajnie czyta, jeżeli są opisane gdzieś tam historyczne wydarzenia w miejscu, w którym się w tej chwili przebywa. Coś tam podnosi atrakcyjność książki. To jak w domu.

In reading such books, the recipients may also be interested in the accuracy of the author in describing places that are familiar to them.

To make the story more coherent and personally meaningful, the reader adapts the author's vision to their current goals. In doing so, they build on what is known and "closest to the reality we know" and correct only what is necessary to maintain coherence in the text.[15] A narrative that is too descriptive can be a limitation because it hinders concretisation (Ingarden, 1960, pp. 60–62). In this way, readers are discouraged from filling in gaps in the text (Gerrig, 2018, p. 21). They may feel overwhelmed or even bored:

> Often, and this is the habit of many modern writers, they try to describe this world down to the last detail... there is no room for the reader... there must be 1,500 adjectives, well there doesn't have to be, I will contribute my imagination to it and build something for myself" [R25].
>
> Często, i to jest nawyk wielu tych współczesnych pisarzy, oni próbują ten świat opisać do reszty szczegółowo... tam nie ma tego miejsca dla czytelnika... musi być 1500 przymiotników, no nie musi, ja już sobie do tego swoją wyobraźnię dołożę i sobie coś zbuduję.

This type of description can also seem insignificant to the progress of the plot, especially if the reader is looking for content that will evoke emotions (need for affect, need for suspense – see Bilandzic et al., 2019, p. 807.)

---

15 For more on how readers reconstruct fictional worlds (*the principle of minimal departure*), see Marie-Laure Ryan, 1980, pp. 403, 405–406. The logic of interference during reading (*the minimalist hypothesis*) is described by McKoon & Ratcliff (1981) and Gerrig, 2018, p. 13, pp. 30–31.

> I look forward to events or descriptions of emotions more than nature or that the plot takes place in some town and that town is being described, but I can already see that this will not make much difference [R92].
>
> Bardziej czekam na akcję albo takie rzeczy o emocjach opisane niż już właśnie przyroda albo że gdzieś się dzieje w jakimś miasteczku i to miasteczko jest opisywane, ale ja już widzę, że to nie będzie miało większego znaczenia.

A certain level of mastery of the author's writing and the coherence of the narrative world presented is then expected, as the right combination of components helps the reader to anticipate subsequent events and/or appreciate the work.

> I think it was Vonnegut who said that each successive sentence is supposed to either develop a character or move the plot forward… one can see this craftsmanship, you can get something out of each sentence for yourself or some thought out of it [R62].
>
> To chyba Vonnegut powiedział, że właśnie każde kolejne zdanie ma albo budować postać, albo posuwać akcję do przodu… widać ten kunszt, z każdego zdania można coś wyjąć dla siebie jako właśnie jakieś tam przemyślenie.

However, familiarity with a story world or story-world logic may not be sufficient for transportation. Just as important is self-reference (Damasio, 2022, p. 109), which can be facilitated by personal resonance with situations familiar to the reader:

> In "Normal People" she captured something, in terms of the generation of contemporary thirty-year-olds… I think I found my problems described there simply [Age].
>
> W „Normalnych ludziach" ona coś złapała, jeśli chodzi o pokolenie współczesnych trzydziestolatków… ja tam chyba znalazł[x]m swoje problemy po prostu.

Sometimes it is not even an image or problem described by the author, but a word or phrase (an associative stimulus) that triggers the appropriate cognitive category, activating a script or a theme in someone's life (Oatley, 2012, p. 98). The activated emotional process, which arises on the grounds of emotionally similar experiences (type-similar, see Kelly as cited in Hogan, 2022, p. 161) and involves perceptual-motor components, may lead to (partial and temporary) identification. This is manifested in a tendency to "empathic identification"[16] with the protagonist ("feel[ing] the emotions of others as if they were our own", "to feel with another", "as if readers have gone through it themselves" [R43]). Readers can also imagine what it would be like to step into the character's shoes (de Vignemont & Singer, 2006, p. 435; Wolf, 2019, p. 43):

---

16 It involves perceptual-motor components (Dvash & Shamay-Tsoory, 2014, p. 285).

> I often think to myself, oh this is just how I would feel. Or that this is how I would behave in such a situation, right? I often identify with the character that way [R35].
>
> Wielokrotnie tak jest, że sobie myślę, oj to tak jak ja. Albo, że jak ja bym się zachował/a w takiej sytuacji, tak? Często utożsamiam się tak z bohaterem.

However, not all readers are familiar with such feeling:

> I don't really identify with the characters, like I don't feel like I'm the one doing such a thing or something, but when my favourite character was going through something, something was happening to him, then I reacted differently… I do not know how I would behave, because this behaviour, in my opinion, is forced by the situation [R32].
>
> Nie bardzo uosabiam się z bohaterami, żebym to akurat ja takie coś robił/a czy coś, ale jak ten ulubiony bohater coś przeżywał, coś mu się działo, to człowiek tak jakoś inaczej reagował… Nie wiem, jakbym się zachował/a, bo to zachowanie, moim zdaniem, wymusza sytuacja.

If there is no reference to the "self" instead of empathizing with the protagonist, the reader will rather sympathize with them (Gerrig & Jacovina, 2009, p. 241), wondering why things happened to them and how they can get out of trouble:

> If I like a character, I cheer for them… I lament that the protagonist receives a blow, that he fails again, because I got attached to this character and I would prefer that he did not have such an uphill struggle… when a good character is caught in an intrigue and cannot extricate themselves from it, then it's a pity that the author does not like them so much… but thanks to this, these mechanisms and the whole plot picks up pace and things keep moving, that's why such a bad thing happened [R57].
>
> Jak polubię, to kibicuję… żałował[x]m, że bohater dostaje w łeb, że znowu mu nie idzie, bo związał[x]m się z tym bohaterem i wtedy wolał[x]bym, żeby on jednak aż tak pod górkę nie miał… jak bohater dobry trafia w intrygę i nie potrafi się z niej wyplątać, to wtedy szkoda, że autor tak go nie lubi… ale dzięki temu te mechanizmy i ta cała fabuła nabiera prędkości i coś się dalej dzieje, po coś się takie zło wydarzyło.

Information about what the literary character thinks, feels, says and does makes the reader more aware of the impact of the event, the challenges the literary character faces and their motivations. A reader who understands the plight of a protagonist facing adversity, names the emotions the protagonist is experiencing and anticipates further developments, has the ability to mentalise, i.e. the kind of empathy that is called cognitive or cognitive-affective (Aue et al., 2021, pp. 8, 10; Hogan, 2022, p. 157). It supports the integration of the worldview that the reader can and wants to accept, and provide behavioural patterns that allow them to test themselves in new roles.

Identifying with the character and finding oneself
Getting to know the protagonist
The experience of detachment from reality comes with a change in the role of the reader:

> In the moment of reading, I can stop being myself and be transported to another world, a world not the one I am in, but one I choose for myself at that moment [R82].
>
> W chwili czytania mogę przestać być sobą i przenieść się w inny świat, w świat nie ten, w którym jestem, tylko taki, który w danym momencie sam/a sobie wybiorę.

The feeling that one stops being oneself occurs not only as a result of disengagement through partial sensory deprivation and silencing of the inner critic, but also of the experience of "thinking someone else's thoughts." Georges Poulet describes reading as "the strange invasion of my person by the thoughts of another. I am a self who I granted the experience of thinking thoughts foreign to him" (as cited in Gerrig, 2018, p. 22).[17] Nathalie Phillips points out that close reading of fiction activates "regions of the brain that are aligned to what the characters are both feeling and doing" (Wolf, 2019, pp. 51–52). The reader gets to know what the protagonist thinks and feels, not just how they behave. This gives the reader the feeling of knowing the character well, or at least gaining more or less access to how they perceive the world and unfolding events. With this insight, reader can make judgments about the character's attitudes and relate them to themselves (Gottschall, 2021, p. 35).

Depending on the way that they gain insight into the character's inner life – from their own perspective, that of another character who is an internal focalizer ("who sees" – Bortolussi & Dixon, 2003, p. 11), or that of an omniscient narrator – the way they evaluate the character's behaviour may change from dispositional attributions, typical of an observer's perspective (3rd-person narration) to situational attributions, typical of an actor's perspective (1st-person narration). Some studies suggest that first-person narration may affect spatial memory of events and the degree of immersion, among other things, by reducing the mental load associated with taking the protagonist's perspective (Hartung et al., 2016, p. 14; 2017, p. 3). The first-person perspective promotes greater emotional engagement with the protagonist compared to the third-person perspective. In experiments conducted by Franziska Hartung et al, third-person narratives were rated as less fascinating and sadder (2017, pp. 7, 10). Geoff Kaufman and Lisa Libby have found that the highest levels of *experience-taking* (the term they use instead of *identification*) and the greatest changes in the participants' behaviour were elicited by the first-person narratives

---
17 It is worth mentioning that some experiments have been conducted on the influence of "Free Indirect Discourse" (FID), which offers the illusion of insight into the character's mind and feelings (Hakemulder & Koopman, 2010).

(2012, p. 2). However, this is not always the case and individual preferences, skills and needs (e.g. more cognitive insight) may come into play. The use of first-person narration can sometimes make readers uncomfortable (Keen, 2007, pp. X–XI). This could also be due to limited reading experience or unfamiliarity with the genre.

> No, I don't identify with the characters yet, absolutely... even to the point where I used to have a very big problem reading books that were written in the first person. I didn't feel it at all, I didn't know how to find my footing in it, but lately I've been reading something and it's already completely different, it's as if with the number of the books I've read, I've started developing maturity and openness to new forms [R56].

> Nie, jeszcze nie utożsamiam się z bohaterami, absolutnie... nawet do tego stopnia, że miał[x]m kiedyś bardzo duży problem z czytaniem książek pisanych w pierwszej osobie. Nie czuł[x]m tego w ogóle, nie umiał[x]m się w tym odnaleźć, ale ostatnio coś tam czytał[x]m też i już zupełnie inaczej, nie, no jakby gdzieś tam z tą ilością tych przeczytanych książek ta dojrzałość i otwartość na nowe formy gdzieś tam mi wchodziła.

Alternatively, the author may have deviated from familiar conventions that the reader has assimilated. Readers' comments suggest that it would also be useful to explore how perspective changes the experience depending on the genre.

> It depends on the book. In fantasy, 1st-person narration doesn't work well very often. The narrator has to explain the world. In other genres, however, this narrowing of perspective is sometimes natural, and introduces mystery, uncertainty [R74].

> To zależy od książki. W fantastyce narracja pierwszoosobowa nie sprawdza się zbyt często. Tam narrator musi tłumaczyć świat. W innych gatunkach jednak to zawężenie perspektywy bywa naturalne, wprowadza tajemniczość, niepewność.

A third-person narrative, while potentially more demanding on the information processing system as it provides insight into the thoughts and behaviours of multiple characters, can in turn improve the anticipation of plot development and understanding of the broad context. To what extent it stimulates reading engagement remains to be studied. What is certain is that not always and not everyone consciously identifies with the protagonist (has the impression of becoming one, or that the protagonist is like them or has something in common with them). This is partially because "Not every text has the potential to resonate with a reader's self-concept" (Loi et al., 2023a, p. 49). The motivation to read can also vary from book to book:

> It depends on what book I'm reading at the time, if I can relate it to my life, but I don't read all books to analyse them so much and look for references [R71].

> To zależy, jaką książkę czytam w danym momencie, czy gdzieś tam mogę to odnieść też do swojego życia, ale nie, jakby nie wszystkie książki też się czyta po to, żeby gdzieś tam tak aż tak je analizować i szukać odniesień.

> There are books that I can't tear myself away from and where I am able to identify with the character and I can experience good or bad moments together with them… laugh or even get emotional or cry, but I don't know how to define this, because not always, not every book is so me as I would like it to be [R96].

> Bywają książki, gdzie nie potrafię się oderwać i gdzie potrafię się identyfikować z postacią i potrafię razem z nią przeżywać dobre czy złe chwile… roześmiać się, czy wręcz wzruszyć albo zapłakać, ale nie wiem, jak to określić, bo nie zawsze, nie każda książka jest w takim stopniu mną, jakbym chciał/a.

Identification of this kind, then, does not seem to be a necessary condition for engagement in reading:

> I think that if I see myself in the character in some way, then I will definitely look through his or her eyes, but if not, then just the world itself is interesting, for example, "The Lord of the Rings", so I can just be in this world and observe it [R84].

> Myślę, że jeśli widzę w bohaterze swój obraz w jakimś stopniu, no to na pewno będę patrzył/a przez jego oczy, ale jeśli nie, to po prostu sam świat ciekawy jest, na przykład, „Władca Pierścieni", że ja mogę po prostu być w tym świecie i to obserwować.

In addition, Kaufman and Libby claim that "a high degree of absorption into a narrative world is likely a necessary but not sufficient factor for experience-taking to occur" (2012, p. 8). The reader can become attached to a literary character, which means that they form an emotional bond with a character and invest themselves in their life, but do not necessary identify with them:

> I've already, let's say, established an emotional bond with the protagonist and some grave harm will happen to her/him, well then it really affects me [R45].

> Już powiedzmy nawiązał[x]m więź emocjonalną z bohaterem i jemu stanie się wielka krzywda, no to wtedy rzeczywiście porusza mnie to.

> Do I think that they are, for example, experiencing similar life dilemmas as me or something like that? No, but I do care about their fate, in the sense that it moves me emotionally. I think about them [R76].

> Czy myślę, że oni przeżywają na przykład podobne rozterki życiowe jak ja albo coś takiego? Nie, ale przejmuję się ich losami, w tym sensie, że poruszają mnie one emocjonalnie. Myślę o nich.

In this case, the distinction between reader and fictional character remains intact (Wojciehowski & Gallese, 2022, p. 63).

Keith Oatley posits that: "For a character to come alive, the reader needs to become emotionally attracted to him or unusual situation" (2012, p. 164). In order for the reader to be able to interact with the fictional character and to experience the congruent emotional state, the character should be antropomorphic (seen as a real person), identifiable (characteristic in some way, easy to distinguish from others) and likeable (they become "people whom we know", "quasi-real friends" – see Bálint & Tan, 2019; Gottschall, 2021, p. 35; Mar et al., 2011, p. 820; Oatley, 2012, pp. 115, 162; Van Laer et al., 2014, pp. 802–803; Zillmann & Cantor, 1977, pp. 163–164):

> It's a character with whom you would want to have a beer and talk, that is, you feel that he's a cool person simply [R81].

> To jest bohater, z którym by się chciało usiąść na piwo i pogadać, czyli czujesz, że on jest fajnym po prostu człowiekiem.

> I think when reading a book, people identify with the character, so it is important whether we like them or dislike them. And I think there were a couple of characters that I liked [R96].

> Myślę, że człowiek, czytając książkę, identyfikuje się z jakimś bohaterem, więc potrzebne jest to, czy go lubimy, czy mniej lubimy. I tak mi się wydaje, że było parę takich postaci, które lubił[x]m.

Certain characteristics or attitudes favour this, others do not. A character, even if they embody the best qualities, should not be free of vulnerabilities, because they make them more human and believable:

> … characters with problems, weaknesses, they are the most convincing, because they are closest to us [R74].

> … postacie z problemami, słabościami, są najbardziej przekonujące, bo są nam najbliższe.

> She needs to be cordial, not to be haughty, not to think she is better than others, to go through the same problems that we as women go through every day. I think it helps a lot to identify with such a person, if we see that she also faces the same things in life that we face, setbacks, stumbling blocks, if we see that she had, for example, a difficult childhood, then it allows us to get closer to such a character and identify with her [Gender].

> Musi być serdeczna, nie wywyższać się, nie uważać się za lepszą od innych, przeżywać te same problemy, które my przeżywamy jako kobiety na co dzień. Myślę, że to bardzo pomaga w utożsamieniu się z taką osobą, jeżeli widzimy, że spotyka ją w życiu też to samo, co nas spotyka, jakieś niepowodzenia, potyczki, jeżeli

widzimy, że miała na przykład trudno w dzieciństwie, to gdzieś tam pozwala zbliżyć się do takiej postaci i się z nią utożsamić.

However, it would be difficult to come up with some fixed catalogue of desirable qualities:

> You know what, I just have to find the character likeable in many ways, he/she doesn't have to have one specific, let's say, trait that wow he's funny, then I like him. No. Sometimes it's the odd characters in the book, but there's something about them that makes me say, I like him, I like her, and let's say I enjoy reading what they do, what they look like, how they behave, I become friends with that character [R45].

> Wiesz co, musi mi przypasować po prostu postać pod wieloma względami. Nie ma jakiejś jednej, określonej powiedzmy cechy, że ooo jest zabawny, to go lubię. Nie. Czasami to są dziwne postacie z książki, ale coś jest takiego, co mówię, lubię go, lubię ją i sprawia mi przyjemność, jak czytam, co robi, jak wygląda, jak się zachowuje. Zaprzyjaźniam się z tą postacią.

Anne Hamby and David Brinberg argue that when a reader identifies some values or beliefs in a story that are consistent with their beliefs, their subsequent acceptance may also include other beliefs implied by the story (2016, p. 499). The study by Kaufman and Libby shows that when a protagonist is perceived as an in-group person, *experience-taking* is more likely and higher than when a character is an out-group person in terms of race, ethnicity or sexual orientation. There is also evidence to suggest that readers may break through the experiential barrier towards an out-group character when their difference is revealed later in the narrative (2012, pp. 8–10).

John S. Sabo and Roger Giner-Sorolla have tested the hypothesis that reading fiction gives readers a "fictional pass" that allows them to mitigate moral condemnation of a protagonist who has done something wrong (harm violation), especially when the behaviour that violates acceptable norms is mild or justifiable and understandable in the circumstances, and the act itself is not a violation of purity (e.g. the human body or a cultural taboo) that indicates the character's moral wickedness (2017, p. 134, 152–153).

> In "The Tattooist of Auschwitz", for example, I liked Lali a lot, because he was basically a good person, helpful, even though he did bad things [R45].

> W „Tatuażyście z Auschwitz" na przykład Lalego polubił[x]m bardzo, no bo w gruncie rzeczy dobry człowiek, pomocny, mimo że robił złe rzeczy.

But if their behaviour cannot be excused or justified, so that there is nothing to mitigate the character's responsibility and no rational or moral basis to support their behaviour in any way, e.g., then reader repulsion follows:

> "Auto-da-fe"… a title that made a profound impression on me in the sense that I read this book, but it was so disagreeable, this main character was so detestable that I had a horrible distaste after reading it, by the way, I think in Updike's "Rabbit Run" the main character is also just very disagreeable, because it's not a situation where, let's say, someone is a negative character for three quarters of the book, and at the end, let's say, they undergo a transformation and in the end it turns out that there is good in him, here there were no positive qualities at all, so I just felt sickened and was asking myself why I'm even reading it [R49].

> „Auto-da-fe"… tytuł, który zrobił na mnie piorunujące wrażenie pod tym względem, że przeczytał[x]m tę książkę, ale ona właśnie była taka nieprzyjemna, ten główny bohater był taki odpychający, że czuł[x]m taki koszmarny niesmak po jej przeczytaniu. Zresztą chyba w „Uciekaj króliku" Updike'a też jest główny bohater właśnie bardzo negatywny, bo tu nie chodzi o taką sytuację, że powiedzmy ktoś tam jest takim negatywnym bohaterem przez trzy czwarte książki, a na koniec dokonuje się przemiana i w rezultacie okazuje się, że jednak gdzieś tam w nim jest to dobre. Tutaj właściwe nie było pozytywnych cech, więc ja po prostu czuł[x]m taki koszmarny niesmak i pytanie właściwie, po co ja to czytał[x]m.

We should also take into account the way that characters perceived as bad can generate more tension and excitement for readers, and lead to greater engagement (Salgaro et al., 2021, p. 9). There is also some evidence that moral judgments are more likely to be evoked when reading non-fiction than fiction (Bermejo-Berros et al., 2022, p. 13). The interviews, which shed light on the context of readers' judgments, suggest that being more judgmental may be determined by "moral evilness" or the lack of perceived good qualities in a fictional character (Salgaro et al., 2021, p. 1). Another possible explanation in that the fictional character was not fully integrated into the plot. In future research, it would be a good idea to test whether a more complex and ambiguous protagonist helps or hinders the reader's ability to identify with them, or at least to feel a sense of kinship (Wirth et al., 2012, p. 411).

Self-expanding through encountering with others

The experience of the other, or as Maryanne Wolf puts it – "thinking beyond ourselves" (2016, p. 3) – is something that can be described in many ways, differentiating between "identification"[18], when the reader imagines being a literary character, feeling what they feel, being in their shoes (first-person perspective can evoke such an attitude, with the domination of "fresh emotions" – spontaneous reaction to the text); feeling "sympathy" for the literary character, when they experience something painful (encouraged by the spectator's perspective; with the dominance of remembered, emotional memories); and feeling "empathy", when the reader, using their mentalising skills, understands what a character is feeling and experiences something similar, but also perceives these feelings

---

[18] "Identification may be interpreted also as empathy. For more on different definitions of "identification", see Wojciehowski & Gallese, 2022, p. 63.

as their own, rather than as having been taken over from the literary character (Cupchik et al., 1998, pp. 363, 365; Mar et al., 2011, pp. 823–824).[19] To make the issue even more complex, we can also consider using a concept of *trans-* or *interpassivity* (Leder, 2014, p. 21). When reading an absorbing book, the reader – passive (Žižek) or disappearing/absent/decentered (Lacan) – takes on the experiences of the characters (*others*) in a trans- or interpassive way: "when the other rejoices, I rejoices with them, my most intimate feelings can be more radically externalised, I can actually laugh and cry through another" (Žižek, 1998, p. 5; see also in Leder, 2014, p. 21).[20] Delegating one's experience to others or objects[21], as Žižek shows with the examples of media entertainment (e.g. sitcom laughs) that are the subject of his critique, can be perceived as reducing (alienating) rather than enriching experience, because it leads to less engagement with real life, conforming to social norms or current trends. In the case of reading, paradoxically, "interpassivity" can be more beneficial because this mental activity involves a number of complex processes such as imagining, emotional engaging, mentalising, judging, predicting, remembering and so on. It allows to vicariously experience a range of emotions, including fear, joy and being moved. The reader can benefit from feeling *as if* they are experiencing a particular emotional state in a safe space without negative physical consequences (Oatley, 2012, p. 51). This mechanism is both safe and energy-saving as the brain does not come into contact with the body. We "learn adaptive emotional responses without having to experience", simply by observing others' reactions to certain objects or situations, judging them and associating a certain emotional expression with them (Hogan, 2022, pp. 152–153). However, it could be debated what is interpassive here, the process of eliciting emotions or the emotions themselves (Wojciehowski & Gallese, 2022, p. 62). What emotions, real or "quasi-emotions", do readers experience during or after reading? Patrick Hogan and Raymond Mar et al., drawing on the Indian tradition, suggest a distinction between "everyday feelings" (*bhavas*) and "literary feelings" (*rasas*). The latter require a deep insight, reflect what has been observed, remembered, rooted in shared experiences and passed on as our collective past (cultural or human) (Hogan, 1996; Mar et al., 2011, p. 825).

What should not be overlooked when discussing what the reader feels when reading is that experiencing 'the other' is an embodied simulation (Oatley, 2011). As Hannah Wojciehowski and Vittorio Gallese explain, "readers reuse the brain-body mechanisms employed in daily life". Feeling what the character feels may be possible by grounding the character's situation in the reader's own mental and physical experiences, their environmental interactions (wider life context), and sensorimotor processes that shape their response (2022, pp. 61–62; Tosi et al., 2024). The key to this is the mirror neuron mechanism, but the authors stress that it is not as simple as an "actual physical imita-

---

19 David Comer Kidd and Emanuele Castano identify two types of theory of mind, *affective* (understanding the emotions of others) and *cognitive* (inferring the beliefs and intentions of others) (2013, p. 377).
20 For a more nuanced analysis of how Andrzej Leder defines "interpassivity", see Turczyn, 2020, p. 225.
21 „Ktoś lub coś doznaje rozkoszy zamiast podmiotu" [Someone or something rejoices instead of the subject] – as Anna Turczyn points out (2020, pp. 223–224).

tion" of what a fictional character is doing. Alvin I. Goldman distinguishes between two types of simulation: "low-level" mindreading, which is characterised by automatic mirroring based on simple matching or similarity, and "high-level" mindreading, which is more effortful and imaginative perspective-taking, depending on working memory and the ability to use the stored information (2009, pp. 246–247). Simulation mode activates part of the cortical motor system without forcing the reader to do any action (Wojciehowski & Gallese, 2022, p. 62). As already mentioned, while reading instead of comparing oneself with others as in a real life, the reader may replace "the self" with "the other" (Kaufman & Libby, 2012, p. 2). This *experience-taking* simulation can be thought of as very similar to what one might experience when dreaming (Oatley, 2011; Damasio, 2022, p. 121). The resemblance to a dream can be supported by the *deictic shift theory*, according to which the reader, transported from the real world to the world of the story and immersed in the life of the protagonist, begins to "perceive the story 'from the inside' and ha[s] the feeling of directly experiencing what is happening" (Busselle & Bilandzic, 2008, pp. 261–263). As who? We might ask. Certainly not merely an observer (a distant spectator or eyewitness), because they feel that they are part of the narrative world. Reading books allows the reader to "reduce their own reality and achieve the duality of inhabiting the real and narrative worlds as a real and narrative character" (Gerrig, 2018, p. 22):

> I get transported there to them, participate in all this life, in their emotions, even sometimes. I would do things differently; I would behave differently [R48].
>
> Przenoszę się tam do nich, uczestniczę w tym całym życiu, w ich emocjach, nawet czasami bym zrobił/a inaczej, inaczej bym się zachował/a.
>
> When I read a book, I feel as if I am participating in the events or, for example, in the conversation that the author of the book is having, and also if I can find something in common with a character in the book, this also encourages me to read… I feel as if I am there, not as the main character or as a character at all, but also not exactly as a neutral observer [R49].
>
> Gdy czytam książkę, to mam wrażenie, że uczestniczę w tych wydarzeniach, czy na przykład w rozmowie, którą przeprowadza autor książki i też jeżeli znajduję w bohaterze książki coś wspólnego, to też zachęca mnie to do czytania… czuję się tak, jakbym tam był/a, nie jako główny bohater czy w ogóle jako postać, natomiast też nie do końca jako neutralny obserwator.
>
> I'm an observer, like I'm participating in these events, watching from a distance [R71].
>
> Jestem obserwatorem, tak jak jakbym uczestniczył/a gdzieś tam w tych wydarzeniach, patrząc z boku.

> In general, I am a… I don't know what to call it, an observer, but not a passive one, rather an involved one [R25].
>
> Generalnie jestem takim… nie wiem, jak to nazwać, takim obserwatorem, ale nie biernym, a zaangażowanym.

The participation is thus "from a side-participant" (Gerrig, 2018, p. 110), or indirect (Leder, 2014, p. 21), and it relies on the assumption that the reader participates in events, neither as an actor – because they are not a performer who can interfere – nor as an observer, because they watch from the inside, they are partially detached from the physical world, and they attribute actions to situation rather than personality (actor-observer bias, see e.g. Gerrig & Jacovina, 2009, p. 230; Oatley, 2012, pp. 28–29). Eric Purchase claims that in the world of the story, „we cease to be passive observers and become the protagonist of our own dreams" (2019, p. 40). Alberto Manguel admits that when he reads he feels like a narrator, in control of the pace of the pages and the time, for example when he decides to postpone the pleasure of reading (2023, p. 217). The reader is certainly not passive (Manguel, 2023, p. 217; Oatley, 2011, p. 62), especially in neuroscientific terms (de Vignemont & Singer, 2006, p. 437). They perform rather than just "observing without acting" (Christiansen & Dalsgård, 2021, p. 292). However, there will be those who will say that this is not a sufficiently active role.

As we already know, identifying with the character does not necessarily happen, even when the reader is immersed in the events of the story world. What is more likely is that they will become attached to the character. However, there is some evidence to suggest that a player of a game is more likely to identify with a character. Wojcichowski and Gallese argue that: "in interactive media such as computer games, attachment may refer to the degree of control one has over a character's actions, identification with the protagonist, or responsibility for the character's safety and interactions with others (Bowman et al.). In the gaming context, the overlap between identification and attachment is particularly pronounced" (2022, p. 64). This is also in line with what some of the research participants said:

> I do not feel like I am the protagonist, I feel more like the protagonist in a video game, I actually identify more with the protagonist then… when reading, I think of myself more as an observer… someone out there who watches, finds out things, but cannot interfere [R74].
>
> Bohaterem się nie czuję, bohaterem czuję się bardziej w grze, rzeczywiście bardziej wczuwam się w bohatera… w czytaniu raczej mam się chyba za obserwatora… kogoś tam, kto patrzy, dowiaduje się rzeczy, ale nie może interweniować.

In the light of research on gamers' experiences, the greater sense of identification with a character may be a result of the fact that playing is seen as acting, due to the greater sense of agency (Wirth et al., 2012, p. 412). However, if playing games is a means of self-expression through creating and customising avatars, taking decisions, achieving goals and jointly planning strategies, and interacting socially with other players, reading is more of an "expressive enactment" (Sikora et al., 1998) of someone else's story, which may be beyond our own experience. A literary character is distinct from the reader. It is not the avatar of the reader through which they express themself. Instead, readers are encouraged to look inward and to imagine themselves in a different role (vicarious experience), to test themselves in some way, and to prepare for what might happen in order to have appropriate control in future (Koopman, 2015, p. 21). It might be an oversimplification to say that the reader completely avoids responsibility for the actions of the fictional characters, as this can manifest itself in the mental rather than the behavioural realm:

> A book can certainly stir up fears, traumas, with the help of a book one can dig down into the very things that are in us, let's say, that are the most gnawing, toxic things [R49].
>
> Książka zdecydowanie może wywołać lęki, traumy, za pomocą książki można się dokopać do właśnie tych rzeczy, które są w nas powiedzmy takie najbardziej uwierające, toksyczne.

Perhaps we should therefore consider using another term with regard to being active while reading. This is how Holland puts it: "When we enjoy movies, books, plays or poems, we do not act, and we consciously know that we cannot change the work. We imagine; and we let literature and other media help our imagining" (2009, p. 43). In doing so, the reader becomes emotionally and cognitively involved in the world of the story by:

- (re)constructing the world depicted in the book, by concretisation (Ingarden, 1960, pp. 60–62) or even world-making/co-creating (Hanich, 2018, p. 440; Oatley, 2011, pp. 39, 60);
- observing events or becoming informed about them, creating expectations and predictions based on this knowledge and re-evaluating predictions (Wolf & Gottwald, 2016, p. 69);
- "giv[ing] substance to the psychological life of characters" (Gerrig, 2018, pp. 2, 17); sympathising with the fictional characters, establishing an emotional bond with them, embodying them (*experience-taking*, which is a spontaneous and experientially driven process), or understanding what they feel (*perspective-taking*, which is more conscious than experience-taking, requires effort and is a more conceptual process) (Bálint & Tan, 2019; Charmaz et al., 2019, p. 53; Kaufman & Libby, 2012, p. 15);
- making moral judgments; when good wins, they rejoice; when evil triumphs, they feel injustice (Oatley, 2012, pp. 48–49; see "affective disposition theory" by Zillmann & Cantor, 1977; see also research by Arthur Raney, 2003);
- considering the protagonist's situation and giving them mental advice;
- giving meaning to the story by relating it to the blueprint of the self and the value system (Martínez, 2014), or "experience[ing] narratives in consonance with their own identity themes" (Gerrig, 2018, p. 22).

All this is aimed at experiencing the book in a personal way (Fuller & Rehberg Sedo, 2013, p. 33). Oatley suggests that reading fiction allows us to "put aside our immediate relationships and concerns and can take on something of the selfhood of an imaginary character" (2012, p. 17). We could also say that the reader may find in a character a suitable "form" for themselves, and when this happens they take on the other's experience rather than identifying with it. The aesthetic distance created by the narrative allows the reader to include of "the self" in "the other" (projection, less conscious, more defensive) or to include "the other" in "the self" (introjection, more conscious and self-expanding). This relational dynamic between "the self" and "the other" can facilitate a deeper self-understanding:

> Certainly there were some female protagonists with whom I could identify in this way and observe how they cope, or just as an observer who sees how it looks from the outside that… Oh Jesus, what a pushover she is, why doesn't she believe in herself, I don't take it personally, but as I look at it from a bystander's point of view, it is the kind of an identification that sometimes someone seems close to me [Gender].

> Na pewno były takie bohaterki, z którymi mogłam się w ten sposób zidentyfikować i obserwować, jak one sobie radzą, albo właśnie jako taki obserwator zobaczyć, jak to z zewnątrz wygląda, że… O Jezu, jaka ona jest sierota, no dlaczego ona w siebie nie wierzy, ja do siebie tego nie biorę, ale tak z boku jak popatrzę, to jest taka identyfikacja, że czasem ktoś taki mi się wydaje bliski.

> Sometimes even when I read a suspense novel, well, you can actually relate it to yourself… there were times when I wondered, when there was a reaction of "how could she have done that! What a mean thing to do," but then… a moment later… I referred this to myself, how I would have behaved in this situation, and I think that even in such a seemingly purely entertaining escapist book you can also find a lot of such references to your own life… however, you can get something out of every book for yourself [Gender].

> Czasem nawet jak czytam thriller, no to rzeczywiście można to odnieść do siebie… zdarzały mi się takie momenty zastanowienia, kiedy była reakcja „Ale jak ona tak mogła! Ale wredota", ale później… chwila… i wtedy było takie odniesienie do siebie, że jak ja bym się zachowała w tej sytuacji i myślę, że nawet niby w takiej czysto rozrywkowej lekturze dla ucieczki też można znaleźć wiele takich odniesień do własnego życia… z każdej lektury można coś jednak wynieść tak dla siebie.

When we read, we experience "narrative feelings/emotions", such as empathy or sympathy with a fictional character. They occur when plot events and character actions relate to readers' personal factors, evoking memories of past experiences, as shown by Gibbs (2006), Sikora et al. (2010), and Koopman (2016), Bálint & Tan (2019). This way of recognising familiar feelings in someone else promotes a sympathetic or empathetic attitude and thus insight into oneself (Koopman, 2014). "Narrative emotions" are involved in imagining, accepting and ultimately interpreting fictional world (Miall & Kuiken,

2002, p. 223). There are also "aesthetic feelings", that come from admiration and appreciation of how characters and events are presented (Koopman, 2015, p. 20; Mar et al., 2011, p. 822). This includes many literary features, such as metaphors, that can influence readers' responses:

> Looking at Škvorecký, for example, there are passages there that are just amazing, that there can be something so well written, so well told, and when I go back to it, I just continue to be enthralled and the enthrallment turns into enjoyment [R76].
>
> Patrząc na tego Skvoreckiego na przykład, tam są takie fragmenty, które w ogóle są niesamowite, że może być coś tak napisane, tak opowiedziane, i jak wracam, to dalej jestem po prostu zachwycon[x] i zachwyt przekłada się na przyjemność.
>
> "Harry Potter" is one of the books that has fantastic language, and it turns out that this is the translator's merit, not the author's… how witty this language is, how cool it is… the difficult issues that were addressed there were talked about in an intelligent and age-appropriate way [R21].
>
> „Harry Potter" to jest jedna z niewielu tych książek, która ma fantastyczny język sam w sobie i okazuje się, że to jest nawet zasługa tłumacza, a nie autorki… dowcipność tego języka, ta taka fajność… o trudnych sprawach, które były tam poruszane jednocześnie mówiono w sposób inteligentny i dostosowany do wieku.

Focusing on the literary aspects of the work allows episodic memories to be evoked, activating more reflective processing. This is a mark of the eudaimonic endeavours of the readers. Some interviewees noted that their appreciation of literary aspects and sensitivity to language improved with age, as their knowledge and reading skills increased (Wimmer et al., 2023, p. 241):

> Now I pay attention to the language, in the past I knew nothing about language… You don't read Proust for the plot, you read Proust for the language, and I think when you're around 40–50, eventually the language starts standing out, that you discover, wow, this is really unique, and so we can read Mickiewicz, "Pan Tadeusz" is nothing special to us, only when you learn more about this, wow, this is a cool book, suddenly it turns out that this is something outstanding [Age].
>
> Teraz zwracam uwagę na język, dawniej nic nie wiedział[x]m o języku… Prousta nie czyta się dla fabuły, jego się czyta dla języka i myślę, że to tak koło 40.–50. w końcu ten język na tyle się przeżre, że odkrywa się, wow, to naprawdę jest wyjątkowe i tak sobie możemy czytać Mickiewicza, dla nas to jest nic wyjątkowego ten „Pan Tadeusz", dopiero jak się zdobędzie wiedzę na ten temat, wow, to jest fajna książka, nagle się okazuje, że to jest coś wybitnego.

Miall and Kuiken have proposed that "aesthetic and narrative feelings interact to produce metaphors of personal identification that modify self-understanding" (2002, pp. 221, 223). Reading about other people's problems and being able to identify with them helps us to see that we are not alone (Bálint & Tan, 2019). "It can give you, that you feel recognized... instead of being alone with it, thinking everyone else feels great" says one of the participants in the study conducted by Charlotte Christiansen and Anne Line Dalsgård says (2022, p. 302). This statement aligns with Emy Koopman's observation that individuals find comfort not only in observing someone who is in a worse situation than themselves (see "downward social comparison theory"[22]), but also when they are experiencing suffering and are aware that others have gone through similar experiences (Koopman, 2015, pp. 20–21; Oliver & Bartsch, 2010, p. 56).

With insight into the world of the protagonist's thoughts and impressions, the perspectives of "self" and "non-self" "overlap easier. The boundary between the reader's "self" and the character may be blurred. The "I" that is diluted in an interactive simulation can take on different forms depending on which of its patterns are activated by the narrative (Loi et al., 2023a; Martínez, 2014). The reader may recognize something in the attitudes or behaviours of the "other" that resonates with their present or past experiences. Confronting such personal feelings may recontextualise them, thereby slightly altering the narrative of who the reader is or has become (Miall & Kuiken, 2002, pp. 229, 238).

> Do I identify with characters? Yes, a little, Ivan was always closer to me than Dimitri, that is, the one who goes to school there and studies, not the one who drinks constantly [Gender].

> Czy się utożsamiam? Trochę tak, trochę tak, zawsze mi ten Iwan był bliższy niż właśnie ten Dimitri, czyli ten, który tam chodzi do szkoły i się uczy, a nie ten, który pije ciągle.

> He too was the kind of person, his parents wanted him to be someone else, and he just wanted to be someone else entirely and work in an unprofitable profession... and from him one can learn strength, persistence, chasing after one's desires, dreams, goals, and so on [R97].

> On też był takim człowiekiem, że jak gdyby rodzice chcieli, żeby był kimś innym, a on po prostu chciał zupełnie być kimś innym w takim niedochodowym zawodzie... i od niego można się uczyć takiej siły, takiego przetrwania, takiego dążenia do swoich pragnień, marzeń, celów i tak dalej.

The reader can perceive in the protagonist the *desired possible self* (*ideal self*) that surpasses them in some respect, the "I" of the hero, spy, scientist or avenger for a just cause, that fulfils the innermost desires, including those that are socially unacceptable (*the dreaded self*). By entering the simulation, the reader has the chance to test it unfettered: "Hannibal Lecter is equally terrifying, but also fascinating and appealing" [RC]. Oatley points out that reading about heroic acts can also give readers the opportunity to experience being heroic (2012, p. 79): "sometimes I like these great heroes, it is beau-

---

[22] See Leon Festinger (1954), Thomas A. Wills (1981) and Valerie Ellen Kretz (2020).

tiful, I need such role models... we also greatly need John Rambo, James Bond, John Wick" [Gender]. *The possible feared-self*, in turn, emerges in response to a confrontation with a vision of oneself that the reader does not approve of, which they fear all the more strongly, the more likely it seems that they could become like the protagonist or behave in a similar way:

> I always promised myself that I wouldn't become the grouchy Barbara from "Nights and Days", who felt unfulfilled and was dissatisfied no matter what... I still remember her from Polish class in high school, and I promised myself that no, I wouldn't be like that [Gender].
>
> Cały czas sobie obiecywałam, że nie mogę być taką gnuśną Barbarą z „Nocy i dni", która czuła jakieś niespełnienie i szukała dziury w całym... pamiętam jeszcze z języka polskiego w ogólniaku i tak sobie przyrzekłam, że nie, ja taka nie będę.

However, seeing an image of oneself in a negative character or one who has done something wicked can help the reader realize what they are capable of and whether it is appalling for them. Readers often analyse their behaviour during and after reading and either accept themselves (Wirth et al., 2012, p. 412) or challenge themselves (self-expansion):

> I was looking for inspiration in books, for mood improvement... I wanted to see different thinking than, for example, how I think about myself, that let's say I have little to say, I don't know much and in general, who am I, and here I had a different outlook, how you can approach yourself, how you can accept yourself, how to like yourself, what are the ways to do it, so such books are an inspiration to me and give me a positive kick that there is hope for me, that it is possible to change this kind of stereotypical thinking, this habitual thinking, to a different kind, one that is more conducive to a sense of satisfaction with one's life and with oneself, so certainly such books just inspired me... my mood was better after reading them [R31].
>
> Szukał[x]m w nich jakieś takiej inspiracji właśnie, też poprawy nastroju... chciał[x]m zobaczyć takie inne myślenie niż na przykład ja myślę o sobie, że powiedzmy właśnie niewiele mam do powiedzenia, niewiele wiem i w ogóle, co to ja jestem, a tutaj miał[x]m takie inne spojrzenie, jak można podejść do siebie, jak można siebie zaakceptować, jak polubić, jakie są na to sposoby, więc takie książki są dla mnie inspiracją i dają takiego pozytywnego kopa, że jest dla mnie nadzieja, że można zmienić to takie stereotypowe myślenie, takie nawykowe, na inne, takie bardziej właśnie sprzyjające poczucie zadowolenia ze swojego życia i z siebie, więc na pewno takie książki mnie właśnie inspirowały... ten nastrój był lepszy po lekturze.
>
> It happened to be Paullina Simons' book "The Bronze Horseman", and the whole series by this author, and all the hardships that the protagonist of this book goes

through, of course, they were not comparable to mine, they were completely different, but the strength of this woman, perhaps exaggerated at times, it was as if she shared this strength with me, and this helped me a lot [Gender].

To była książka Paulliny Simons „Miedziany jeździec", akurat i cała seria tej autorki i tak jakby wszystkie trudności, które bohaterka tej książki przeżywa, oczywiście one nie były porównywalne do moich, one były zupełnie inne, ale siła tej kobiety, być może nawet czasami przerysowana, jakby ona się tą siłą ze mną dzieliła i to mi bardzo pomagało.

Dealing with negative emotions
Feeling pain or being in pain
If the book the reader is reading does not allow them to meet their needs, contradicts their world view and values, or is unbearably cruel, this will evoke a whole range of negative emotions, from anger or dissatisfaction towards the author, whom the reader may hold responsible for the death of a beloved character, through disgust or annoyance or discouragement at their behaviour, to sadness resulting from the end of the story:

> It happens very often that I understand that he had to die for the sake of the novel, but I've become so attached to him that I wish that it hadn't happened, that it's so upsetting… when in Harry Potter the author killed off Sirius Black, I thought I'd just get on the train and give her a talking to, that I already understand that she had to kill off a few characters, but she could have spared him that [R21].

> Bardzo często mam tak, że rozumiem, że dla powieści on musiał umrzeć, ale ja się z nim tak związał[x]m, że ja bym nie chciał/a, że to jest takie przykre… jak Harry'emu Potterowi zabiła Syriusza Blacka, to myślał[x]m, że po prostu wsiądę w pociąg i jej powiem parę nieładnych słów, że już ja rozumiem, że ona musiała pozabijać paru bohaterów, ale już tej szpili mogła mu oszczędzić.

Attributing blame to the character or author can lead to anger, but the pattern of activation varies among readers (Kuppens et al., 2007, as cited in Smith & Kirby, 2009, p. 1356). When the character suffers, this may evoke sympathetic or empathic response. "Empathizing with the pain of others does not involve the activation of the whole pain matrix, but is based on activation of those second-order representations containing the subjective affective dimension of pain" – explain Jerome Singer et al. (2004, p. 1161). Some further research has shown that it also "triggers an internal sensorimotor simulation of the observed somatic experience" (Dvash & Shamay-Tsoory, 2014, p. 290).[23] According to the enactive approach, the process of evaluation (both cognitive and emotional) is not separate from bodily events.[24] Emotions are embodied and evoked by the agent's (reader's) interactions with the environment. This approach postulates "a deep

---
23 See also review by Riečanský & Lamm, 2019, pp. 966, 970.
24 See Prinz and Colombetti's interpretations described by Caracciolo, 2022, p. 58.

integration of action and perception (sensorimotor integration)"(Colombetti, 2007, p. 529). Empathy can therefore be conceptualised as a graded phenomenon, entailing intricate bodily representations and neural simulations. It "extends beyond the affective-cognitive dichotomy while triggering a graded cascade of rhythmic representations of simulation, affect, mentalisation, cognitive control and subjective-experience" (Zebarjadi et al., 2021, pp. 3, 7). Observing someone's expression of pain or pleasure activates emotional or episodic memories by associating and retrieving relevant (emotionally similar) information from memory (Bortolussi & Dixon, 2003, pp. 12, 18) and then, through automatic and/or reflexive processing (mentalising and perspective-taking), the reader is led into an embodied simulation "running in their head", which helps them to engage with narrative fiction and understand others, and may help to instil more prosocial behaviour (Hogan, 2022, pp. 152, 154; Oatley, 2011, pp. x, 18–19).[25] If the character is seen as good, honest and like-minded, the reader mainly feels sympathy (compassion or empathic concern) for them. The level of experiential pleasure may be much higher if the outcome of the action (the ending of the story) is morally correct in terms of the reader's internalised norms (Oliver, 2010, p. 55). Therefore, reader may enjoy seeing the guilty punished because it meets their expectation of righting wrongs (Oatley, 2012, p. 133):

> In one book from Larsson's Millennium saga, when the main character took revenge on her superintendent, I had a feeling of satisfaction that this *** got what he deserved [R57].

> W książce tej sagi Millenium Larssona, jak główna bohaterka zemściła się tym swoim kuratorze, to czuł[x]m taką satysfakcję, że taki *** dostał to, na co zasłużył.

> In general, I don't like haughty characters, I don't like hubris, both in life and in books, such characters don't speak to me, I'd rather that they fail, so that in the end this hubris is their downfall [R74].

> Generalnie nie lubię postaci pysznych, nie lubię pychy i w życiu i w książkach takie postacie mnie nie przekonują, wolał[x]bym, żeby przegrały, by w końcu ta pycha została ukruszona.

If the reader's expectations about the development of the plot or the character's situation are not met, and if they have no hope of a positive outcome, their reluctance to continue reading may be reinforced by their exasperation:

> For me, "Game of Thrones" by G. G. Martin is a classic example of a story without hope, it was plainly horrendous, because even if there was a spark of hope, the heroine or hero found a haven for a while, allies, friends... Bam! Everyone dies on the next page... the book is fascinating, the narrative is engaging, fantastic,

---

25 However, as Suzanne Keen points out, building on Kruger's findings (*Evolution and Altruism*), prosocial behaviour influenced by fiction may be limited by a lack of reciprocity resulting from an inability to interact with the fictional world (2007, p. 16).

> the universe imaginatively conceived, deep human bonds, but at some point the level of cruelty, unjust, wanton cruelty, the level of taking away hope on every step, became too much to bear, and I remember that I was so put off that I just closed the book and never came back to it again… I was so terribly tormented, anguished as a reader with hope taken away from me at every turn, with cruelty, with injustice, that even the displays of solidarity between people, even the small victories that happened there, did not offset the overall tone of the book [R49].

> Dla mnie „Gra o Tron" G. G. Martina to jest taki sztandarowy przykład opowieści bez nadziei, to po prostu było koszmarne, bo nawet jeśli tam pojawiała się iskierka nadziei, bohaterka czy bohater gdzieś na chwilę odnalazł przystań, sprzymierzeńców, przyjaciół… Sru! Na następnej stronie giną wszyscy… książka fascynująca, narracja wciągająca, fantastyczna, świat fantastycznie wykreowany, głębokie więzi międzyludzkie, ale w którymś momencie poziom tego okrucieństwa, niesprawiedliwego, bezsensownego, poziom odbierania nadziei na każdym kroku, osiągnął punkt kulminacyjny i pamiętam, że ja już czuł[x]m takie obrzydzenie, że po prostu zamkn[x]ł[x]m tę książkę i już nigdy więcej do niej nie wrócił[x]m… był[x]m tak strasznie umęczon[x], udręczon[x] jako czytelnik zabieraniem mi nadziei na każdym kroku, okrucieństwem, niesprawiedliwością, że nawet przejawy tej solidarności pomiędzy ludźmi, nawet te drobne zwycięstwa, które się tam pojawiły, nie rekompensowały ogólnej wymowy tego tekstu.

This can lead to them putting the book down, doubting the purpose of reading, or experiencing mood swings, loss of motivation due to lack of positive reinforcement, and even emotional breakdown:

> The sadness of this book ["Let's Go Play at the Adams'"] was roiling in me, I was sick after reading this book for two or three days, I could not get it out of my head… in a psychological sense, this book really made me sick… not with some descriptions of torture, I read a lot of horror stories, including varieties of extreme horror, this does not faze me one bit, but how the narrative was handled… also the fact that these were children, and the fact that there was no punishment for what happened [R74].

> Smutek tej książki ["Zabawmy się u Adamsów"] gdzieś we mnie wił, ja po tej książce był[x]m dwa czy trzy dni chor[x], ja jej nie mogł[x]m wyrzucić z głowy… w takim sensie psychicznym ta książka mnie naprawdę struła… nie tam jakimiś opisami tortur, czytam bardzo dużo horrorów, także takie odmiany horroru ekstremalnego, to mnie w ogóle nie bierze, ale właśnie to, jak tam była prowadzona ta relacja… też fakt, że to były dzieci, też fakt, że nie było kary za to, co się wydarzyło.

Respondents' reactions to the unsatisfactory ending were twofold: firstly, deep sadness, and secondly, indignation or even disgust, especially if they felt that the way things were going was unfair. Reader's frustration may also be due to the additional processing

required to minimise cognitive dissonance or the lack of coherence. However, the interpretation of the situation may change (Charmaz et al., 2019, p. 8).[26]
Unlike anger, where reasoning is mainly through forward chaining to achieve retribution, reasoning in sadness is through backward chaining to understand how it could have happened (Oatley, 2012, p. 95). If a book does not bring the immediate desired results, it can be the subject of reflection at a later time:

> I have a sense of injustice, it's happened many times, then why, when she's already gotten so many kicks and punches from life, it can't be like this… But it's the books that I think about long after I've read or listened to them that are the most valuable to me, because I nevertheless feel that they touch my life in some way, that I think about them, that I don't just think about having to go to work, coming back, making dinner and cleaning up, I just am emotionally affected by them [R35].

> Takie poczucie niesprawiedliwości, tak, to wielokrotnie, że dlaczego, że tyle już dostała w kość od życia i znowu i po prostu nie, to nie może tak być… Ale właśnie te książki, o których gdzieś tam myślę jeszcze długo po ich przeczytaniu czy wysłuchaniu są dla mnie najbardziej wartościowe, bo jednak czuję, że coś tam w jakiś sposób poruszają moim życiem, że o nich myślę, że nie myślę tylko o tym, że trzeba pojechać do pracy, wrócić, zrobić obiad i posprzątać, tylko gdzieś tam ciągle je przeżywam.

It is worth considering that sadness or tearfulness is not necessarily a simple response to the loss that has affected fictional characters, but the result of feeling moved (Koopman, 2015, p. 20), "feeling ourselves in the presence of something larger than ourselves, something that takes us out of our egoistic concerns, something that prompts reflectiveness, something that makes room for insight" (Oatley, 2012, p. 97; see also "self-transcendent media experiences" in Oliver et al., 2018). Such a feeling, evoked in a transgressive way by axiological concepts, could be called "eudaimonic"[27] (moving and thought-provoking). Emy Koopman, following Mary Beth Oliver, describes eudaimonic motivations for reading as those driven by a need to understand and gain greater insight, to stimulate self-reflection and to learn, so it is not as simple as satisfying the need for justice. It takes concentration, challenge and competence to experience eudaimonic happiness (Oliver et al., 2018, p. 382; Figure 3).

---

26 With regard to film adaptations, the disappointment often reported by study participants may reflect the need for congruence between the reader's concretisation (what the reader imagined while reading), and a film visualisation, which is not as close to and controlled by the reader (Hanich, 2018, pp. 426, 430).
27 Some researchers have suggested, however, that "eudaimonia" is not a feeling, mental state or cognitive evaluation, but rather a way of living (Ryan et al., 2006, p. 143).

Facing our fears
Readers may explore fear through literature in a safe setting (Oatley, 2011, p. 38). However, confronting something that causes resistance or is uncomfortable, unfamiliar or incompatible with one's image of the self and the world activates the self's defence mechanisms. Too much similarity can also be a source of disconcerting feelings and may be perceived as threatening, leading to distancing from the situation or fictional character and experience of "personal distress". It refers to feelings of anxiety, worry or discomfort when a character with whom the reader sympathises or identifies experiences something negative (Tosi et al., 2024). It is "accompanied by a desire to withdraw from a situation in order to protect oneself from excessive negative feelings" (Singer & Klimecki, 2014, p. 875; Keen, 2007, pp. 4–5). In such a situation, the reader may want to avoid or reduce overwhelming emotions such as grief or shame. This "overdistancing" is a kind of psychological defence (see Thomas Scheff cited by Mar et al., 2011, p. 825; see also Djikic et al., 2009a, p. 14). Some readers may even refuse to acknowledge painful emotions or, conversely, may not be able to modulate them at all (Hogan, 2022, p. 154). However, they can be alleviated, fully understood and assimilated thanks to the aesthetic values of the book as suggested by Raymond Mar et al. or Lessa Lamb, the narrator of Erica Berry's *Wolfish: Wolf, Self, and the Stories We Tell About Fear* (Mar et al., 2011, pp. 824–825; Flatiron, 2023).[28] It seems that the mechanisms behind this are affective-cognitive processes of balancing homeostasis[29] to achieve wellbeing and self-understanding.

Negatively valenced content may not be an inhibiting factor, as tension and suspense can also be a stimulus to engagement (Lehne & Koelsch, 2015, pp. 1, 4) if the balance between uncertainty and curiosity is "just right"[30] for the reader: "although it all got so gritty and so dark, I was soaking it up, I really had to read it to the end, because I couldn't put it down" [R74]. Moritz Lehne and Stefan Koelsch define *tension* and *suspense* as affective states associated with conflict or uncertainty, evoking emotional concern and desire for resolution, hence anticipation and prediction (2015, p. 2). Such "recreational fear" is a mixture of fear and enjoyment (Andersen et al., 2020, p. 1497). As Oatley says, "suspense itself is an emotion enjoyment" (2012, p. 54). It appears to be an essential component of narrative, leading to affective, cognitive and physiological involvement (increased pupil dilation, see Riese et al., 2014, pp. 212, 225). If the reader is seeking a sensation, then they will enjoy the uncertainty that accompanies reading. If they have specific expectations about the outcome, then the surprise or confirmation model comes into play. The reader enjoys solving problems or being right, attitudes which are rooted in the need for cognition as a personality trait and are related to their self-esteem. If they have low self-esteem, a surprising ending that does not

---

28 "She said she had heard from listeners who found catharsis in getting to re-experience, through the safety of narration, moments adjacent to their life. Part of her goal with my book, she said, was trying to help the listener "renegotiate their contract" with fear." (Erica Berry..., 2024).
29 For more on the role of homeostasis, see Damasio 2022.
30 Women may be more likely than men to report fear rather than enjoyment (Andersen et al., 2020, p. 1505).

confirm their suspicions may lead to dislike (fear of failure) (Knobloch-Westerwick & Keplinger, 2006, pp. 194–195, 198).[31]

Chun-Ting Hsu et al. have provided evidence that "although emotional content such as descriptions of vicarious fear is not necessary for immersive reading experience, arousing, negatively valenced texts do indeed facilitate immersive processes" (2014, p. 1359). Following Oatley, we might ask how it is that, when we read – unlike in real life – we eagerly engage with characters who are having some difficulties (2012, p. 16). It appears that this mainly occurs when the events, characters' issues or traits of their selfhood do not reflect our own fears, violate any of our standards and our sense of safety. If the character's suffering triggers a traumatic experience (fearful memories) in the reader, it may lead them to a more aversive response. The reader may be afraid of confronting too deeply the problems they experience on a daily basis, or those that they have repressed (unwanted intrusion into the self). Thus, discovering similarities to people or events is not always welcome. Under the pressure of rising or sustained tension that draws the reader into the simulation, the line between fiction and reality becomes partially blurred, as the reader is somehow in two places at once:

> Läckberg published another book, and I had already read all of her previous titles. I sat down to read this book and I'm reading the description of the corpse of this four-year-old girl, what beautiful eyes and hair she has, so nicely combed, and at that moment my daughter walks into my room, and she perfectly matches the description of this corpse I had just been reading about, then my Kindle flew across the room and hit the wall… I started to get too emotional about it and had to take a break, so I switched to another book, and since then I started reading two at the same time, I just had to give myself a break, because I was terribly stressed by all the lurking dangers threatening the lives of the characters, who I had grown attached to [R56].

> Läckberg wydała kolejną książkę, której wszystkie już pozycje wcześniejsze miał[x]m przeczytane. Siadł[x]m do tej książki i czytam opis zwłok tej czteroletniej dziewczynki, jakie to ma piękne te oczy i włosy tak ułożone i wchodzi mi w tym momencie do pokoju moja córka, która idealnie odpowiada opisowi tego trupa, o którym właśnie tutaj przeczytał[x]m, to ten mój Kindle przeleciał przez cały pokój i zatrzymał się na ścianie… zaczął[x]m za bardzo emocjonalnie do tego podchodzić i musiał[x]m sobie zrobić taką przerwę, więc przeskakiwał[x]m na inną książkę, no i stąd się zaczęło czytanie dwóch jednocześnie, że po prostu musiał[x]m gdzieś tam odpocząć, bo był[x]m strasznie zestresowan[x] tym czyhaniem na życie moich bohaterów, z którymi się zżył[x]m.

> Very engaging, I read "Silence of the Lambs" shuddering at every little rustle in the room [R71].

---

31 These findings are based on research into the mystery genre, not thrillers or horror stories.

> Bardzo wciągająca, „Milczenie owiec" przeczytał[x]m, drżąc na każdy szelest w pokoju.

Long-term exposure to stressful stimuli can even cause people to temporarily give up reading or change their habits, for example by starting a second book to distract themselves from the previous one that is too deeply affecting or boring: "I had such a terrible reading hangover after all those crime novels that I couldn't bring myself to read anything" [R56].

Csíkszentmihályi argues that the lack of skills appropriate to a challenge causes anxiety (feeling overwhelmed, and discouraged) (2014; 221; 2022, pp. 130–131). Within the domain of reading, it is often associated with the school system, especially reading aloud, reading books that are often unsuitable for a students' age, knowledge and sensitivity and the expectation of a certain interpretation, which leads to the fear of failing at the task and being judged unfavourably:

> There were always these two sides fighting inside me, on the one hand finding this key and answering in a way that would make the teacher exclaim "yes, that's what it was all about!," and on the other hand what I had to offer in these explanations, what the author meant to say, what was my opinion, resulted from my thoughts, very often turned out not to be in line with what was supposed to be taught to us, so this made me very disheartened [R49].

> Zawsze walczyły we mnie te dwie opcje, z jednej strony znalezienia tego klucza i odpowiedzenia na lekcji języka polskiego tak, żeby pani polonistka wykrzyknęła „tak, właśnie o to chodziło!", a z drugiej strony to, co miał[x]m do zaproponowania w tych wyjaśnieniach, co autor chciał powiedzieć, co było moje, wynikało z moich przemyśleń, bardzo często okazywało się, że nie jest zgodne z tym, co miało zostać przerobione na tej lekcji języka polskiego, więc to mnie bardzo zniechęcało.

Something that transcends the knowledge or skills of the reader, but has not been imposed, will, at best, create a sense of the book's unsuitability to the needs, abilities or circumstances[32] rather than the fear or shame or embarrassment that comes from being judged by others:

> I tried to read this author's book, and I think he uses such a difficult language, I think a bit like, I do not know if that's the right word for it, philosophical, a bit, well, not for me [R97] [about Olga Tokarczuk's book]

> Próbował[x]m czytać i uważam, że bardzo trudnym takim językiem pisze, trochę chyba takim, nie wiem, czy dobrze określę, filozoficznym, troszkę takim no nie dla mnie [o książce Olgi Tokarczuk]

---

32 See the primary appraisal of positive, negative/dangerous, or irrelevant stimuli in Richard Lazarus' transactional model of stress and coping (Lazarus & Folkman, 1987, p. 144–147; Lazarus, 1991, p. 830).

> I have to spend a lot of time to enhance my knowledge in a given area, which I don't have, and only then I can get deeper into it, at this point in my life, I don't have time for that [R56].
>
> Ja muszę poświęcić mnóstwo czasu, żeby uzupełnić moją wiedzę z danego zakresu, której nie mam i dopiero mogę gdzieś tam brnąć dalej, no na tę chwilę w moim życiu, ja nie mam na to czasu.

At the same time, however, readers often make judgments about fictional characters, authors, other readers and themselves, which can also be a source of shame or remorse:

> I'm not proud of it, but I thought that if I read more difficult books, I would be better in some way [RD].
>
> Nie jestem z tego dumn[x], ale myślał[x]m, że jak czytam cięższe książki, to jestem lepsz[x] w jakiś sposób.
>
> When I was younger, back in college, in high school, I don't know why, I thought men wrote better books… and when I think about it now, I feel ashamed [RE].
>
> Jak był[x]m młodsz[x] na studiach jeszcze, w szkole średniej, nie wiem dlaczego, wydawało mi się, że mężczyźni piszą lepiej… jak teraz o tym wspominam, to się tego wstydzę.
>
> I like to observe. I also like to analyse… To be honest, sometimes, and this is probably my biggest vice, I judge people. This is the worst thing. I am working on myself to accept people for who they are [RF].
>
> Lubię obserwować. Lubię też analizować… Szczerze mówiąc, czasami, i to jest chyba moją największą przywarą, że ja tych ludzi oceniam. To jest najgorsze. Pracuję nad sobą, żeby akceptować to takim, jakim kto jest.

However, judging a character's choices, actions or beliefs is also inherent to reading (Oatley, 2012, pp. 48–49). As Wolf puts it: "experiencing of other lives… forces us to examine our own prior judgments and the lives of others" (2019, p. 48). Thus, evaluating literary characters can have a positive outcome in terms of understanding ourselves.

Dissapointment can be triggered by the thought of rereading a book that the reader once enjoyed. If it does not meet the reader's needs, and they now see the situation differently, they may react to the same circumstances with different emotions, and this may negatively affect their "self" (Smith & Kirby, 2009, p. 1353):

> – You wouldn't want to taint that memory, right?
> – Right, I would prefer to leave it in an airtight package, so that it sits here quietly [R57].

- Nie chciał[x]by Pan/i skazić tego wspomnienia, tak?
- Tak, wolał[x]bym zostawić je w takim opakowaniu hermetycznym, żeby tu sobie spokojnie siedzi[ało].

- I'm afraid to go back to some of the books that I remember as just mine, ones that somehow touched me, ones which I remember fondly…
- You feel as if you are interfering with your past, or is it something else?
- With my past, with my past experiences, so I fear that this rapture over the book might turn out to be a delusion… this second attempt after several years was disappointing because I actually didn't know myself what I was more disappointed with, myself or this book [R49].

- Boję się sięgać do niektórych książek, które pamiętam jako takie właśnie moje, takie, które jakoś tam mnie poruszyły, takie, do których wracam wspomnieniem, z przyjemnością.
- Czuje Pan/i jakby ingerował/a w swoją przeszłość, czy to jest coś innego?
- W swoją przeszłość, w swoje doświadczenia z przeszłości, więc jest strach, że ten zachwyt nad tekstem w którymś momencie mógłby się okazać ułudą… to drugie podejście po kilku latach to było jakoś rozczarowujące z tego względu, że właściwie sam/a nie wiedział[x]m, czym jestem bardziej rozczarowan[x], sobą czy tą książką.

Readers may differ in their arousal in response to the events and decisions of the characters in the story because they have different predispositions, attachment styles, levels of sensitivity and episodic memories for activating certain emotions in certain situations (Hogan, 2022, p. 151). Some experiments have shown that readers who tend to be emotionally detached in real life (have an avoidant attachment style) may experience greater changes in their emotions when reading fiction (Djikic et al., 2009a, p. 17; Oatley, 2012, pp. 122–124).

On the basis of what the participants in the study said, we can conclude that:

- reluctance to read a particular book may be caused by external pressure, intrusive marketing, challenging literary language, unfamiliar subject matter or genre, stereotypes about certain genres or types of books, predicted plot, or unacceptable viewpoints of the author, narrator, or literary character;
- dissatisfaction can arise from a number of factors, including but not limited to the quality of the work, its editorial or graphic design. Disdain is a stronger feeling expressed when a work is perceived as lacking literary quality and depth, although this is often ascribed by default to certain genres, particularly popular fiction;
- annoyance is caused by a certain protagonist's trait or behaviour, too detailed descriptions, frequent flashbacks, or interruptions of the reading by others; while frustration is caused by deviations from the pattern, the determination of the protagonist's fate, e.g. by revealing in the first chapter that the protagonist is going to die;

- disgust is caused by cruelty to people and animals, violation of purity, deformation of the body, unacceptable moral stances of the author/narrator/character;
- anger and moral indignation are caused by the violation of the formed self-image and the world, its coherence with the reader's knowledge and imagination, their value system, acquired cognitive patterns, predictions. It is a common reaction to the death of one of the protagonists with whom the reader has sympathised or empathised, an ending that is premature, hasty or perceived as negative and unjust because evil triumphs over good and the perpetrators are not punished; it can also be experienced when the reader witnesses the destruction or throwing away of books;
- disappointment comes from the failure to fulfil a need (an unhappy ending or ending without a proper closure, rereading beloved books after years);
- remorse can be caused by having succumbed to stereotyping;
- sadness is a reaction to the death of the protagonist, the breakdown of a relationship, the end of the reading and the need to say goodbye to the characters and leave the world of the story;
- fear or rather personal distress is triggered when the distance to reality is reduced or blurred and the reader is forced to confront the painful and repressed that has not yet been processed;
- anxiety is an emotional response to events in the novel, caused by the tension created by plot turns that increase uncertainty about the protagonist's fate. Anxiety can also be caused by a lack of skills appropriate to a challenge and a sense of being judged by what one reads or how one interprets. If one has already been judged, it will cause embarrassment or shame. The latter is also often triggered by reading or talking about certain topics (e.g. sexual matters), especially if it takes place in a specific setting and in the presence of others.

Negative emotions have both a defensive and a modifying effect. Moreover, the regulatory mechanisms of the mind allow one to control the vision one imagines, unlike, for example, in a movie:

> What we see in a movie is someone else's vision, someone else's imagination, and it can be sort of more intense than what we imagine, so our imagination based on the book can probably be more gentle, safer for us [71].[33]
>
> To, co widzimy w filmie, to jest czyjaś wizja, czyjeś wyobrażenie i ono może być jakby intensywniejsze od tego, co my sobie wyobrazimy gdzieś tam, więc nasze wyobrażenie na podstawie książki może być chyba może być bezpieczniejsze.

Experiencing fear, anger or sadness makes us aware of what is really important and encourages us to think or act, to defend values or seek clarification. Pain, suffering and the awareness of death are, as Antonio Damasio says, a more powerful driving force than pleasure and wellbeing (2022, p. 104). These can also help develop qualitatively new emotions.

---

[33] See also Hanich, 2018.

After reading

Looking for compensation

Readers often look for books that not only let them enter their world, but also keep them inside for a long time. This explains the popularity of epics, cycles and series of novels, or even books written by the same author.

Readers do not want to stop being involved in the events of a novel while they are still being entertained (Riggs & Knobloch-Westerwick, 2023, p. 2). If they are in a rush to know how it ends and are deeply absorbed in reading, they do not want to be interrupted, so they may deliberately avoid interacting with others:

> I am on a walk and I am there listening to this book so intently that it annoys me to have people greet me, so I try, if I see someone familiar, to go past so that they do not notice me, so that I do not have to turn off the book [R76].

> Jestem na spacerze i jednak jestem tam zasłuchan[x] w tę książkę na tyle, że irytuje mnie, że ludzie pozdrawiają mnie, więc staram się, jeżeli widzę kogoś znajomego, tak przejść, żeby mnie nie zauważył, żebym nie musiał/a wyłączać książki.

If they have to put the book down and stop reading, the moment of gratification is postponed. On the one hand, this encourages them to imagine possible scenarios, thereby maintaining a mental connection with the book; on the other hand, it spoils the fun and they risk losing track of the plot:

> I like to start reading a book and just read it, and I keep some kind of continuity in my mind, that even if I'm not reading it at a given moment, I'm thinking about that book [R71].

> Lubię zacząć czytać książkę i ją po prostu przeczytać i gdzieś tam jakąś taką ciągłość w głowie zachować, że nawet jeżeli nie czytam w danym momencie, to gdzieś tam o tej książce myślę.

Sometimes readers delay the return to reality and the end of the "adventure", as they call reading:

> When the book drew me in and I enjoyed reading it, I would put off the pleasure until later more often, that when I finished a chapter, I could continue reading, but no, put it down, take care of something else and come back [R57].

> Jak książka mnie wciągnęła i cieszył[x]m się lekturą, to bardziej odkładał[x]m przyjemność na później, że jak kończył[x]m rozdział, mógł[x]m dalej czytać, to jednak odłóż, zajmij się czymś innym i wróć.

Despite their many responsibilities, they constantly look for opportunities to return to reading:

> When I don't know who killed and I'm on the penultimate chapter for example… then I have to listen. And then I do everything… even say to my son, "darling, I have to go out shopping." – "But mom, you just went!" But he knows that I have to go out, because at home there is no way for me to listen. I have to go out, because I forgot something, and to listen to this passage some more, whether this is really what it is, so the book really affects me, it really makes me addicted [Gender].

> Jak nie wiem, kto zabił i jest już przedostatni na przykład rozdział… to ja muszę posłuchać. I wtedy robię wszystko… nawet mówię do mojego syna, „syneczku, ja muszę wyjść na zakupy" – „Ale mamo, przed chwilą byłaś!" Ale on wie, że ja muszę wyjść, bo w domu nie ma opcji, żebym przesłuchała. Ja muszę wyjść, bo jeszcze czegoś tam zapomniałam i żeby jeszcze posłuchać ten kawałek, czy rzeczywiście to jest to, więc jak ona na mnie działa, jak ona mnie uzależnia ta książka.

Books that "pull you in" arouse the need for instant consumption of the next volumes or even of other media products related to them:

> It's been a long time since any book sucked me in so much that I would run to the store for the next volumes and the next books by this author and even go to see the movie [R88].

> Dawno mnie tak żadna książka nie wciągnęła, żeby biegać po następne tomy i po następne książki tej autorki i nawet pójść na film.

An idiosyncratic mental representation of the narrative world, characters and events is fully available only while reading, as the reader uses it to understand the story (Zwann, 1999, p. 15 as cited in Gerrig, 2018). After the reading is over, especially when absorption was mainly emotional, it diminishes. We can remember certain images, feelings and impressions, but not every aspect of the story in great detail (Andersen & Hakemulder, 2024, pp. 5, 14):

> I would not, for example, be able to describe to you in detail, visualize this world… this world exists for me when I am reading, I am immersed in it very deeply, so the boundaries between reality and this imaginary world are blurred, but when I leave it, I finish reading, all that is left is an impression, an emotion, while very few facts, information are left in me [R49].

> Ja bym nie był/a w stanie na przykład opowiedzieć ze szczegółami, zwizualizować tego świata… ten świat istnieje dla mnie wtedy, kiedy czytam, jestem w nim bardzo głęboko, tak że zacierają się granice pomiędzy rzeczywistością a tym światem wyobrażonym. W momencie, kiedy go opuszczam, kończę lekturę, to z tego wszystkiego zostaje mi wrażenie, emocja, natomiast bardzo niewiele zostaje we mnie faktów, informacji.

> I don't remember the books I've read in general, I remember moments… just as we probably remember things from life, we never know what we will remember, so it's probably the same with books [R92].
>
> Ja w ogóle nie pamiętam książek, które przeczytał[x]m, pamiętam momenty… tak jak pewnie z życia pamiętamy, nigdy nie wiemy, co zapamiętamy, tak pewnie z książki.

The inevitable return to reality therefore comes with some loss, and can even evoke a sense of distress at the break with a story friend with whom one feels a strong and authentic connection (Gottschall, 2021, p. 35):

> As an ending is associated with some sadness, the end of the story, no more, it's a shame, it was good, it was cool, but well, it's over [R74].
>
> Zamknięcie wiąże się z pewnym smutkiem, koniec historii, nie ma już więcej, szkoda, to było dobre, fajne, ale no cóż, skończyło się.

Positive endings have been shown to increase global reflection and lead to more story-consistent beliefs in the reader (Hamby & Brinberg, 2016, pp. 498–499, 503). Books that have aroused emotions and identification empathy (causing an emotional resonance) leave a certain trace of memory:

> I read it about 20 years ago, but I still remember Prince Myshkin, in "The Idiot", Ivan, Dmitri and Alosha in "Brothers Karamazov", while I do not remember others, I do not remember what happened in "The Witcher", these characters are in general a little cartoonish, the stories are hardly memorable, and I read "The Witcher" at the same time as Tolkien and Dostoevsky… I turned on the game and there were these characters, but I remembered nothing of it, only from the game, and I remember Dostoevsky to this day [R81].
>
> Ja to czytał[x]m ze 20 lat temu, ale do dzisiaj pamiętam tego księcia Myszkina, w „Idiocie", Iwana, Dymitra i Aloszę w „Braciach Karamazow", podczas gdy innych nie, nie pamiętam, co się działo w „Wiedźminie", te postacie są w ogóle takie trochę papierowe, historie jakoś nie zapadają w pamięć, a czytał[x]m tego „Wiedźmina" w tym samym czasie co Tolkiena i Dostojewskiego… włączył[x]m sobie grę i tam takie postacie były, ale nic z tego nie pamiętałem, dopiero z gry, a Dostojewskiego pamiętam do dzisiaj.

Some of the compensatory activities after the "loss" include rereading, looking for information about the book or the author, reaching for other books by the author, and reading derivative works:

> I was so engrossed in the story, and it bummed me out that it was the end of the trilogy, there was no further story, that I even read up on the historical threads,

what happened afterwards, I looked it up in Wikipedia to sort of say goodbye to these characters [R76].

Tak był[x]m bardzo wkręcon[x] w historię i zasmuciło mnie, że to już koniec trylogii, już nie ma dalej historii, że nawet sobie doczytywał[x]m wątki historyczne, jak to tam dalej potem było, w Wikipedii sprawdzał[x]m, żeby tak jakby się pożegnać z tymi bohaterami.

To relieve tension, a reader may also want to share their experiences with others or to seek affirmation, confirmation of their impressions from the opinions of other readers (need for social acknowledgement, see in Hanich, 2018, p. 440):

I pester my husband, I say, listen, you know, because here is this character, and he behaved this way" and, for example, I am still affected by it and share that I do not like certain things [Gender]

Ja męczę mojego męża, mówię, „Słuchaj, wiesz, bo tu jest ten bohater, on i tak zachował" i na przykład przeżywam i dzielę się z tym, że pewne rzeczy mi się nie podobają.

Discussing books with friends can also broaden one's perspectives. However, even when readers agree on the overall judgment of a book, they tend to give different weight to different aspects of it:

The interpretations were the same, while the perception of what was more interesting to us differed, for example, X found the third volume verbose, while for me it was all right in terms of the pace of the plot, also other character traits of the main character were more important to me than to X, who treated it holistically [R57].

Interpretacje były takie same, natomiast różnił się odbiór tego, co było dla nas ciekawsze, na przykład X uznała, że trzeci tom był przegadany, kiedy dla mnie był całkiem w porządku, jeśli chodzi o szybkość akcji, też inne cechy charakteru głównego bohatera były dla mnie bardziej istotne niż dla X, która traktowała to całościowo.

Reading books allows readers to gain an appropriate aesthetic distance from themselves and their not-quite-assimilated feelings (Oatley, 1994, p. 63; 2012, p. 33; Schindler et al., 2022, p. 24) by entering another's feelings and thoughts and confronting the patterns they have learnt at home. Thanks to the retrospective reflection that results from the integration of information from the book and one's own world view (Gottschall, 2021, p. 55), readers may return with a better understanding or acceptance of themselves, with a self that is somehow expanded (in knowledge and experience) and empowered (with more self-esteem). They may also be less judgmental and more aware of the context of someone's actions, see things around them differently, and define their real-life situation differently than before (Wolf, 2019, pp. 43–45). It is therefore possible that the reader will be changed in some way by the "journey" (Gerrig, 2018, p. 16; Oatley, 2012, pp. 113, 116):

> Now when I read, it's like I became aware of this life a short time ago simply as if I woke up and I am a completely different person... now I understand that books were missing in my life. In general, I think that my life would have been completely different, better, wiser, I would have been able to solve various problems even life problems [Age].

> Teraz jak czytam, to po prostu to życie sobie tak jak gdyby uświadamiam... od niedawna po prostu jak gdybym się przebudził/a i jestem zupełnie inną osobą... teraz rozumiem, że zabrakło książek w moim życiu. Ogólnie myślę, że moje życie wyglądałoby zupełnie inaczej, lepiej, mądrzej, po prostu bym potrafił/a rozwiązywać różne problemy takie nawet życiowe.

Some studies have shown that "transportation affects the impact of a story on readers' story implicated beliefs and on their evaluation of protagonists" (Green & Brock, 2000, p. 703). However, the question of whether this leads to a better understanding of other people in real life and changes our behaviour remains unanswered. The assumption that this is the case does not take into account the asymmetry of the knowledge we have about other people compared to that we have gained about the novel's characters (especially the protagonist) by observing their actions, analysing their statements or learning about their mindset. We can only hope that, since the book encourages us to go beyond ourselves, the reader will take its advice and open up to the perspective of the "other" also in that life that is not a dream or a simulation.

A tale of two systems

Defining the situation

In reading mode, instead of behaviour (e.g. fleeing from a dangerous situation), the reader responds with an emotional reaction and an affective-cognitive judgment, and in some cases a physical reaction that can be directly experienced by the reader (e.g. accelerated heartbeat, laughing, crying). Experiencing specific emotions depends on how one interprets a situation in context. "How people define situation matters" – says Charmaz. Something that would cause fear in real life may cause excitement in the narrative world. This can also change over a lifetime as we "learn different ways to define our situation" (Charmaz et al., 2019, pp. 35, 38). However, it is worth noting that researchers disagree on when the cognitive evaluation of a stimulus occurs. According to the *James-Lange theory* (1884), an external stimulus causes a physiological response (arousal), which we then interpret as an emotion, such as fear when we see something threatening ("emotions resulting from bodily feedback" – Otis, 2022, p. 16). In the *Cannon-Bard theory* (1920), physiological arousal and emotional sensation are simultaneous but independent. We do not need to experience physiological changes to feel an emotion; rather, physiological arousal is responsible for the intensity of the sensation but does not condition the experience of the emotion (Otis, 2022, p. 16). In the *Schachter-Singer two-factor theory of emotion*, interpreting physiological arousal in context is necessary for experiencing emotion (identifying the cause of arousal and the event); for example, if the stimulus is not interpreted as threatening, it will not cause fear (Schachter-Singer, 1962, pp. 91–92; Dror, 2017). In *Lazarus' cognitive-motivational-relational theory*, emotions are not automatic responses, but are determined by the appraisal of the stimulus (which precedes physiological response and emotion), such as the degree of threat, harm or challenge (primary appraisal of the significance of the stimulus) and the ability to cope with it (secondary appraisal). A reappraisal strategy is also employed, with the aim of reframing and thereby regulating emotions (Lazarus & Folkman, 1987, pp. 144–147, Lazarus, 1991, 830). Thus, the feeling of emotion is a function of one's interpretation of the situation in context. According to the transactional model of stress and coping, the secondary appraisal of the situation is twofold, through a problem-focussed strategy (such as planning or restraining (cognitive) or taking actions (behavioural)) – is the ability to change the situation itself – or an emotion-focussed strategy (such as denial or social support seeking), the ability to change the relationship to the situation[34] (Lazarus, 1991; Smith & Kirby, 2009, p. 1357; Garnefski et al., 2001, p. 1312–1313). The mechanism of regulation also allows the reader to control the imagined vision to a certain extent.

The excitation-transfer theory suggests that a stimulus first triggers a physiological and psychological arousal. This arousal can then transfer to a subsequent, less intense stimulus, influencing and potentially amplifying our emotional reaction. *The three-factor theory of emotion*, developed by Dolf Zillmann and Joanne Cantor, expands on this by suggesting three key factors that contribute to our emotional experience: dispositional factors, the excitatory factor (level of physiological arousal), and the experimental factor (our interpretations of the situation) (Bryant & Miron, 2003). In the relational model of appraisal and emotion proposed by Smith and Kirby, the focus is not on *what is appraised*, as in Lazarus' structural model, but on *how people evaluate* the emotional stimuli ("situational and dispositional antecedents of appraisals" (2009, p. 1352). The researchers suggest that emotional experience involves three processes: perceptual stimulation (observing and experiencing fear or pleasure), associative processing (activating memories), and reasoning (slower than immediate appraisal, involving critical thinking).

With regard to empathy, there are also two models: *the late appraisal model* and the *early appraisal model*. The first one stands for the automatic activation of empathy through perception of an emotional cue. The empathic response can be modulated by contextual appraisal. The second model suggests that the empathic response is elicited through appraisal, taking into account both external and internal information. As Frederique de

---

34 There is a difference between cognitive (planning) and behavioural (taking actions) emotion regulation. Garnefski et al. analyse the former, such as: self blame, blaming others, acceptance, refocus on planning, positive refocusing, rumination or focus on thought, positive reappraisal, putting into perspective, catastrophizing (2001, pp. 1314–1316, 1319–1320). See also Stanisławski, 2019.

Vignemont and Tania Singer put it, "in this model there are two independent systems working in parallel, empathic resonance and appraisal processes" (2006, p. 438).
According to the model proposed by Joseph Le Doux, when emotions are felt in response to an external stimulus, the signal is transmitted along the so-called lower primary emotion pathway from the thalamus (decoding) to the amygdala (recognising and responding, as well as emotional memory) and then via ascending pathways to the prefrontal cortex (awareness of the emotion) (Jarymowicz & Imbir, 2010). When reader makes conscious judgments, the process of signal transmission here follows from the thalamus via the cortex to the amygdala (Jarymowicz & Imbir, 2010, pp. 445–446). It must be said that an oversimplification of these processes can lead to the assumption that they work sequentially, when in fact some of them can work in parallel ("low" and "high" roads of information processing), with feedback loops between structures.
A more automatic, primary System 1 may have an advantage over secondary, reflexive System 2 in threatening situations (the role of the amygdala in dealing with imminent danger). It also exhibits greater activity in people with depression, because their prefrontal cortex is thinner and synaptic connections are reduced (Csabai et al., 2018; Kang et al., 2012). The cingulate cortex, which synaptically receives signals from both systems, may enhance emotional over cognitive reactions. In moral cognition and conscious emotional regulation, the ventromedial prefrontal cortex plays a critical role. It receives information from the amygdala and cortical regions, integrates it and helps to make judgments based on social values (Young & Koenigs, 2007, p. 71).

Liking and judging

The transportation to the imaginary world changes one's sense of one's body: "the rest of the body doesn't exist, I disconnect from it, I don't need it" [R49]. Readers experience things as if in a dream, "surrendering to the author's vision" [R45]. Although our bodies are more relaxed during fluent reading in the *flow* state (Thissen et al., 2021) with a limited ability to respond to external stimuli[35], we remain conscious, our brain activity is high, and our eye movements are purposeful (saccades, and fixation periods), unlike, for example, the NREM phase. The body is actively involved in reading. What is familiar (consistent with past experience or environmental demands and known to the reader)[36] and desirable is accepted (an approach system), and what is unknown (a source of tension) and undesirable (a source of disgust, aversion) or inconsistent with existing knowledge may be rejected (an avoidance system) or eventually accepted after some reduction,

---

35 A variety of studies on psychophysiological responses to reading have been conducted, providing evidence that heart rate (HR) or heart rate variability (HRV) may be associated with the ability to regulate emotions (modify their expression) and cognitive performance (text comprehension). However, it should be noted that the results may vary depending on the text material (e.g. a novel or web pages used in the experiment), its length, and the age and level of literacy of the reader, as well as the time at which the heart rate (HR) or heart rate variability (HRV) is measured (before reading, during reading, or after reading) (Brouwer et al., 2015; Mason et al., 2018; Williams et al., 2015).
36 The hippocampus plays an important role in recognising and orienting towards situations (Broadbent et al., 2004, p. 14519).

such as putting in perspective (Bermejo-Berros et al., 2022, p. 13; Hamby & Brinberg, 2016, p. 499; Jarymowicz & Imbir, 2010, pp. 450–451; Vorderer et al., 2004, p. 388). This process of approaching or inhibiting happens automatically, hence the problem of identifying the source of excitation, naming emotions, and restraining expression:

> I am not speaking, for example, of some clearly identifiable emotions: joy, sadness, sorrow, because I do not know if I would be able to name these emotions that way, if I would be able to distinguish them, it is rather a wave of emotions [49].
>
> Nie wspominam na przykład o jakichś emocjach jednoznacznie się kojarzących, radość, smutek, żal, bo nie wiem, czy ja nawet bym był/a w stanie tutaj tak nazywać te emocje i nawet nie wiem, czy był[x]bym w stanie je wyróżnić, to jest raczej taka fala emocjonalna.

It may not be clear where they come from or which episodic memories are associated with them (Hogan, 2022, p. 153). Emotions spread to all aspects of the book (and, according to the *excitatory transfer theory*, to other objects as well), making it difficult for the reader to justify their liking or disliking of certain aspects of the book (Jarymowicz & Imbir, 2010, p. 447). Readers' reactions can also be hard to stop:

> Jeez, when I was reading this book, I cried and laughed, and this was at work to boot [R92].
>
> Jezu, ja na tej książce i płakał[x]m i śmiał[x]m się i to jeszcze był[x]m w pracy.
>
> When I'm reading "Harry Potter", I can cry for half an hour [R21].
>
> Nad "Harrym Potterem" potrafię ryczeć przez pół godziny.
>
> Sometimes I found myself crying from laughter on the bus [R45].
>
> Czasami zdarzało mi się płakać ze śmiechu w autobusie.
>
> Recently I was reading a book, and I cried a lot, because it moved me so much... I couldn't contain my tears, and I remember, it was a beautiful summer, the garden, the sun, my husband was reading some newspaper, in between I would even mutter one-word answers like "yes" or "no," but at a certain point I was not able to interrupt the book and I read and cried and I think I even sobbed [Gender].
>
> Ostatnio też czytałam książkę i bardzo płakałam, bo mnie bardzo wzruszyła... Nie umiałam opanować łez i pamiętam, to było piękne lato, ogród, słońce, mąż sobie czytał jakąś gazetę, nawet w międzyczasie coś tam odburknęłam „tak" albo „nie", ale już w pewnym momencie nie byłam w stanie książki przerwać i czytałam i płakałam i chyba nawet zaszlochałam.

They are influenced by external stimuli that arouse them and encourage them to maintain contact and to consume books or repeat readings that evoke desired feelings or help to distract from daily sorrows (hedonic disengagement – Stanisławski, 2019). Reading in this mode is controlled by System 1 in the dual-processing hypothesis of the mind. It works on the "associative-intuitive processor".[37] Unwanted content, such as that which evokes disgust, can be automatically inhibited, reduced if reader uses any coping strategy, or accepted after reappraisal in the secondary, reflexive system.[38] The process of activation or inhibition, regulated by the appraisal, which is an "evaluative component of emotion", as Giovanna Colombetti says (2007, p. 527), and known as appraisal of the compatibility of the content, relevant to the reader's needs and congruent with the reader's knowledge, goals and environmental demands)[39], ensures the stimulation to explore (hedonic motivation) and the satisfaction of basic emotional and psychological needs (gaining/restoring homeostasis) (Figure 2). As an automatic system of appraisal, it seems closely linked to the formation of daily habits ("I read in the morning/evening", "I read a series", "I read more books by the author", "I skip long descriptions", "I don't finish reading a book that…").

More complex emotions and states emerge as a result of conscious mental processes. Readers follow the plot, make inferences based on clues embedded in the text, relate the story events in which they are emotionally involved to their internalised value system (the world of axiological concepts of right and wrong), imagine the situation as if they were in the character's shoes, and take an 'interpersonal stance' towards the character's emotions, which may lead to empathy or sympathy. Reflections on the self, others and the world are constantly interwoven. Readers form judgments regarding a book by noting specific features thereof, such as the cover, the plot, the characters and the language. They may also re-evaluate some aspects at a later stage or when they read the book again. Subsequent evaluations involve a juxtaposition of the reader's initial impressions with their later reflections, both during and after the reading process. Conscious judgments engage a complex neural network that enables readers to assess their skills and abilities to cope with the challenge, threat, harm or loss, not just the significance of the stimulus as in System 1. This appears to be regulated by the second, much newer, language processor, which operates sequentially, yet not in complete isolation, as it is interdependent on System 1 (Clark as cited in Oatley, 2011, pp. 77, 214).[40] System 2 activates a mechanism for controlling the standards of the "self", especially the degree of compliance with social norms and the compatibility of "self" (seen as a continuous process of experiencing and

---

37 See for example Sergio Da Silva, 2023. More also in Andy Clark's research on the "hybrid mind" (2006), as cited in Oatley, 2011, pp. 76–77.
38 Krzysztof Stanisławski claims, on the basis of the findings of Lazarus, Folkman, Skinner and Wellborn, that "coping refers to both volitional and automatized, cognitive, emotional, and behavioral responses to stress" (2019, pp. 4–5).
39 See Richard Lazarus' primary appraisal in the structural model of appraisal (Lazarus 1991, p. 827; Smith & Kirby, 2009, p. 1357).
40 For further information regarding the so-called *unified model*, please refer to the works of Kruglanski & Gigerenzer (2011) and Laura F. Mega et al. (2015).

developing) with "self-concept" (what the reader can define as their own and what tends to be stable). Typical phrases used by study participants that indicate such a comparison or formation of opinion included: "I read faster/more than others", "I read what others read or the opposite (avoid bestsellers, award-winning books)", "I read something difficult", "I want to understand", "I don't read a certain genre/type of books", "I don't read when…", "I buy something that others may like, something to be proud of, something useful", "I participate in reading challenges", "I read books in the canon", "I talk to others about books", "I wonder what I would do in the character's shoes", "I am inspired by them", "I identify with some characters"). It is all the result of assimilated standards of *ought-own self* or *ought-other self* and formed *ideal self* or *desired self* (Martínez, 2014, pp. 118–119, 123). Readers may attempt to maintain social order and conform to cultural expectations (Charmaz et al., 2019, pp. 7–8). When they feel shame, guilt, frustration or boredom they try to restore the disturbed balance. However, the realisation of the duty-based standards of the self brings rather relief than pleasure. Satisfaction and a sense of self-efficacy come from "pursuing intrinsic goals and values" (Ryan, 2005, p. 139) by voluntarily engaging in activities that meet the challenges. It can lead to personal growth, promote greater awareness and contribute to a broadened view of the world of others. However, this can only be achieved through an ongoing dialogue with them, rather than a self-focused approach. Understanding the motivations of fictional characters requires both systems to work together. Automatic emotional mirroring and rapid affective response are supported by reflective *perspective-taking* resulting from more deliberate cognitive reasoning. Data from both the real and fictional worlds, as well as the reader's memories and beliefs, are integrated and emotions can be regulated in the process of reappraisal.

Both systems – the first, which is more intuitive, automatic, associative and based on mental shortcuts (heuristics), and the second, which is more reflective, effortful and slower, able to produce long-term effects – work together to enhance the reading experience. The first system provides content/reading material that is deemed sufficiently "safe" and that meets the reader's immediate needs. It motivates readers to read, stimulates engagement and encourages continued reading, repetition and reaching for more books, which can or should be pleasurable or help to restore homeostasis (Miall & Kuiken, 2002, pp. 223–224). The second system enables reader to process more or less unfamiliar vocabulary, to decipher metaphorical meanings, to think in a more abstract way, to categorise, judge and evaluate more critically, to predict events (Da Silva, 2023, p. 1063). It helps to face challenges to gain understanding, increase the complexity of the self (self-expansion), strengthen its structures, order the state of consciousness and solidify the self.

It seems that, regardless of the type of book and whether the reader's current motivational force is hedonic, homeostatic or eudaimonic, both systems are at work when reading a book. However, the balance between them can shift depending on the situation, the complex of information being processed, the cognitive resources available or the pressure of time (Da Silva, 2023, p. 1057). Crucial here is determining "the motivations we have for altering or sustaining a current state" (Hogan, 2022, p. 157). Over time, with practice, if some processes become too automatic, readers may feel unchallenged and experience less engagement or satisfaction. In such cases, they may seek out more complex narratives or consider different genres, to elicit optimal cognitive and emotional engagement that matches their increased skills.

Satisfying needs

Leisure reading needs not be defined as a strictly hedonic activity, as it involves the reader at many levels and they pursue various motivations throughout the process. Caution is also needed when using what is known as the *mood management theory* to interpret the motivation of the media user.[41] Given this theory, we might want to argue that the reader chooses what to read to maintain a positive mood, maximising pleasure and minimising discomfort (Koopman, 2015, p. 19; Mar et al., 2011, p. 819). Many studies mention the so-called "tragic (drama) paradox", which is defined as a situation in which media users, instead of choosing content to maximise their pleasure, choose to read or watch sad or tragic novels/films (Bartsch et al., 2014; Koopman, 2015; Oatley, 2012; Oliver & Bartsch, 2010). "Sad books" can increase feelings of discomfort. And even when they end happily, as Emy Koopman argues against the *excitation transfer theory*, this does not seem to be enough to compensate for the negative content experienced for a long time while reading. Moreover, many of these novels do not have happy endings. A more nuanced view of this issue is presented by Mary Beth Oliver and Arthur A. Raney or Kate T. Luong and Silvia Knobloch-Westerwick. Those last ones, after comparison *mood management theory* and the *selective exposure self- and affect-management model*, conclude that users not only want to manage their mood, but also to satisfy other needs related to the search for truth and moral beauty and self-development (Luong & Knobloch-Westerwick, 2021; Oliver, 2003, p. 986). This leads to the following conclusions, people read sad books not because they want to *feel good* while reading or *feel better* after reading them[42], but because they want to *feel more*, experience different states, learn new ways of coping with their feelings (e.g. anxiety) and problems, gain recognition, insight or even catharsis. Sad books "have the potential to move us more intensely than joyful media", as Koopman claims (2015, pp. 20–21, 27, see also Damasio, 2022, p. 104).

The very nature of an experience like reading is that it unfolds over time. The reader must therefore constantly regulate their state in response to what is happening in the story, how they define it and how they can deal with it (emotional or problem-focused coping). In some cases, they consume the content that is emotionally compatible with their current needs. It is then a routine activity that runs smoothly because there is no need to interpret deeply, just follow the story as it unfolds (Charmaz et al., 2019, p. 27). Consuming books minimises the need for deep processing, conserves strength and enables recovery, but does not transform the reader. It does not require the reader to put themselves in completely new situations or to experience mixed feelings. The intention

---

41 Raymond Mar argues that "distinct cognitive processes are required for the comprehension of literary fiction compared to television and film" (2010, p. 821).
42 However to some extent the *downward social comparison theory* applies here too.

behind such reading is to satisfy the emotional needs and cravings for new content (novelty bias, see Wolf, 2019, 70), to go beyond the limits of one's own experience, to experience a sense of excitement (Ryan et al., 2006, pp. 140, 159; Wirth et al., 2012, p. 410). Standards of the self may also come into play, forcing the reader to fulfil their obligation in order to maintain their self-esteem and feel relief rather than shame, guilt or disappointment. In this mode of reading, readers may feel that they need validation (external approval) rather than challenge. As one of the participants puts it:

> Readers reach for a book to get away from their daily problems for a while, to be entertained, to be delighted by something, to be moved by something, and they treat this book very instrumentally, like it's a short-term remedy, something very pop, meaning something to be consumed, devoured mindlessly, something that I need at the moment, but let's say it doesn't rearrange my intellect too much and doesn't require too much effort and competence, it's something easy, enjoyable, entertaining, something that offers solace, but also provides pleasure, maybe temporary, but extremely important [R49].

> Czytelnicy sięgają po tę książkę, żeby na chwilę się oderwać od codziennych problemów, żeby się rozerwać, żeby coś ich zachwyciło, żeby coś ich wzruszyło i traktują tę książkę tak bardzo instrumentalnie, doraźnie, bardzo pop, czyli jako coś, co można skonsumować, przeżuć, coś, co w tej chwili jest mi potrzebne, ale powiedzmy jakoś nie przemeblowuje za bardzo mojego intelektu i nie wymaga ode mnie aż takiego wysiłku i kompetencji, jest czymś łatwym, przyjemnym, rozrywkowym, czymś, co daje ukojenie, ale też zapewnia przyjemność, może i doraźną, ale niezwykle ważną.

It seems as though the content is absorbed more passively. Consumption exhausts the product, leaving no content for further processing and no long-lasting effects. After reading a book once, it is "used up" (Bloom, 2019b, p. 42):

> It was a cool book, an awesome book, I read it very quickly, it had me glued to the pages, I read it twice, but it's not a book that will tug at my viscera or emotions… in horror or detective stories very often the moment that disappoints is that moment of resolution, it's often the case, however, I look forward to the ending, look for something, and here is… so, this is what he contrived… endings often disappoint me… I don't know, maybe they are too simple, maybe I wanted something more, maybe I imagined that God knows what will happen, or maybe they just affect me too little, but I would like the book to stay with me, to move something in me. The monster appears, the villain, the mystery is explained, the villain is defeated, and that's how it all ends, and that's generally disappointing to me [R74].

> To była fajna książka, super książka, przeczytał[x]m ją bardzo szybko, wciągnęła mnie, przeczytał[x]m ją dwa razy, ale to nie jest książka, która poszarpie moimi trzewiami czy emocjami… w horrorach czy w kryminałach bardzo często momentem, który rozczarowuje, jest ten moment wyjaśnienia, często tak jest,

że jednak człowiek dążył, szukał czegoś, a tu... aaa to tak sobie wymyślił... zakończenia często mnie rozczarowują... Nie wiem, może są zbyt proste, może ja chciał[x]m czegoś więcej, może sobie wymyślił[x]m, że nie wiadomo, co się stanie, a może po prostu za słabo oddziałują, ja bym jednak chciał/a, żeby książka we mnie zostawała, żeby coś we mnie poruszała. Pojawia się potwór, ten zły, zagadka jest wyjaśniona, zło jest pokonane i tak się to wszystko kończy i to jest dla mnie z reguły rozczarowujące.

If the books we read do not challenge us (they do not lead us to cross the "conventionally scripted boundaries" (Miall & Kuiken, 2002, p. 227), do not provoke us to reflect on what we have experienced (reflective emotions – see Oatley, 2012, p. 101), and do not induce self-modifying feelings, we may feel bored or disappointed after some time. It should be emphasised, however, that reading something "light" or in a consumption-oriented mode can be beneficial for the reader. It brings a short-lived satisfaction that comes from the gratification of needs, reduced tension or getting rid of unwanted thoughts, and as a result "can in the long run affect health" (as Pennington & Waxler put it, paraphrasing Pico Iyer, 2018, p. 100). Pleasure reading allows readers to mentally distance themselves from their responsibilities, escape into suspense or distract themselves from everyday worries[43]:

> I find this book so engrossing that it lets me turn off thinking... my head works nonstop, I can't turn it off, I can't stop thinking, figuring things out, counting, planning, I can't turn it off with anything but a book. And it must be a good book [R56].

> Ta książka jest dla mnie na tyle wciągająca, że ona pozwala mi wyłączyć myślenie... mi głowa non stop pracuje, ja nie umiem się wyłączać, nie umiem przestać myśleć, kombinować, liczyć, planować, nie umiem tego wyłączyć przy niczym tylko przy książce. I to musi być dobra książka.

> It was a way to relax a little, read a little, to have some sort of privacy, peace and quiet for myself [R25].

> Była jakimś tam sposobem na relaks, trochę przeczytać, trochę jakby mieć takiej prywatności, ciszy dla siebie.

> I prefer books that lift me up emotionally or give me relief, joy [R97].

> Wolę książki, które mnie podnoszą psychicznie czy dają taką ulgę, radość.

> I have already forgotten about my misfortunes, and there is such relaxation, and while reading the words of this book, sometimes delving into them fully, I dream a little, that if things were like this, it would be better, it would be easier [R32].

---

43 See Koopman, 2014 and what Oatley notes, based on the reading of Janice Radway's Reading the Romance, 2012, p. 77.

> Zapomniał[x]m już o tych swoich jakichś nieszczęściach i takie odprężenie następuje i wczytując się w słowa tej książki, no nieraz tak całkowicie, człowiek jeszcze coś pomarzy, że ach, jakby to tak było, no to by było lepiej, byłoby lżej.

A book constitutes a *psychological (imaginative, intimate) space* in which the reader can be alone for a while (Fuller & Rehberg Sedo, 2013, p. 32). The idiosyncratic act of concretisation is why the book seems to be the most intimate medium. One of the interviewees confirmed this by saying: "a relationship with a book is the most intimate relationship of my life" [R49].[44] What can be added to this is Julian Hanich's remark that the reading of a book "amplifies a sense of mineness" (2018, p. 431, see also Damasio, 2022, p. 165–166). The metaphors of what a book can be for readers and what needs it can fulfil are shown in Figure 1. There are three domains here: *empirical* (action-based or physical), *cognitive* (based on knowledge, abstract thinking and language use) and *affective* (emotion-based). Each can be characterised by a gerund describing activities, processes or states in which the book is involved. For example, the empirical sphere can by described by *producing* (a book perceived as material), *owning* (a book as a product that can be purchased and collected), *consuming* (a book as food[45]), *using* (a book as a tool) or *measuring* (a book perceived by its size, thickness or number of pages).

Reading engagement, driven by the excitement and curiosity generated by emotions, internal needs (consistency with acquired knowledge, sense of belonging, recognition by others) and standards of self, such as *ought-other self, ought-own self* requires relevant content (e.g. familiar in type or genre, desirable or at least not aversive) that brings pleasure, hope and a kind of validation. Books to consume, or consuming them as a mode or phase of reading, can have a regulating and restorative effect, firstly by stimulating exploration (hedonic mechanism), and secondly by helping to restore the balance (psychological or cognitive) that has been disturbed in daily life (homeostatic mechanism). This conclusion seems to be somewhat in line with *mood management theory* (Vorderer, 2003, p. 131; Vorderer et al., 2004, p. 389).

Books could also have a more modifying effect, contributing to the psychological development and expansion of the self (Csíkszentmihályi, 2022, pp. 84–89). In order to satisfy more eudaimonic needs for personal growth, self-understanding or truth-seeking, evoked by axiological concepts and standards of the self (mainly the *ideal self* or the *actual self*, as the *ought-own self* is more oriented towards maintaining current self-esteem), and ultimately to find truth and achieve self-expansion (being able to overcome self-limitations, including those in the moral domain, such as stereotypical thinking), the reader needs to use a more conscious, slower, reflective style of processing and a set of skills appropriate to the challenge.

Mary Beth Oliver and Arthur A. Raney argue that entertainment can be both pleasurable and meaningful, satisfying both hedonic and eudaimonic needs (2011, p. 985).

---

44 See also in Purchase, 2019, pp. 79–80.

45 Metaphors of reading as eating were common in the interviews, as in the literature on reading experience. See for example Manguel, 2023, pp. 243, 246.

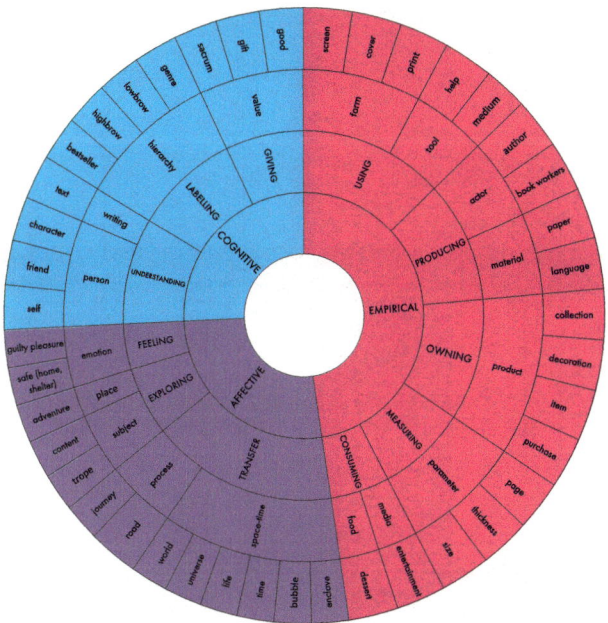

Figure 1. Books as metaphors – a schema of the reader's needs

In contrast to the *dual-processing hypothesis of the mind*, according to the *unified model*: "judging intuitively or deliberately both rely on similar or same mental processes following similar processing rules, while differentially engaging divergent mental structures ... any rule can be easier (or more difficult) to process, used consciously or non-consciously, and its use is not determined by the operation of one distinct system over another but rather the amount of available resources" argues Laura Mega et al. (2015, p. 13). It appears that the hedonic, homeostatic and eudaimonic mechanisms may be interconnected, potentially operating at varying levels during the act of reading, depending on a reader's motivation, which is driven by current needs (quick gratification or satisfaction of higher-order needs), skills, mentalising competencies, and potential for emotional or problem-focused coping, rather than the specific type or genre of book being read.[46] Figure 2 shows the affective-cognitive processes involved in the act of reading according to the regulatory system. The conceptual framework is based on that described and structured by Maria Jarymowicz and Kamil Imbir (2010, p. 457, see Table 1). My extension of the framework is on the basis of the results of this study.

---

46 See also Antonio Damasio, 2022, pp. 35, 109, who states that coordinating three modes of processing, related to being, feeling and knowing, helps to integrate mental images with our body. This kind of self-reference is essential for the evocation of personal experience.

Evaluation system	Source of emotion		Stimuli	Feeling/state	Response	Elicitation mechanisms	Purpose
System 1 (automatic, primary)	external	arousal	positive	pleasure, happiness, hope	approaching, consuming, repeating	**hedonic** (experience pleasure)	to act / to explore
			negative	reluctance, anxiety, personal distress, disgust	inhibiting		
	internal	drive	desired	consistency with prior knowledge, recognition by others, sense of belonging	satisfying needs		to sustain existence / to achieve well-being
			unwanted	inconsistency with prior knowledge, feeling rejected, judged, different	reducing distortions		
System 2 (reflexive, secondary)	standards of self	*ought-own self, ought-other self,* other-focused standards	adapting behaviour to standards, fulfilling obligations	moderately positive emotions	feeling relief	**homeostatic** (self-regulation)	to maintain positive self-esteem (cognitive balance)
			deviations from the norm, failing to comply with the obligations imposed	shame, guilt, disappointment, remorse, low self-esteem	applying emotion- or problem-focussed strategies (defining oneself in a new way, putting in perspective, blame-others, catastrophizing etc.)		
		actual self ideal self	skills (moderately) exceed challenge	relaxation or boredom	(un)voluntary engaging in the activity		
			challenge and skills are low	boredom or apathy			
			challenge greater than skills	anxiety, worry			
			challenge meets skills	*flow state* enjoyment (satisfaction, pride, sense of efficacy, self-acceptance)	voluntary engaging in the activity, pursuing intrinsic goals		to achieve insight, personal growth
	axiological concepts		expressions of kindness, goodness, justice, virtue, righteousness, beauty	admiration, appreciation, being moved, moral elevation	redefining needs, overcoming limitations and stereotypes, getting to know oneself and others better, becoming more aware	**eudaimonic** meaning-making (self-expansion self-understanding truth-seeking)	
	transgressive		expressions of injustice, immorality, malice, wickedness	anger, moral indignation, frustration, repulsion, disappointment, sadness	looking for causes, motives, solutions, reinterpreting		to pursue a cause greater than yourself

Figure 2. Affective-cognitive processes involved in the act of reading

Further studies

In the context of our daily lives, we are exposed to numerous changes. Some of them can be regarded as revolutionary, including the transitions between life stages, major and difficult life events such as leaving university, entering the workforce, starting a family, having a child or facing a medical issue. Such events can have a profound impact on an individual's lifestyle, personal interests, self-esteem, motivation, and goals. Only through the use of longitudinal research, including in-depth qualitative interviews, can this be fully explored. However, we should also bear in mind that there are some almost imperceptible shifts in our daily routines that are taking place all the time. To a certain extent, these can be attributed to a number of external factors. Greater access to the cultural offerings and job markets of other countries may encourage individuals to read books from other cultures in order to learn something useful and experience personal growth. However, it appears that the influence of social media and audio-video streaming platforms is even more powerful, as they are changing the way we communicate and consume cultural goods. The plethora of distractions offered by today's digital world affects not only "what" we watch, listen to, play or read, but also "how" we do it. It is harder to focus on one thing at a time than it was five or ten years ago. Given the rapid development of technology in recent years, we should address how it affects certain aspects of our lives, including reading, which may be particularly threatened in the face of multitasking and hyperattention (more about "switch costs" in Wolf & Gottwald, 2016, p. 146).

It would be beneficial for future studies to apply an observational approach in a natural setting to collect data on the reading habits and practices of avid readers in real time. The study could use a self-reporting tool (a digital diary) installed on a mobile phone to collect self-reported data from readers about their experiences while reading books or afterwards (not based on psychometrics such as Csíkszentmihályi's Experience Sampling Method, 2014, pp. 21–34). The study would not look at how people say they usually read, or how they used to read; it would instead focus on their current reading practices. The use of digital diary apps to collect data at different points in time allows for a more reliable analysis of fluctuations in reading practices than is possible with data obtained from surveys or interviews. This is because there is no recall bias or social desirability bias. Furthermore, readers report on specific readings that are still vivid in their minds, rather than on their preferences or aggregated experiences.

When I talk about a change or something more subtle, a "shift" in reading behaviour (such as a change in mood), I talk about an observed deviation (fluctuations) in someone's reading habits, short-term adjustments in behaviour that can be tracked over a period of weeks, not in the context of someone's entire life. Investigating reading practices means looking at how someone's reading activity manifests itself in their actions, motivations and evaluations.

One of the possible outcomes of such a study could be to identify clusters of people with similar reading patterns. However, we may be interested not only in whether readers who identify themselves as avid readers share common characteristics, how many books they read, what genres they read, how they choose books and whether they prefer print books to e-books or audiobooks, but most importantly, how their reading practices might fluctuate over short periods of time. It seems reasonable to measure the frequency of new reads, rereads and unfinished books, as well as the frequency with which readers move between different genres, book formats, devices and locations while reading a single book and subsequent books. Such measurements could yield insights into the reading behaviours of a particular cohort of readers. It would be beneficial to ascertain how frequently they deviate from their typical reading preferences and habits. How often, if ever, and when do they change the source of books, e. g. borrowing instead of buying? How do their reading motivations and needs change with each book they read? How do their reading immersion (being drawn into the world of the story) and evaluations differ (how do they rate the different elements of a work?), as well as the subjectively perceived effects of reading? Do reading engagement, motivation, book evaluations, and reading effects change over time as readers reread, continue reading, move on to the next book in a series or follow the same author?

My future research interests lie in the twofold aspect of reading: the first, behavioural, encompassing reading routines and habits, and the second, affective-cognitive, which pertains to mental strategies, such as imagining the characters and events in a text, engaging emotionally with the protagonist, establishing personal connections, predicting and evaluating various elements of the book.

Getting to know the reader[1]

One of the interviewees started our conversation with those memorable words:

> Nowadays there's such a terrible pressure to be a writer, to be a creator who is admired by millions, if not billions, but somehow we terribly underestimate the readers [R49].
>
> W dzisiejszych czasach to jest taki straszny nacisk na to, żeby być autorem, żeby być twórcą, którym się będą zachwycać miliony, jeżeli nie miliardy, ale jakoś strasznie nie doceniamy czytelników.

I did my best to capture the full range of experiences described by study participants during the interviews. The readers' stories were multi-layered, but all followed a similar structure – either presenting the interviewee's reading biography or focusing on a particular stage of it. When people share their experiences of reading books, they often temporalise their reading experience, dividing it into periods marked by gradual or radical life events. These periods may be characterised by types or genres of books they read, formats, motivation, intensity and ways of reading. It indicates changes in the reader's needs, life and self. In telling their reading biographies, readers compare not only the books they have read in the past with those they are reading now, but also their impressions and reactions, the pace and depth of reading, as well as comparing themselves with other readers of a similar age. They often admit that they used to read more and for longer than they do now. They were also less selective about what they read. There is a time in every reader's life when they are exploring, discovering who they are and what their needs are. At this *exploration stage*, reader seeks out titles of different types and genres and reads them intensively, even several books a week, often experiencing deep immersion. This usually happens in high school, but if access to books is somehow limited, books are not easily accessible at home or through the public library, or a family situation discourages reading, it can happen in adulthood, even in retirement. When reader feels empowered enough to follow their own needs, they regain their autonomy in deciding what to read and how. It is a liberating experience that can have a profound impact on their future reading lives. It improves the quality of their reading experience, because reading on one's own terms (voluntarily) can satisfy current needs, help to find rest, feel enjoyment, experience adventure, maintain self-esteem, be moved (moral elevation), and gain a new perspective on a given issue. Reading free from external pressures

---

1 The title of this section is borrowed from a chapter in a textbook on librarianship by Jacek Wojciechowski, *Podstawy pracy z czytelnikiem* [*Fundamentals of working with a reader*] 1991, p. 97.

can also help reader to confront past reading failures (unfinished books) and overcome the inherited school-reading shame of not understanding a book. Reader can return to books that they once dismissed, perhaps because they were too difficult to read. With greater literacy and emotional maturity, understanding is now easier. The more books a reader reads, the more they enter a universe of related cultural works (not only books, but also films, series and games), among which they can find some similar motifs and satisfy their needs, whether emotional, psychological, social, transcendental or physical (relaxation, distraction, recognition, insight, owning the books etc.).

As reader gains autonomy in deciding what to read and how, their perception of books may change. Having explored, reader already has a relatively well-formed literary taste and knows what they like to read. It can narrow down the reading in terms of the types or genres of books that are read. Intensive reading experience makes reader more selective and discerning, paying also more attention to literary features. To avoid the disappointment of being challenged by new content that may not be satisfying, they may reread their favourites more often. Beloved books are therefore a kind of guarantee that reading expectations will be fulfilled. In some cases, however, rereading can also be a source of disappointment, because we never really read the same book again. Each time we remember or forget something else, using our expanded knowledge and paying attention to different aspects of the book (Manguel, 2023, p. 101).

Despite the fact that adult readers may become more selective, this does not mean they stop experimenting for good. They do so when they feel that reading the same type of books does not bring the expected results, e.g. does not surprise them, arouse emotions or provide new knowledge. Some life events, such as starting a family, having a baby, getting diagnosed with an illness, or disruptions, such as moving house or commuting, can affect someone's reading in terms of genres, types of books and its formats. Although adult avid readers often claim that they do not read certain genres (e.g. fantasy or romance) that they feel are not for them (disparity between their self-concept and the idea of who reads such books or how they are written or what benefits they bring), they may overcome this reluctance and explore less favoured types of books when encouraged by friends' recommendations, literary awards, pop culture influence, or specific circumstances. Transformative moments for readers are often associated with the end of one phase of life and the beginning of a new one, becoming aware of one's needs, a change of environment (home/work), the birth of a child, an illness or a difficult personal/family situation that changes priorities. In these moments books become a tool for changing the habits and the way readers think about themselves or the world. Whether the willingness to take on challenges and face one's own limitations or unknowns diminishes with age needs to be explored further. Analysis of the collected material provides anecdotal evidence that it may be more related to when the exploration phase occurs, in childhood, school or later in the reader's life.

An analysis of the quoted statements of the interviewees reveals three mechanisms that are involved in the reading process: hedonic (pleasure-seeking), homeostatic (balance-seeking) and eudaimonic (insight- and truth-seeking). We can also briefly characterise them as *feeling more, feeling just right* and *understanding more*. Reading for pleasure or self-regulation is related to the more or less unconscious (or automated through internalisation) control of resources (content relevant and congruent with needs) and standards of the self (*ought-own self, ought-other self*) in relation to social norms, whereas reading for self-understanding and truth-seeking is related to management, *actual* and *ideal* self-concepts, axiological concepts, and the ability and skills to face challenges (providing a sense of agency). Many of the participants' statements indicated that readers seek hedonic stimuli derived from consuming the "known unknown", i. e. content that is consistent with their experience (e. g. familiar genre or author). However, eudaimonic needs were also often expressed, including when reading popular fiction, providing evidence that affective-cognitive processes operate simultaneously and independently of the genre of the book. Feelings evoked by standards of "self" tended to be communicated by pointing to a role model (*an ideal self*) or by confessing which ambivalent character attracted their attention (*a feared self*).

Engagement in reading, or more broadly in consuming media narratives, can be seen as a form of simulation or "trance-like experience" (Holland, 2009; Mar et al., 2006; Mar & Oatley, 2008; Oatley, 2011, 2012), which facilitates the development of mentalising skills and socio-moral reasoning, thereby strengthening the reader's theory of mind (Bartsch et al., 2014; Kidd & Castano, 2013; Loi et al., 2023b; Oliver et al., 2012, 2018). When the reader identifies with a fictional character, their response is dominated by "fresh emotions" (spontaneous reactions to the text). Emotional memories, on the other hand, are more likely to characterise the attitude of an aesthetically distanced spectator who tends to focus more on their own reactions and who evokes pleasurable past memories in response to the descriptive text (Cupchik et al., 1998, pp. 363, 365). Coding and analysis of quotes provides some evidence that emotions are not only related to judgements (evaluative feelings), but are actually expressed as judgements or preferences (Michalik-Jeżowska, 2013, p. 8; Oatley, 2012, p. 36). In some cases it seemed difficult to separate the codes labelled emotions and judgments, as well as to manage the quotations that could be used as examples in many contexts of the provided analysis (see *Liking and judging* subsection).

Thanks to my conversations with the interviewees, I have come to realise that the process of reading is a constant change of tensions between controlling the self and liberating oneself from this obligation. Freeing oneself from the obligation to read what is imposed, such as school readings or books considered valuable because they are in the canon or because everyone is talking about them (instrumental motivation), or to read in a certain way changes the quality of the reading experience. Firstly, this happens when the reader can satisfy their immediate needs and recuperate their energy; secondly, when they want to improve their sense of efficacy or even expand the self with new qualities. When they encounter challenging emotions, they may try to distance themselves (Scheff as cited in Oatley, 2012, p. 33). If the emotions are presented at the right aesthetic distance, as in literature, reader may experience them by engaging in a simulation. This requires overcoming the habit of being oneself by entering into relationships with fictional characters. The reader adopts their perspective and sees or feels the world as they do. This can paradoxically lead to self-discovery (Oatley, 2012, pp. 125–126).

As a readers, we are all *subjects in process*, to borrow a term coined by Julia Kristeva and used in grounded theory studies such as Linsey Howie's study of women's reading communities (2011). When we encounter "the other" in reading or talking about books, we engage emotionally and cognitively, exploring differences and thus constantly negotiating our own identities. We develop "a sense of self through [the] relationship to the author, characters and text" (Howie, 2011, p. 148). In a book club meeting, this can even be enriched by self-expression, validation of experience (seeing oneself "reflected in others") and "creating connections between members of the group and the group itself", as Howie points out (2011, p. 151; see also Christiansen & Dalsgård, 2021). It strikes me that when we talk about books, we are really talking about ourselves and how we relate to others, not about the author or the character or the plot itself. We try in vain to demarcate this story of *the self* and *the other*, and the blurry space in between.[2] We assign subjective meanings to objects in interpretive processes that enable us to act, to deal with problems and to understand how we behave. We do not define things but indicate how we perceive and interpret them in a given situation. Christiansen and Dalsgård point out that restructuring the reading experience in conversation is not directly healing but can be a stimulus for change (2021, pp. 303–304). That is also my hope, that thanks to reading, we will be able to look at our family members, colleagues or neighbours and, instead of "mangl[ing them] with our ignorance every day", as Roth says in *American Pastoral* (2016, p. 35), we will see how vulnerable they are and try to put ourselves in their shoes or sympathise with them, as we do with all those strangers in the novels. It seems to me that we all need to read more closely in real life. One way of doing this, in the absence of the omniscient narrator, is to ask questions and listen to the answers. So who are you now, dear reader, in your 20s, 40s or 60s? And what would you like to say to me, to us or, most importantly, to yourself?

---

2   See Holland's psychological theory of reader response, 2009 and the concept of "narrative self" in Hogan, (2019) and McAdams (2011).

Acknowledgements

I just want to say a huge thank you to everyone who took part in this study. I was so touched by how many of you were willing to help me! You chose to trust me enough to be vulnerable and share your stories with me. It has meant the world to me! It is easy to lose sight of how deeply the books and other cultural products we consume permeate our everyday lives. They influence what we think about ourselves and others, what we say and how we express ourselves. You might even say that our relationship with them is intimate. That is why I am so grateful that you all had the courage to speak with me, and that no-one escaped from Room 207 when I started recording and asking questions that were sometimes not so easy to answer. I was genuinely surprised to see how you opened up as the interviews progressed. One of you even confessed to me that when we finished you felt like you were coming out of the zone, so we had a *flow*, which made me really happy to hear. We had to stop two of the interviews and continue on the second day because you had so much to say and every word was a pearl of wisdom, so I got greedy and wanted more and more. My apologies for that. I could not control myself. You really impressed me! You made me smile, you made me think, you challenged me in many ways. I really appreciate all of that! It has been such a fascinating journey! But as much as I love it, it could not last forever. I came home, sat down and started to transcribe everything you said, word for word. Then came the coding stage, where I took what you said and tagged it, emphasising the processual aspect of your experience to understand what was really going on, and in the second stage tagging it more theoretically to compare it with what other participants were saying. It took me an enormous amount of time, so the crisis was lurking around the corner. All that information was too overwhelming and not numbers, but words and emotions, from a real person whom I had the chance to meet personally and whom I do not want to hurt, but I have to somehow describe their experience, understand it and put it into a proper academic framework. I asked myself, how can I put it all together? What is the thread that runs through all these stories? Could I find it and make it all clearer? I had some doubts, but I kept going. There was a time when your words were ringing in my ears, I could quote them with incredible precision. And then I asked myself, "So what does it all mean?" I pondered in my mind. "What are you really telling me? Come on, you can do it! Think outside the box" – I tried to encourage myself. But nothing really happened. One day just slipped into the next and I found myself coding, integrating, diagramming and repeating the whole process over and over again.

It was frustrating at the time. I told myself and others who asked me about the result: "Well, you know what, I believe in the process. It has to take time. I have to be more patient." Easier said than done! Where the end is, I can't even see. My family, who patiently endured my moods, asked me every day what I was doing. I always had the same answer! "Guess what? I am doing research! After several months, I finally wrote something that looked like a research article. Then I corrected it seven or eight time, or rather ninety-nine times! Each time the text grew, I made a few more changes. And that is the end result! Now it is a book.

A big thank you to the University of Wroclaw for making this possible. So much academic work has been done by people who support research at my alma mater. I have been awarded the IDUB grant (BPIDUB.36.2022), which provides me with substantial technical, publishing and logistical support, enabling me to connect with a research community of scholars. I would like to express my deepest gratitude to my esteemed and kind reviewers, Professor Dr. Gerhard Lauer from Johannes Gutenberg University Mainz and Professor Dr. Mihael Kovač from the University of Ljubljana, who provided invaluable scholarly feedback that helped me polish my manuscript and improve its overall quality. My heartfelt thanks extend to Dr. Jaka Gerčar of the University of Ljubljana, who read an early draft of this manuscript and offered constructive insights. I am also sincerely thankful to the delegates of the By the Book and SHARP conferences who asked thought-provoking questions after my presentations and listened with remarkable patience as I frequently exceeded the allocated time. I am deeply indebted to my colleagues, family, and friends, whose unwavering support and generous insights have been crucial throughout my research journey. I have referred to so many studies by so many scholars in so many different fields that it is not easy to keep track – all to make a more useful index in the book, even in the e-book version.

In this book, I have tried to collect all the most important words from you, organise them in a way that makes sense for academic research and then tell a story about "us" because, guess what, I'm in this story, too. You will find me between the lines and in the structure. I have named the chapters and referred to some of the research of many scholars from different backgrounds. I hope they will all forgive me for simplifying their findings. I have so much to learn to gain their knowledge and to interpret what they have said more subtly and accurately. But I can assure you that I did my best at the time. I will try to do better in the future by learning from my mistakes or making them more acceptable to myself – my biggest – inner critic.

Oh dear, see, it was supposed to be a tribute to you, my dear reader, and it ended up being a story about me and the hardships of academic work. But wait, it was all because of you. You were the reason. Reader.

References

Andersen, M. M., Schjoedt, U., Price, H., Rosas, F. E., Scrivner, C., & Clasen, M. (2020). Playing With Fear: A Field Study in Recreational Horror. *Psychological Science, 31*(12), 1497–1510. https://doi.org/10.1177/0956797620972116

Andersen, T. R., & Hakemulder, F. (2024). "The poem has stayed with me": Continued processing and impact from shared reading experiences of people living with cancer. *Poetics, 102*, 101847. https://doi.org/10.1016/j.poetic.2023.101847

Aue, T., Bührer, S., Mayer, B., & Dricu, M. (2021). Empathic responses to social targets: The influence of warmth and competence perceptions, situational valence, and social identification. *PloS one, 16*(3), e0248562. https://doi.org/10.1371/journal.pone.0248562

Augustyn, K., Liguzinski, M., & Siwecka, D. (2024). Digital books in Polish public libraries: Case study of partnership with the commercial distributor Legimi. *Public Library Quarterly, 43*(6), 691–723. https://doi.org/10.1080/01616846.2024.2317073

Baker, L., & Scher, D. (2002). Beginning readers' motivation for reading in relation to parental beliefs and home reading experiences. *Reading Psychology, 23*(4), 239–269. https://doi.org/10.1080/713775283

Bal, P. M., & Veltkamp, M. (2013). How does fiction reading influence empathy? An experimental investigation on the role of emotional transportation. *PloS one, 8*(1), e55341. https://doi.org/10.1371/journal.pone.0055341

Bálint, K., & Tan, E. (2019). Absorbed character engagement: From social cognition responses to the experience of fictional constructions. In J. Riis & A. Taylor (Eds.), *Screening characters. Theories of character in film, television, and interactive media* (pp. 209–230). Routledge.

Bandura, A. (1977). Self-efficacy: Toward a unifying theory of behavioral change. *Psychological Review, 84*(2), 191–215. https://doi.org/10.1037/0033-295X.84.2.191

Baron, N. S. (2015). *Words onscreen: The fate of reading in a digital world*. Oxford University Press.

Baron, N. S. (2021). *How we read now: Strategic choices for print, screen, and audio*. Oxford University Press.

Baron-Cohen, S., & Wheelwright, S. (2004). The empathy quotient: An investigation of adults with Asperger syndrome or high functioning autism, and normal sex differences. *Journal of Autism and Developmental Disorders, 34*, 163–175. https://doi.org/10.1023/B:JADD.0000022607.19833.00

Baron-Cohen, S., Wheelwright, S., Hill, J., Raste, Y., & Plumb, I. (2001). The "reading the mind in the eyes" test revised version: A study with normal adults, and adults with Asperger syndrome or high-functioning autism. *The Journal of Child Psychology and Psychiatry and Allied Disciplines, 42*(2), 241–251. https://doi.org/10.1017/S0021963001006643

Bartlett, F. C. (1995). *Remembering: A study in experimental and social psychology*. Cambridge University Press.

Bartsch, A., Kalch, A., & Oliver, M. (2014). Moved to think: The role of emotional media experiences in stimulating reflective thoughts. *Journal of Media Psychology, 26*(3), 125–140. doi: 10.1027/1864-1105/a000118

Baumeister, R. F., & Vohs, K. D. (2007). Self-Regulation, ego depletion, and motivation. *Social *and personality psychology compass, 1*(1), 115–128. https://doi.org/10.1111/j.1751-9004.2007.00001.x

Berglund, K. (2024). *Reading audio readers: Book consumption in the streaming age.* Bloomsbury Publishing.

Bermejo-Berros, J., Lopez-Diez, J., & Martínez, M. A. G. (2022). Inducing narrative tension in the viewer through suspense, surprise, and curiosity. *Poetics, 93,* 101664. https://doi.org/10.1016/j.poetic.2022.101664

Bilandzic, H., & Busselle, R. W. (2008). Transportation and transportability in the cultivation of genre-consistent attitudes and estimates. *Journal of Communication, 58*(3), 508–529. https://doi.org/10.1111/j.1460-2466.2008.00397.x

Bilandzic, H., Sukalla, F., Schnell, C., Hastall, M. R., & Busselle, R. W. (2019). The narrative engageability scale: A multidimensional trait measure for the propensity to become engaged in a story. *International Journal of Communication, 13,* 32, 801–832.

Bloom, H. (2019a). *Jak czytać i po co? (oryg. How to read and why?)* (A. Kunicka, Trans.). Aletheia.

Bloom, H. (2019b). *Zachodni kanon. Książki i szkoła wieków (The Western canon: The books and school of the ages)* (B. Baran & M. Szczubiałka, Trans.). Aletheia.

Boddice, R., & Smith (2020). *Emotion, sense, experience.* Cambridge University Press.

Bortolussi, M., & Dixon, P. (2003). *Psychonarratology: Foundations for the empirical study of literary response.* Cambridge University Press.

Bortolussi, M., & Dixon, P. (2015). Memory and mental states in the appreciation of literature. In P. F. Bundgaard, F. Stjernfelt (Eds.), *Investigations into the phenomenology and the ontology of the work of art: What are artworks and how do we experience them?* (pp. 31–49). Springer Nature.

Brewer, W. F., & Lichtenstein, E. H. (1982). Stories are to entertain: A structural-affect theory of stories. *Journal of Pragmatics, 6*(5–6), 473–486. https://doi.org/10.1016/0378-2166(82)90021-2

Brewer, W. F., & Treyens, J. C. (1981). Role of schemata in memory for places. *Cognitive Psychology, 13*(2), 207–230. https://doi.org/10.1016/0010-0285(81)90008-6

Broadbent, N. J., Squire, L. R., & Clark, R. E. (2004). Spatial memory, recognition memory, and the hippocampus. *Proceedings of the National Academy of Sciences, 101*(40), 14515–14520. https://doi.org/10.1073/pnas.0406344101

Brouwer, A. M., Hogervorst, M., Reuderink, B., van der Werf, Y., & van Erp, J. (2015). Physiological signals distinguish between reading emotional and non-emotional sections in a novel. Brain-Computer Interfaces, 2(2–3), 76–89. https://doi.org/10.1080/2326263X.2015.1100037

Bryant, J., & Miron, D. (2003). Excitation-transfer theory and three-factor theory of emotion. In J. Bryant & D. Miron (Eds.), *Communication and emotion* (pp. 31–59). Routledge. https://doi.org/10.4324/9781410607584

Burman, J. T., Green, C. D., & Shanker, S. (2015). On the meanings of self-regulation: Digital Humanities in service of conceptual clarity. *Child development, 86*(5), 1507–1521. https://doi.org/10.1111/cdev.12395

Busselle, R., & Bilandzic, H. (2008). Fictionality and perceived realism in experiencing stories: A model of narrative comprehension and engagement. *Communication theory, 18*(2), 255–280. https://doi.org/10.1111/j.1468-2885.2008.00322.x

Busselle, R., & Bilandzic, H. (2009). Measuring narrative engagement. *Media Psychology, 12*(4), 321–347. https://doi.org/10.1080/15213260903287259

Caracciolo, M. (2022). Cognitive science: Literary emotions from appraisal to embodiment. In In P. C. Hogan, N. J. Irish, L. Pandit Hogan (Eds.), *The Routledge companion to literature and emotion* (pp. 50–60). Routledge. https://doi.org/10.4324/9780367809843

Carpenter, P. A., & Just, M. A. (2013). Reading comprehension as eyes see it. In *Cognitive processes in comprehension* (pp. 109–139). Psychology Press.

Charmaz, K. (2014). *Constructing grounded theory* (Second edition). SAGE Publications.

Charmaz, K., Harris, S. R., & Irvine, L. (2019). *The social self and everyday life: Understanding the world through symbolic interactionism*. Wiley Blackwell.

Charmaz, K., Komorowska, B., & Konecki, K. (2013). *Teoria ugruntowana: praktyczny przewodnik po analizie jakościowej*. Wydawnictwo Naukowe PWN.

Chelsea, D., & Joseph, V. (2022). User preferences towards select attributes of digital reading: An exploratory study post pandemic. *International Journal of Health Sciences, 6*(S3), 11995–12007. https://doi.org/10.53730/ijhs.v6nS3.9235

Christiansen, C. E., & Dalsgård, A. L. (2021). The day we were dogs: Mental vulnerability, shared reading, and moments of transformation. *Ethos, 49*(3), 286–307. https://doi.org/10.1111/etho.12319

Clark, A. (2006). Language, embodiment, and the cognitive niche. *Trends in Cognitive Sciences, 10*(8), 370–374. https://doi.org/10.1016/j.tics.2006.06.012

Colombetti, G. (2007). Enactive appraisal. *Phenomenology and the Cognitive Sciences, 6*, 527–546. https://doi.org/10.1007/s11097-007-9077-8

Coplan, A. (2004). Empathic engagement with narrative fictions. *The Journal of Aesthetics and Art Criticism, 62*(2), 141–152. https://doi.org/10.3389/fncel.2018.00024

Csabai, D., Wiborg, O., & Czéh, B. (2018). Reduced synapse and axon numbers in the prefrontal cortex of rats subjected to a chronic stress model for depression. *Frontiers in Cellular Neuroscience, 12*, 24. https://doi.org/10.3389/fncel.2018.00024

Csíkszentmihályi, M. (2014). *Applications of flow in human development and education. The collected works of Mihaly Csikszentmihalyi*. Dordrecht: Springer.

Csíkszentmihályi, M. (2022). *Flow. Stan przepływu: zanurzyć się w doświadczeniu, płynąć z jego nurtem, smakować życie* (oryg. *Flow: The Psychology of Optimal Experience*) (A. Haduła, Trans.). Feeria Wydawnictwo.

Cupchik, G. C. (1995). *Emotion in aesthetics: Reactive and reflective models. Poetics, 23*(1–2), 177–188.

Cupchik, G. C. (2011). The role of feeling in the entertainment= emotion formula. *Journal of Media Psychology, 23*(1), 6–11. doi: 10.1027/1864-1105/a000025

Cupchik, G. C., Oatley, K., & Vorderer, P. (1998). Emotional effects of reading excerpts from short stories by James Joyce. *Poetics, 25*(6), 363–377. https://doi.org/10.1016/S0304-422X(98)90007-9

Damasio, A. (2022). *Odczuwanie i poznawanie. Jak powstają świadome umysły* (oryg. *Feeling & Knowing. Making Minds Conscious*) (A. Binder, Trans.). Copernicus Center Press.

Davis, M. H. (1983). Measuring individual differences in empathy: Evidence for a multidimensional approach. *Journal of Personality and Social Psychology, 44*(1), 113–126. https://doi.org/10.1037/0022-3514.44.1.113

De Mulder, H. N., Hakemulder, F., Klaassen, F., Junge, C. M., Hoijtink, H., & van Berkum, J. J. (2022). Figuring out what they feel: Exposure to eudaimonic narrative fiction is related to mentalizing ability. *Psychology of Aesthetics, Creativity, and the Arts, 16*(2), 242–258. https://doi.org/10.1037/aca0000428

De Vignemont, F., & Singer, T. (2006). The empathic brain: How, when and why?. *Trends in cognitive sciences, 10*(10), 435–441. https://doi.org/10.1016/j.tics.2006.08.008

Decety, J. (2005). Perspective taking as the royal avenue to empathy. In B. F. Malle & S. D. Hodges (Eds.), *Other minds: How humans bridge the divide between self and others* (pp. 143–157). The Guilford Press.

Decety, J. (2007). A social cognitive neuroscience model of human empathy. In E. Harmon-Jones, P. Winkielman (Eds.), *Social neuroscience: Integrating biological and psychological explanations of social behavior*. The Guilford Press.

Decety, J., & Batson, C. D. (2009). Empathy and morality: Integrating social and neuroscience approaches. In: J. Verplaetse, J. Schrijver, S. Vanneste, & J. Braeckman, (Eds.), *The Moral Brain. Essay on the evolutionary and neuroscientific aspects of morality*. Springer, Dordrecht. https://doi.org/10.1007/978-1-4020-6287-2_5

Delgado, P., Vargas, C., Ackerman, R., & Salmerón, L. (2018). Don't throw away your printed books: A meta-analysis on the effects of reading media on reading comprehension. *Educational Research Review, 25*, 23–38. https://doi.org/10.1016/j.edurev.2018.09.003

Djikic, M., Oatley, K., & Moldoveanu, M. C. (2013). Reading other minds: Effects of literature on empathy. *Scientific Study of Literature, 3*, 28–47. https://doi.org/10.1075/ssol.3.1.06dji

Djikic, M., Oatley, K., Zoeterman, S., & Peterson, J. B. (2009a). Defenseless against art? Impact of reading fiction on emotion in avoidantly attached individuals. *Journal of Research in Personality, 43*(1), 14–17. https://doi.org/10.1016/j.jrp.2008.09.003

Djikic, M., Oatley, K., Zoeterman, S., & Peterson, J. B. (2009b). On being moved by art: How reading fiction transforms the self. *Creativity Research Journal, 21*(1), 24–29. https://doi.org/10.1080/10400410802633392

Dror, O. E. (2017). Deconstructing the "two factors": The historical origins of the Schachter–Singer theory of emotions. *Emotion Review, 9*(1), 7–16. https://doi.org/10.1177/1754073916639966

Duman, R. S., & Aghajanian, G. K. (2012). Synaptic dysfunction in depression: Potential therapeutic targets. *Science, 338*(6103), 68–72. https://doi.org/10.1126/science.1222939

Dvash, J., & Shamay-Tsoory, S. G. (2014). Theory of mind and empathy as multidimensional constructs: Neurological foundations. *Topics in Language Disorders, 34*(4), 282–295. https://doi.org/10.1097/TLD.0000000000000040

Ellis, D. (2020, August 10). A 2x, 1.5x or 1x Audiobook listener? Book Riot. https://bookriot.com/audiobook-speed/

Erica Berry on the Polyamorous Intimacy of reader, author, and audiobook narrator. (2024, February 20). Literary Hub. https://lithub.com/erica-berry-on-the-polyamorous-intimacy-of-reader-author-and-audiobook-narrator/

Etkin, A., Egner, T., & Kalisch, R. (2011). Emotional processing in anterior cingulate and medial prefrontal cortex. *Trends in Cognitive Sciences, 15*(2), 85–93. https://doi.org/10.1016/j.tics.2010.11.004

Fenigstein, A., Scheier, M. F., & Buss, A. H. (1975). Public and private self-consciousness: Assessment and theory. *Journal of Consulting and Clinical Psychology, 43*(4), 522. https://doi.org/10.1037/h0076760

Fernandez-Blanco, V., Prieto-Rodriguez, J., & Suarez-Pandiello, J. (2015). A quantitative analysis of reading habits (No. AWP-05-2015). *Association for Cultural Economics International*.

Festinger, L. (1954). A theory of social comparison processes. *Human relations, 7*(2), 117–140. https://doi.org/10.1177/001872675400700202

Fischer, S. R. (2003). *A history of reading*. Reaktion books.

Fish, S. (1980). *Is there a text in this class? The authority of interpretive communities*. Harvard University Press.

Fuller, D., Rehberg Sedo, D. R. (2013). *Reading beyond the book: The social practices of contemporary literary*. (1st ed.). Routledge. https://doi.org/10.4324/9780203067741

Fuller, D., & Rehberg Sedo, D. R. (2023). *Reading bestsellers: Recommendation culture and the multimodal reader*. Cambridge University Press. https://doi.org/10.1017/9781108891042

Garnefski, N., Kraaij, V., & Spinhoven, P. (2001). Negative life events, cognitive emotion regulation and emotional problems. *Personality and Individual differences, 30*(8), 1311–1327. https://doi.org/10.1016/S0191-8869(00)00113-6

Gerčar, J., & van der Weel, A. (2023). Reading health and the Reading Health Index. *Societies, 13*(4), 86. https://doi.org/10.3390/soc13040086

Gerrig, R. J. (2018). *Experiencing narrative worlds: On the psychological activities of reading*. Routledge. https://doi.org/10.4324/9780429500633

Gerrig, R. J., & Bernardo, A. B. (1994). Readers as problem-solvers in the experience of suspense. *Poetics, 22*(6), 459–472. https://doi.org/10.1016/0304-422X(94)90021-3

Gerrig, R. J., & Jacovina, M. E. (2009). Reader participation in the experience of narrative. *Psychology of learning and motivation, 51*, 223–254. https://doi.org/10.1016/S0079-7421(09)51007-9

Gibbs, R. W. (2006). Metaphor interpretation as embodied simulation. *Mind and Language, 21*, 434–458. http://dx.doi.org/10.1111/j.1468-0017.2006.00285.x

Goldman, A. (2009). Mirroring, simulating, and mindreading. *Mind and Language, 24*, 235–252. https://doi.org/10.1111/j.1468-0017.2008.01361.x

Goldman, S. R., & Varma, S. (1995). Caping the construction-integration model of discourse comprehension. In C. A. Weaver, S. Mannes, C. R. Fletcher (Eds.), *Discourse comprehension: Essays in honor of Walter Kintsch* (pp. 337–358). Routledge. https://doi.org/10.4324/9780203052921

Góralska, M. (2018). Zwrot afektywny a współczesne badania nad książką i czytelnikiem. Rekonesans badawczy. *Przegląd Biblioteczny, 86*(2), 219–233. https://doi.org/10.36702/pb.431

Góralska, M. (2021a). Przyjemność czytania, udręka wyboru. O niektórych technologiach wykrywalności i rekomendacji książek w sieci. *Roczniki Biblioteczne, 65*(1), 253–269. https://doi.org/10.19195/0080-3626.65.12

Góralska, M. (2021b). Wykorzystanie danych z serwisów społecznościowych LibraryThing, Goodreads i Anobii w badaniach naukowych w latach 2006–2019. *Przegląd Biblioteczny, 89*(1), 23–40. https://doi.org/10.36702/pb.825

Gottschall, J. (2012). *The storytelling animal: How stories make us human*. Houghton Mifflin Harcourt.

Gottschall, J. (2021). *The story paradox: How our love of storytelling builds societies and tears them down* (First Edition). Basic Books, Hachette Book Group.

Green, M. C. (2004). Transportation into narrative worlds: The role of prior knowledge and perceived realism. *Discourse processes, 38*(2), 247–266. https://doi.org/10.1207/s15326950dp3802_5

Green, M. C., & Brock, T. C. (2000). The role of transportation in the persuasiveness of public narratives. *Journal of Personality and Social Psychology, 79*(5), 701–721. https://doi.org/10.1037/0022-3514.79.5.701

Guthrie, J. T., Seifert, M., & Kirsch, I. S. (1986). Effects of education, occupation, and setting on reading practices. *American Educational Research Journal, 23*(1), 151–160. https://doi.org/10.3102/00028312023001151

Hakemulder, F. (2004). Foregrounding and its effects on readers' perception. *Discourse Processes, 38*, 193–218. http://dx.doi.org/10.1207/

Hakemulder, F. (2020). Finding meaning through literature: Foregrounding as an emergent effect. *Anglistik: International Journal of English Studies, 31*(1), 91–110. https://doi.org/10.33675/ANGL/2020/1/8

Hakemulder, F., & Koopman, E. (2010). Readers closing in on immoral characters' consciousness. Effects of free indirect discourse on response to literary narratives. *Journal of the Literary Theory, 4*(1), 41–62. https://doi.org/10.1515/jlt.2010.004

Hakemulder, F., & Mangen, A. (2024). Literary reading on paper and screens: Associations between reading habits and preferences and experiencing meaningfulness. *Reading Research Quarterly, 59*(1), 57–78. https://doi.org/10.1002/rrq.527

Hamby, A., & Brinberg, D. (2016). Happily ever after: How ending valence influences narrative persuasion in cautionary stories. *Journal of Advertising, 45*(4), 498–508. https://doi.org/10.1080/00913367.2016.1262302

Hanich, J. (2018). Great expectations: Cinematic adaptations and the reader's disappointment. *New Literary History, 49*(3), 425–446. https://doi.org/10.1353/nlh.2018.0027

Hartley, J. & Turvey, S. (2001). *Reading Groups*. Oxford University Press.

Hartung, F., Burke, M., Hagoort, P., & Willems, R. M. (2016). Taking perspective: Personal pronouns affect experiential aspects of literary reading. *PloS one, 11*(5), e0154732. https://doi.org/10.1371/journal.pone.0154732

Hartung, F., Withers, P., Hagoort, P., & Willems, R. M. (2017). When fiction is just as real as fact: No differences in reading behavior between stories believed to be based on true or fictional events. *Frontiers in Psychology, 8*, 1618. https://doi.org/10.3389/fpsyg.2017.01618

Hayles, N. K. (2010). How we read: Close, hyper, machine. *ADE Bulletin, 150*(18), 62–79. https://doi.org/10.1632/ade.150.62

Hogan, P. C. (1996). Toward a cognitive science of poetics: Ānandavardhana, Abhinavagupta, and the theory of literature. *College Literature, 23*(1), 164–178.

Hogan, P. C. (2003). *Cognitive science, literature, and the arts: A guide for humanists*. Routledge. https://doi.org/10.4324/9780203475881

Hogan, P. C. (2011). *Affective narratology: The emotional structure of stories*. University of Nebraska Press. https://doi.org/10.2307/j.ctt1df4gnk

Hogan, P. C. (2015). The idiosyncrasy of beauty: Aesthetic universals and the diversity of taste. In P. F., Bundgaard & F. Stjernfelt (Eds.), *Investigations into the phenomenology and the ontology of the work of art: what are artworks and how do we experience them?* (pp. 109–127). Springer Nature. https://doi.org/10.1007/978-3-319-14090-2_7

Hogan, P. C. (2019). *Personal identity and literature*. Routledge. https://doi.org/10.4324/9780429265228

Hogan, P. C. (2022). *Literature and moral feeling: a cognitive poetics of ethics, narrative, and empathy*. Cambridge University Press. https://doi.org/10.1017/9781009169509

Holland, N. N. (1976). Transactive criticism: Re-creation through identity. *Criticism, 18*(4), 334–352.

Holland, N. N. (2009). *Literature and the brain*. PsyArt Foundation.

Howie, L. (2011). Speaking subjects: Developing identities in women's reading communities. In D. Rehberg Sedo (Ed.), *Reading communities from salons to cyberspace* (pp. 140–158). Palgrave Macmillan. https://doi.org/10.1057/9780230308848_8

Hsu, C. T., Conrad, M., & Jacobs, A. M. (2014). Fiction feelings in Harry Potter: haemodynamic response in the mid-cingulate cortex correlates with immersive reading experience. *Neuroreport, 25*(17), 1356-1361. 10.1097/WNR.0000000000000272

Illouz, E. (2010). *Uczucia w dobie kapitalizmu*. (Z. Simbierowicz, Trans.). Oficyna Naukowa (oryg. *Cold intimacies: the making of emotional capitalism*, Polity Press 2007).

Ingarden R. (1960). *O dziele literackim. Badania z pogranicza ontologii, teorii języka i filozofii literatury*. Państwowe Wydawnictwo Naukowe.

Inzlicht, M., Werner, K. M., Briskin, J. L., & Roberts, B. W. (2021). Integrating models of self-regulation. *Annual review of psychology, 72*(1), 319–345. https://doi.org/10.1146/annurev-psych-061020-105721

Iser, W. (1978). *The act of reading: a theory of aesthetic response*. Johns Hopkins University Press.

Jacovina, M. E., & Gerrig, R. J. (2010). How readers experience characters' decisions. *Memory and Cognition, 38*(6), 753–761. https://doi.org/10.3758/MC.38.6.753

Jarymowicz, M., & Imbir, K. (2010). Próba taksonomii ludzkich emocji. *Przegląd Psychologiczny, 53*(4), 439–461.

Johnson, D. R. (2012). Transportation into a story increases empathy, prosocial behavior, and perceptual bias toward fearful expressions. *Personality and Individual Differences, 52*(2), 150-155. https://doi.org/10.1016/J.Paid.2011.10.005

Jørgensen, H., Mosewich, A. D., McHugh, T. L. F., & Holt, N. L. (2024). A grounded theory of personal development in high-performance sport environments. *Psychology of Sport and Exercise, 71*, 102568. https://doi.org/10.1016/j.psychsport.2023.102568

Just, M. A., & Carpenter, P. A. (1992). A capacity theory of comprehension: individual differences in working memory. *Psychological Review, 99*, 122–149. https://doi.org/10.1037/0033-295X.99.1.122

Kang, H. J., Voleti, B., Hajszan, T., Rajkowska, G., Stockmeier, C. A., Licznerski, P., … & Duman, R. S. (2012). Decreased expression of synapse-related genes and loss of synapses in major depressive disorder. *Nature Medicine, 18*(9), 1413–1417. https://doi.org/10.1038/nm.2886

Kaufman, G. K., & Libby, L. K. (2012). Changing beliefs and behavior through experience-taking. *Journal of Personality and Social Psychology, 103*, 1–19. https://doi.org/10.1037/a0027525

Keen, S. (2007). Empathy and the novel. Oxford University Press. tps://doi.org/10.1093/acprof:oso/9780195175769.001.0001

Kendeou, P., Muis, K. R., & Fulton, S. (2011). Reader and text factors in reading comprehension processes. *Journal of Research in Reading, 34*(4), 365–383. https://doi.org/10.1111/j.1467-9817.2010.01436.x

Kidd, D. C., & Castano, E. (2013). Reading literary fiction improves theory of mind. *Science, 342*(6156), 377–380. https://doi.org/ 10.1126/science.1239918

Kintsch, W. (1988). The role of knowledge in discourse comprehension: A construction-integration model. *Psychological Review, 95*, 163–182. https://doi.org/10.1037/0033-295X.95.2.163

Kirsch, I. S., & Guthrie, J. T. (1984). Adult reading practices for work and leisure. *Adult Education Quarterly, 34*(4), 213–232. https://doi.org/10.1177/00018481840340040

Kneepkens, E. W., & Zwaan, R. A. (1995). Emotions and literary text comprehension. *Poetics, 23*(1-2), 125–138. https://doi.org/10.1016/0304-422X(94)00021-W

Knobloch, S., Patzig, G., Mende, A. M., & Hastall, M. (2004). Affective news: effects of discourse structure in narratives on suspense, curiosity, and enjoyment while reading news and novels. *Communication Research, 31*(3), 259–287. https://doi.org/10.1177/0093650203261517

Knobloch-Westerwick, S., & Keplinger, C. (2006). Mystery appeal: Effects of uncertainty and resolution on the enjoyment of mystery. *Media Psychology, 8*(3), 193–212. https://doi.org/10.1207/s1532785xmep0803_1

Koopman, E. M. (2011). Predictors of insight and catharsis among readers who use literature as a coping strategy. *Scientific Study of Literature, 1*(2), 241–259. https://doi.org/10.1075/ssol.1.2.04koo

Koopman, E. M. (2013). The attraction of tragic narrative: Catharsis and other motives. *Scientific Study of Literature, 3*(2), 178–208. https://doi.org/10.1075/ssol.3.2.03koo

Koopman, E. M. (2014). Reading in times of loss: An exploration of the functions of literature during grief. Scientific Study of Literature, 4(1), 68–88. https://doi.org/10.1075/ssol.4.1.04koo

Koopman, E. M. (2015). Why do we read sad books? Eudaimonic motives and meta-emotions. *Poetics, 52*, 18–31. https://doi.org/10.1016/j.poetic.2015.06.004

Koopman, E. M. (2016a). Effects of "literariness" on emotions and on empathy and reflection after reading. *Psychology of Aesthetics, Creativity, and the Arts, 10*(1), 82–98. https://doi.org/10.1037/aca0000041

Koopman, E. M. (2016b). Reading suffering: An empirical inquiry into empathic and reflective responses to literary narratives. RMeCC, Erasmus Research Center for Media, Communication and Culture. hdl.handle.net/1765/93344

Koopman, E. M., & Hakemulder, F. (2015). Effects of Literature on empathy and self-reflection: A theoretical-empirical framework. *Journal of Literary Theory, 9*(1), 79–111. https://doi.org/10.1515/jlt-2015-0005

Koryś, I. (2018). Książki bardziej książkowe od innych. Społeczne atrybuty prototypu książki. *Rocznik Biblioteki Narodowej XLIX*, 65–100.

Kovač, M., & van der Weel, A. (2020). Paper versus screen reading: what difference does it make? In Å. Hegdal (Ed.), *Paper and Digital. Current research into the effectiveness of learning materials*, (pp. 9-12). International Publishers Association and Norwegian Publishers Association.

Kretz, V. E. (2020). Social Comparison Theory. In *The International Encyclopedia of Media Psychology*, J. Bulck (Ed.). https://doi.org/10.1002/9781119011071.iemp0156

Kristjánsson, K. (2010). *The self and its emotions*. Cambridge University Press. https://doi.org/10.1017/CBO9780511676000

Kruglanski, A. W., & Gigerenzer, G. (2011). Intuitive and deliberate judgments are based on common principles. *Psychological Review, 118*(1), 97–109. https://doi.org/10.1037/a0020762

Kuijpers, M. M., Hakemulder, F., Tan, E. S., & Doicaru, M. M. (2014). Exploring absorbing reading experiences. Developing and validating a self-report scale to measure story world absorption. *Scientific Study of Literature, 4*(1), 89–122. https://doi.org/10.1075/ssol.4.1.05kui

Kuijpers, M., Lendvai, P., Lusetti, M., Rebora, S., Ruh, L., Tadres, J., … & Vogelsanger, J. (2023). Absorption in online reviews of books: Presenting the English-Language AbsORB metadata corpus and annotation guidelines. *Journal of Open Humanities Data, 9*, 13. https://doi.org/10.5167/uzh-253365

Kuiken, D., Miall, D. S., & Sikora, S. (2004). Forms of self-implication in literary reading. *Poetics Today, 25*(2), 171–203. https://doi.org/10.1215/03335372-25-2-171

Kuppens, P., Van Mechelen, I., Smits, D. J., De Boeck, P., & Ceulemans, E. (2007). Individual differences in patterns of appraisal and anger experience. *Cognition and Emotion, 21*(4), 689–713. https://doi.org/10.1080/02699930600859219

Lazarus, R. S. (1991). Progress on a cognitive-motivational-relational theory of emotion. *American Psychologist, 46*(8), 819. https://doi.org/10.1037/0003-066X.46.8.819

Lazarus, R. S., & Folkman, S. (1987). Transactional theory and research on emotions and coping. *European Journal of Personality, 1*(3), 141–169. https://doi.org/10.1002/per.2410010304

Leder, A. (2014). *Prześniona rewolucja. Ćwiczenia z logiki historycznej*. Wydawnictwo Krytyki Politycznej.

Lehne, M., & Koelsch, S. (2015). Toward a general psychological model of tension and suspense. *Frontiers in Psychology, 6*, 118396. https://doi.org/10.3389/fpsyg.2015.00079

Loi, C., Hakemulder, F., Kuijpers, M., & Lauer, G. (2023a). On how fiction impacts the self-concept: Transformative reading experiences and storyworld possible selves. *Scientific Study of Literature, 12*(1), 44–67. https://doi.org/10.61645/ssol.181

Loi, C., Kuijpers, M., Ensslin, A., & Lauer, G. (2023b). Paths to transformation across contemporary reading practices: The role of motivations and genre preferences. *Psychology of Aesthetics, Creativity, and the Arts*. https://doi.org/10.1037/aca0000622

Lu, A. S., Green, M. C., & Alon, D. (2024). The effect of animated sci-fi characters' racial presentation on narrative engagement, wishful identification, and physical activity intention among children. *Journal of Communication, 74*(2), 160–172. https://doi.org/10.1093/joc/jqad030

Łukaszewicz, B. (2022). Kulturowa (nie) przetłumaczalność emocji w języku – na przykładzie emocji negatywnych. *Język a Kultura, 29*, 59–68.

Luong, K. T. & Knobloch-Westerwick, S. (2021). Selection of entertainment media: From mood management theory to the SESAM model. In P. Vorderer, Ch. Klimmt (Eds.), *The Oxford Handbook of Entertainment Theory*, (pp. 158-180). Oxford Academic. https://doi.org/10.1093/oxfordhb/9780190072216.013.10

Maio, G. R., & Esses, V. M. (2001). The need for affect: Individual differences in the motivation to approach or avoid emotions. *Journal of Personality, 69*(4), 583–614. https://doi.org/10.1111/1467-6494.694156

Mangen, A. (2009). *The impact of digital technology on immersive fiction reading: A cognitive-phenomenological study*. VDM Verlag Dr. Müller.

Mangen, A., & Van der Weel, A. (2016). The evolution of reading in the age of digitisation: An integrative framework for reading research. *Literacy, 50*(3), 116–124. https://doi.org/10.1111/lit.12086

Manguel, A. (2023). Historia czytania (H. Jankowska, Trans.). PIW.

Mar, R. A., & Oatley, K. (2008). The function of fiction is the abstraction and simulation of social experience. *Perspectives on Psychological Science, 3*(3), 173–192. https://doi.org/10.1111/j.1745-6924.2008.00073.x

Mar, R. A., Oatley, K., Djikic, M., & Mullin, J. (2011). Emotion and narrative fiction: Interactive influences before, during, and after reading. *Cognition & Emotion, 25*(5), 818–833. https://doi.org/10.1080/02699931.2010.515151

Mar, R. A., Oatley, K., Hirsh, J., Dela Paz, J., & Peterson, J. B. (2006). Bookworms versus nerds: Exposure to fiction versus non-fiction, divergent associations with social ability, and the simulation of fictional social worlds. *Journal of Research in Personality, 40*(5), 694–712.

Mar, R. A., Oatley, K., & Peterson, J. B. (2009). Exploring the link between reading fiction and empathy: Ruling out individual differences and examining outcomes. *Communications, 34*,4, 407–428. https://doi.org/10.1515/COMM.2009.025

Martínez, M. A. (2014). Storyworld possible selves and the phenomenon of narrative immersion: Testing a new theoretical construct. *Narrative, 22*(1), 110–131. http://www.jstor.org/stable/24615412

Mason, L., Scrimin, S., Zaccoletti, S., Tornatora, M. C., & Goetz, T. (2018). Webpage reading: Psychophysiological correlates of emotional arousal and regulation predict multiple-text comprehension. *Computers in Human Behavior, 87*, 317–326. https://doi.org/10.1016/j.chb.2018.05.020

Mathiesen, S. L., Hedger, S. C. V., Irsik, V. C., Bain, M. M., Johnsrude, I. S., & Herrmann, B. (2024). Exploring age differences in absorption and enjoyment during story listening. *Psychology International, 6*(2), 667–684. https://doi.org/10.3390/psycholint6020041

McKoon, G., & Ratcliff, R. (1981). The comprehension processes and memory structures involved in instrumental inference. *Journal of Verbal Learning and Verbal Behavior, 20*(6), 671–682. https://doi.org/10.1016/S0022-5371(81)90238-3

McQuillan, J., & Conde, G. (1996). The conditions of flow in reading: Two studies of optimal experience. *Reading Psychology: An International Quarterly, 17*(2), 109–135. https://doi.org/10.1080/0270271960170201

Mega, L. F., Gigerenzer, G., & Volz, K. G. (2015). Do intuitive and deliberate judgments rely on two distinct neural systems? A case study in face processing. *Frontiers in Human Neuroscience, 9*, 456. https://doi.org/10.3389/fnhum.2015.00456

Miall, D. S. (2006). *Literary reading: Empirical & theoretical studies.* P. Lang.

Miall, D. S. (2015). Temporal aspects of literary reading. In P. F. Bundgaard, F. Stjernfelt (Eds.), *Investigations into the phenomenology and the ontology of the work of art. Contributions to phenomenology* (pp. 15–30). Springer Nature. https://doi.org/10.1007/978-3-319-14090-2_2

Miall, D. S., & Kuiken, D. (1994). Foregrounding, defamiliarization, and affect: Response to literary stories. *Poetics, 22*(5), 389–407. https://doi.org/10.1016/0304-422X(94)00011-5

Miall, D. S., & Kuiken, D. (1995). Aspects of literary response: A new questionnaire. *Research in the Teaching of English*, 37–58. https://doi.org/10.58680/rte199515356

Miall, D. S., & Kuiken, D. (1999). What is literariness? Three components of literary reading. *Discourse Processes, 28*(2), 121–138. https://doi.org/10.1080/01638539909545076

Miall, D. S., & Kuiken, D. (2002). A feeling for fiction: Becoming what we behold. *Poetics, 30*(4), 221–241. https://doi.org/10.1016/S0304-422X(02)00011-6

Michalak, D. (2018). Czytanie książek – ujęcie jakościowe. *Rocznik Biblioteki Narodowej XLIX*, 31–64.

Michalik-Jeżowska, M. (2013). *Emocje a praktyka moralna w refleksji Marthy C. Nussbaum.* Wydawnictwo KORAW.

Młynarczyk, M. (2006). Ja idealne vs Ja powinnościowe. Analiza emocjonalnych konsekwencji rozbieżności w systemie „ja" na podstawie teorii autoregulacji ET Higginsa. Studia z psychologii w KUL, 13, 189–206.

Murray, S. (2018). Reading online: Updating the state of the discipline. *Book History, 21*(1), 370–396. https://doi.org/10.1353/bh.2018.0012

Murray, S. (2021). Secret agents: Algorithmic culture, Goodreads and datafication of the contemporary book world. *European Journal of Cultural Studies, 24*(4), 970–989. https://doi.org/10.1177/13675494198860

Nick Hornby: The older you get, the less time you have for bad books. (2024, October 30). Literary Hub. https://lithub.com/nick-hornby-the-older-you-get-the-less-time-you-have-for-bad-books/

Norrick-Rühl, C. (2019). *Book clubs and book commerce.* Cambridge University Press. https://doi.org/10.1017/9781108597258

Nowak, A., Winkowska-Nowak, K., & Brée, D. (Eds.). (2013). *Complex human dynamics: From mind to societies.* Springer. https://doi.org/10.1007/978-3-642-31436-0

Oatley, K. (2004). *Emotions: A brief history.* Blackwell Publishing. https://doi.org/10.1002/9780470776322

Oatley, K. (2011). *Such stuff as dreams: The psychology of fiction.* Wiley-Blackwell. https://doi.org/10.1002/9781119970910

Oatley, K. (2012). *The passionate muse: Exploring emotion in stories.* Oxford University Press.

Oliver, M. B. (2003). Mood management and selective exposure. In In J. Bryant, D. R. Roskos-Ewoldsen, J. Cantor (Eds.), *Communication and emotion* (pp. 85–106). Routledge. https://doi.org/10.4324/9781410607584

Oliver, M. B., & Bartsch, A. (2010). Appreciation as audience response: Exploring entertainment gratifications beyond hedonism. *Human Communication Research, 36*, 53–81. doi:10.1111/j.1468-2958.1993.tb00304.x

Oliver, M. B., Hartmann, T., & Woolley, J. K. (2012). Elevation in response to entertainment portrayals of moral virtue. *Human Communication Research, 38*(3), 360–378. https://doi.org/10.1111/j.1468-2958.2012.01427.x

Oliver, M. B., & Raney, A. A. (2011). Entertainment as pleasurable and meaningful: Identifying hedonic and eudaimonic motivations for entertainment consumption. *Journal of Communication, 61*, 984–1004. doi:10.1111/j.1460-2466.2011.01585.x

Oliver, M. B., Raney, A. A., Slater, M. D., Appel, M., Hartmann, T., Bartsch, A., ... & Das, E. (2018). Self-transcendent media experiences: Taking meaningful media to a higher level. *Journal of Communication, 68*(2), 380–389. https://doi.org/10.1093/joc/jqx020

Otis, L. (2022). Affective neuroscience: The symbiosis of scientific and literary knowledge. In P. C. Hogan, N. J. Irish, L. Pandit Hogan (Eds.), *The Routledge Companion to Literature and Emotion* (pp. 15–25). Routledge. https://doi.org/10.4324/9780367809843

Pawley, C. (2002). Seeking "significance": Actual readers, specific reading communities. *Book History, 5*(1), 143–160.

Pennington, M. C., & Waxler, R. P. (2018). *Why reading books still matters: The power of literature in digital times*. Routledge.

Perfetti, C., & Stafura, J. (2014). Word knowledge in a theory of reading comprehension. *Scientific Studies of Reading, 18*(1), 22–37. https://doi.org/10.1080/10888438.2013.827687

Pianzola, F., Rebora, S., & Lauer, G. (2020). Wattpad as a resource for literary studies. Quantitative and qualitative examples of the importance of digital social reading and readers' comments in the margins. *PloS one, 15*(1), e0226708. https://doi.org/10.1371/journal.pone.0226708

Price, L. (2019). *What we talk about when we talk about books: The history and future of reading* (First edition). Basic Books.

Purchase, E. (2019). *The future of reading*. Routledge.

Raney, A. A. (2003). Disposition-based theories of enjoyment. In J. Bryant, D. R. Roskos-Ewoldsen, J. Cantor (Eds.), *Communication and emotion: Essays in Honor of Dolf Zillmann (1st ed.)* (pp. 61–84). Routledge. https://doi.org/10.4324/9781410607584

Rehberg Sedo, D. (2011). *Reading communities: From salons to cyberspace*. Palgrave Macmillan.

Reinke, O., & Bläsi, C. (2023). "Read much?"—"Depends. Who wants to know?": A closer look at time as one possible parameter to quantify European reading habits. *Reception: Texts, Readers, Audiences, History*, 15, 73–78. https://doi.org/10.5325/reception.15.1.0073

Riečanský, I., & Lamm, C. (2019). The role of sensorimotor processes in pain empathy. *Brain topography, 32*(6), 965–976. https://doi.org/10.1007/s10548-019-00738-4

Riese, K., Bayer, M., Lauer, G., & Schacht, A. (2014). In the eye of the recipient: Pupillary responses to suspense in literary classics. *Scientific Study of Literature, 4*(2), 211–232. https://doi.org/10.1075/ssol.4.2.05rie

Riggs, E. E., & Knobloch-Westerwick, S. (2023). Losing awareness of our surroundings? The role of attention during transportation into audio narratives. *Journal of Media Psychology: Theories, Methods, and Applications, 36*, 3, 199–213. https://doi.org/10.1027/1864-1105/a000400

Rose, J. (1992). Rereading the English common reader: A preface to a history of audiences. *Journal of the History of Ideas, 53*(1), 47–70.

Rosenblatt, L. M. (1985). Viewpoints: Transaction versus interaction: A terminological rescue operation. *Research in the Teaching of English*, 96–107. https://doi.org/10.58680/rte198515656

Roth, P. (2016). *American Pastoral*. Vintage.

Ruby, P., & Decety, J. (2004). How would you feel versus how do you think she would feel? A neuroimaging study of perspective-taking with social emotions. *Journal of Cognitive Neuroscience, 16*(6), 988–999. https://doi.org/10.1162/0898929041502661

Russell, J. A., & Barrett, L. F. (1999). Core affect, prototypical emotional episodes, and other things called emotion: dissecting the elephant. *Journal of Personality and Social Psychology, 76*(5), 805. https://doi.org/10.1037/0022-3514.76.5.805

Ryan, M. L. (1980). Fiction, non-factuals, and the principle of minimal departure. *Poetics, 9*(4), 403–422. https://doi.org/10.1016/0304-422X(80)90030-3

Ryan, R. M., Huta, V., & Deci, E. L. (2006). Living well: A self-determination theory perspective on eudaimonia. *Journal of Happiness Studies, 9*, 139–170. https://doi.org/10.1007/s10902-006-9023-4

Sabo, J. S., & Giner-Sorolla, R. (2017). Imagining wrong: Fictitious contexts mitigate condemnation of harm more than impurity. *Journal of Experimental Psychology: General, 146*(1), 134–153. https://doi.org/10.1037/xge0000251

Salgaro, M., Wagner, V., & Menninghaus, W. (2021). A good, a bad, and an evil character: Who renders a novel most enjoyable? *Poetics, 87*, 101550. https://doi.org/10.1016/j.poetic.2021.101550

Scapin, G., Loi, C., Hakemulder, F., Bálint, K., & Konijn, E. (2023). The role of processing foregrounding in empathic reactions in literary reading. *Discourse Processes*, 273–293. https://doi.org/10.1080/0163853X.2023.2198813

Schachter, S., & Singer, J. (1962). Cognitive, social, and physiological determinants of emotional state. *Psychological Review, 69*(5), 379–399. https://doi.org/10.1037/h0046234

Scheier, M. F., & Carver, C. S. (1985). Optimism, coping, and health: Assessment and implications of generalized outcome expectancies. *Health Psychology, 4*(3), 219–247.

Scherer, K. R. (2005). What are emotions? And how can they be measured? *Social Science Information, 44*(4), 695–729. https://doi.org/10.1177/0539018405058216

Schindler, I., Wagner, V., Jacobsen, T., & Menninghaus, W. (2022). Lay conceptions of "being moved"("bewegt sein") include a joyful and a sad type: Implications for theory and research. *Plos one, 17*(10), e0276808. https://doi.org/10.1371/journal.pone.0276808

Schmidt, F. T., & Retelsdorf, J. (2016). A New measure of reading habit: Going beyond behavioral frequency. *Frontiers in Psychology, 7*, 216067. https://doi.org/10.3389/fpsyg.2016.01364

Schwabe, A., Brandl, L., Boomgaarden, H. G., & Stocker, G. (2021). Experiencing literature on the e-reader: The effects of reading narrative texts on screen. *Journal of Research in Reading, 44*(2), 319–338. https://doi.org/10.1111/1467-9817.12337

Schwabe, A., Kosch, L., Boomgaarden, H. G., & Stocker, G. (2023). Book readers in the digital age: Reading practices and media technologies. *Mobile Media and Communication, 11*(3), 367–390. https://doi.org/10.1177/20501579221122208

Seilman, U., & Larsen, S. F. (1989). Personal resonance to literature: A study of remindings while reading. *Poetics, 18*(1-2), 165–177. https://doi.org/10.1016/0304-422X(89)90027-2

Sikora, S., Kuiken, D., & Miall, D. (1998). Enactment versus interpretation: A phenomenological analysis of readers' experience of Coleridge's rime of the ancient mariner. In 6th conference of IGEL (International Association for the Empirical Study of Literature) Utrecht, The Netherlands.

Sikora, S., Kuiken, D., & Miall, D. S. (2010). An uncommon resonance: The influence of loss on expressive reading. *Empirical Studies of the Arts, 28*(2), 135–153. https://doi.org/10.2190/EM.28.2.b

Šileris, A. (2023). Digital social reading: motivation and reading behaviour during literature classes. *Logos, 34*(2), 40–52. https://doi.org/10.1163/18784712-03104065

Silvestri, J. A., & Wang, Y. (2018). A grounded theory of effective reading by profoundly deaf adults. *American Annals of the Deaf, 162*(5), 419–444. https://www.jstor.org/stable/26382402

Singer, T., & Klimecki, O. M. (2014). Empathy and compassion. *Current Biology: CB, 24*(18), R875–R.878. https://doi.org/10.1016/j.cub.2014.06.054.

Singer, T., Seymour, B., O'Doherty, J., Kaube, H., Dolan, R. J., & Frith, C. D. (2004). Empathy for pain involves the affective but not sensory components of pain. *Science, 303*(5661), 1157–1162. https://doi.org/ 10.1126/science.1093535

Sinykin, D. (2023). Big fiction: How conglomeration changed the publishing industry and American literature. Columbia University Press.

Smith, C. A., & Kirby L. D. (2009) Putting appraisal in context: Toward a relational model of appraisal and emotion, *Cognition and Emotion, 23*:7, 1352–1372. http://doi.org/10.1080/02699930902860386

Smith, M. C. (1990). Reading habits and attitudes of adults at different levels of education and occupation. *Literacy Research and Instruction, 30*(1), 50–58. https://doi.org/10.1080/19388079009558033

Smith, M. C., & Stahl, N. A. (1999). Adults' reading practices and activities: Age, educational and occupational effects. (ERIC Document Reproduction Services No. ED450339.

Soederberg Miller, L. M., & Gagne, D. D. (2008). Adult age differences in reading and rereading processes associated with problem solving. *International Journal of Behavioral Development, 32*(1), 34–45. https://doi.org/10.1177/01650254070840

Sosnoski, J. (1999). Hyper-readers and their reading engines. In G. E. Hawisher, C. L. Selfe (Eds.), *Passions Pedagogies and 21st Century Technologies* (pp. 161–177). University Press of Colorado. https://doi.org/10.2307/j.ctt46nrfk.12

Stanovich, K. E., Toplak, M. E., & West, R. F. (2021). Rationality and Intelligence.

Stanovich, K. E., & West, R. F. (1989). Exposure to print and orthographic processing. *Reading Research Quarterly*, 402–433. https://doi.org/10.2307/747605

Stine-Morrow, E. A., Gagne, D. D., Morrow, D. G., & DeWall, B. H. (2004). Age differences in rereading. *Memory and Cognition, 32*, 696–710. https://doi.3758/BF03195860

Stockwell, P. (2019). *Cognitive poetics: An introduction* (2nd ed.). Routledge. https://doi.org/10.4324/9780367854546

Tangerås, T. M. (2020). *Literature and transformation: A narrative study of life-changing reading experiences*. Anthem Press.

Thissen, B. A., Menninghaus, W., & Schlotz, W. (2018). Measuring optimal reading experiences: The reading flow short scale. *Frontiers in Psychology, 9*, 2542. https://doi.org/10.3389/fpsyg.2018.02542

Thissen, B. A., Schlotz, W., Abel, C., Scharinger, M., Frieler, K., Merrill, J., … & Menninghaus, W. (2021). At the heart of optimal Reading experiences: Cardiovascular activity and flow experiences in fiction Reading. *Reading Research Quarterly, 57*(3), 831–845. https://doi.org/10.1002/rrq.448

Thompson, J., Teasdale, B., van Emde Boas, E., Budelmann, F., Duncan, S., Maguire, L., & Dunbar, R. (2023). Does believing something to be fiction allow a form of moral licencing or a 'fictive pass' in understanding others' actions? *Frontiers in Psychology, 14*, 1159866. https://doi.org/10.3389/fpsyg.2023.1159866

Thumala Olave, M. A. (Eds.). (2022). *The cultural sociology of reading: The Meanings of reading and books across the world*. Palgrave Macmillan.

Tosi, G., Bonali, N., & Romano, D. (2024). Finding oneself in someone else's shoes: The role of perspective in literary texts. *Consciousness and Cognition, 125*. https://doi.org/10.1016/j.concog.2024.103767

Towey, C. A. (2000). Flow: The benefits of pleasure reading and tapping readers' interests. *The Acquisitions Librarian, 13*(25), 131–140. https://doi.org/10.1300/J101v13n25_11

Turczyn, A. (2020). *Lacan: projekt lektury*. Uniwersytet Jagielloński. https://ruj.uj.edu.pl/entities/publication/4808abde-98dc-4cc3-a5d7-532db3b0cac2

Typotheque: Words On Screens article on Typotheque by Max Bruinsma. (2004, November 29). Typotheque.com. https://www.typotheque.com/articles/words-on-screens

van de Ven, I., Hakemulder, F., & Mangen, A. (2023). 'TL;DR' (Too long; didn't read)? Cognitive patience as a mode of reading: Exploring concentration and perseverance. *Scientific Study of Literature, 12*(1), 68–86. https://doi.org/10.61645/ssol.176

van der Weel, A. (2011). *Changing our textual minds: Towards a digital order of knowledge.* Manchester: Manchester University Press.

van Dijk, T. A., & Kintsch, W. (1983). *Strategies of discourse comprehension.* Academic Press.

van Laer, T., De Ruyter, K., Visconti, L. M., & Wetzels, M. (2014). The extended transportation-imagery model: A meta-analysis of the antecedents and consequences of consumers' narrative transportation. *Journal of Consumer Research, 40*(5), 797–817. https://doi.org/10.1086/673383

van Peer, W., & Pander Maat, H. (1996). Perspectivation and sympathy: Effects of narrative point of view. *Advances in Discourse Processes, 52,* 143–156.

Verplanken, B. (2006). Beyond frequency: Habit as mental construct. *British Journal of Social Psychology, 45*(3), 639–656. https://doi.org/10.1348/014466605X49122

Vorderer, P. (2003). Entertainment theory. In J. Bryant, D. Roskos-Ewoldsen, & J. Cantor (Eds.), *Communication and emotion: Essays in honor of Dolf Zillmann* (pp. 131–153). Lawrence Erlbaum Associates Publishers. https://doi.org/10.4324/9781410607584

Vorderer, P., Klimmt, C., & Ritterfeld, U. (2004). Enjoyment: At the heart of media entertainment. *Communication Theory, 14*(4), 388–408. https://doi.org/10.1111/j.1468-2885.2004.tb00321.x

Waters, S. J., Keefe, F. J., & Strauman, T. J. (2004). Self-discrepancy in chronic low back pain: Relation to pain, depression, and psychological distress. *Journal of pain and symptom management, 27*(3), 251–259. https://doi.org/10.1016/j.jpainsymman.2003.07.001

Watson, D., Clark, L. A., & Tellegen, A. (1988). Development and validation of brief measures of positive and negative affect: the PANAS scales. *Journal of Personality and Social Psychology, 54*(6), 1063–1070. https://doi.org/10.1037/0022-3514.54.6.1063

Webster, D. M., & Kruglanski, A. W. (1994). Individual differences in need for cognitive closure. *Journal of Personality and Social Psychology, 67*(6), 1049–1062.

Wierzbicka, A. (1999). *Emotions across languages and cultures: diversity and universals.* Cambridge University Press.

Williams, D. P., Cash, C., Rankin, C., Bernardi, A., Koenig, J., & Thayer, J. F. (2015). Resting heart rate variability predicts self-reported difficulties in emotion regulation: A focus on different facets of emotion regulation. *Frontiers in psychology, 6,* 1–8. https://doi.org/10.3389/fpsyg.2015.00261

Williamson, P., Carnahan, C. R., & Jacobs, J. A. (2012). Reading comprehension profiles of high-functioning students on the autism spectrum: A grounded theory. *Exceptional children, 78*(4), 449–469. https://doi.org/10.1177/001440291207800

Wills, T. A. (1981). Downward comparison principles in social psychology. *Psychological Bulletin, 90*(2), 245–271. https://doi.org/10.1037/0033-2909.90.2.245

Wimmer, L., El-Salahi, L., Lee, H. W., & Ferguson, H. J. (2023). Narrativity and literariness affect the aesthetic attitude in text reading. *Empirical Studies of the Arts, 41*(1), 231–258. https://doi.org/10.1177/027623742210954

Wirth, W., Hofer, M., & Schramm, H. (2012). Beyond pleasure: Exploring the eudaimonic entertainment experience. *Human Communication Research, 38*(4), 406–428. https://doi.org/10.1111/j.1468-2958.2012.01434.x

Wojciechowski, J. (1991). *Podstawy pracy z czytelnikiem.* Stowarzyszenie Bibliotekarzy Polskich.

Wojciechowski, J. (2000). *Czytelnictwo*. Wydawnictwo Uniwersytetu Jagiellońskiego.
Wojciehowski, H., & Gallese, V. (2022). Embodiment: Embodied simulation and emotional engagement with fictional characters. In In P. C. Hogan, N. J. Irish, L. Pandit Hogan (Eds.), *The Routledge companion to literature and emotion* (pp. 61–73). Routledge. https://doi.org/10.4324/9780367809843
Wolf, M. (2019). *Reader, come home: The reading brain in a digital world* (First Harper paperbacks edition). Harper.
Wolf, M., & Gottwald, S. (2016). *Tales of Literacy for the 21st Century*. Oxford University Press.
Wood, P., & Kardash, C. M. (2002). Critical elements in the design and analysis of critical thinking studies. In B. K. Hofer & P. R. Pintrich (Eds.), *Personal epistemology: The psychology of beliefs about knowledge and knowing* (pp. 231–260). Lawrence Erlbaum Associates Publishers. https://doi.org/10.4324/9780203424964
Woolley, G. (2011). Reading Comprehension. In: *Reading Comprehension*. Springer, Dordrecht. https://doi.org/10.1007/978-94-007-1174-7_2
Young, L., & Koenigs, M. (2007). Investigating emotion in moral cognition: A review of evidence from functional neuroimaging and neuropsychology. *British Medical Bulletin, 84*(1), 69–79. https://doi.org/10.1093/bmb/ldm031
Zasacka, Z. (2023). Czytelnicy i społeczne obiegi książek. *Annales Universitatis Paedagogicae Cracoviensis. Studia de Cultura*, 15(2), 7–23.
Zebarjadi, N., Adler, E., Kluge, A., Jääskeläinen, I. P., Sams, M., & Levy, J. (2021). Rhythmic neural patterns during empathy to vicarious pain: Beyond the affective-cognitive empathy dichotomy. *Frontiers in human neuroscience, 15*, 708107. https://doi.org/10.3389/fnhum.2021.708107
Zhang, H., McKay, D., & Buchanan, G. (2021, March). I've got all my readers with me: A model of reading as a social activity. In *Proceedings of the 2021 Conference on Human Information Interaction and Retrieval* (pp. 185–195). https://doi.org/10.1145/3406522.3446022
Zillmann, D. & Cantor, J. R. (1977). Affective responses to the emotions of a protagonist. *Journal of Experimental Social Psychology, 13*(2), 155–165. https://doi.org/10.1016/S0022-1031(77)80008-5
Žižek, S. (1998) The interpassive subject. Centre Georges Pompidou, *Traverses*. Available at: www.lacan.com/zizek-pompidou.htm

Supplementary material
The Supplementary material for this book can be found online at: https://doi.org/10.18150/QL-ROKU, RepOD

Appendix

Tables 1 and 2 present a schedule of the interviews, along with some general characteristics of the interviewees: their profession (if indicated) and gender. To avoid any risk of identification based on the order of the interview, the gender or the profession of the reader, all quotes from readers embedded in the text have been marked with randomly generated numbers. In the case of particularly sensitive quotations, I decided to use letters (Reader "A" see RA) rather than numbers in order to avoid links to other quotes from the same participants. Quotes disclosing gender, occupation or age are marked with the appropriate label.

Table 1. Calendar of interviews

Known / unknown to the researcher	Who told you about this study?	Month	Form	Gender
known	researcher	May	in-person	male
known	researcher	May	in-person	female
known	researcher	May	in-person	male
known	researcher	May	in-person	female
known	researcher	May	online	female
known	other participant	June	in-person	male
known	other participant	June	in-person	female
known	bookshop (fb)	July	online	male
unknown	bookshop (fb)	July	online	female
unknown	other participant	July	online	female
unknown	bookshop (fb)	July	online	female
unknown	bookshop (fb)	July	online	male
known	researcher	July	in-person	female
known	other participant	July	online	male
unknown	other participant	July	online	female
unknown	other participant	August	online	female
unknown	bookshop (fb)	August	online	male
unknown	other participant	August	online	female
unknown	other participant	August	online	female

Known / unknown to the researcher	Who told you about this study?	Month	Form	Gender
unknown	library (fb)	August	in-person	female
known	researcher	August	in-person	male
unknown	library (fb)	August	online	female
unknown	researcher's family	September	online	female
unknown	other participant	September	online	male
unknown	other participant	September	online	female
unknown	other participant	September	online	female
unknown	researcher's family	September	online	female
unknown	other participant	September	in-person	male
known	researcher	September	in-person	female
unknown	other participant	October	in-person	male

Table 2. Professions indicated by respondents

Profession	Number
academic faculty	6
x – not specified	6
librarian	3
retiree	2
student	2
architect	1
blue-collar worker	1
ceramic artist	1
economist	1
electroradiology technician	1
journalist, bookseller	1
museologist	1
notary public	1
nurse	1
soldier	1
trader	1

Table 3. Authors mentioned in interviews with readers

No.	Author	Cultural affiliation
1	Alex Joe	Polish
2	Alexievich Svetlana Alexandrovna	Belarusian
3	Allende Isabel	Chilean-American
4	Amelina Wiktoria	Ukrainian
5	Andersen Hans Christian	Danish
6	Applebaum Anne	American
7	Atwood Margaret	Canadian
8	Augé Marc	French
9	Austen Jane	British
10	Bachelard Gaston	French
11	Baczyński Krzysztof Kamil	Polish
12	Bahdaj Adam	Polish
13	Barańczak Stanisław	Polish
14	Barbaro Natalia de	Polish
15	Barnes Julian	British
16	Bator Joanna	Polish
17	Beckett Samuel	Irish
18	Boček Evžen	Czech
19	Bonda Katarzyna	Polish
20	Bradbury Ray	American
21	Broch Hermann	Austrian
22	Brodski Iosif	Russian
23	Broniewski Władysław	Polish
24	Brontë Emily Jane	British
25	Brown Dan	American
26	Brzechwa Jan	Polish
27	Bulgakov Mikhail	Russian
28	Cabré Jaume	Catalan
29	Camus Albert	French
30	Canetti Elias	German
31	Čapek Karel	Czech
32	Capote Truman	American
33	Card Orson Scott	American
34	Carroll Jonathan	American
35	Carroll Lewis	British

No.	Author	Cultural affiliation
36	Cegielski Max	Polish
37	Cejrowski Wojciech	Polish
38	Celan Paul	French
39	Cendrars Blaise	Swiss-French
40	Centkiewicz Czesław	Polish
41	Cervantes Miguel de	Spanish
42	Chandler Raymond	American
43	Cherezińska Elżbieta	Polish
44	Chmielarz Wojciech	Polish
45	Chmielewska Joanna	Polish
46	Christie Agatha	British
47	Coben Harlan	American
48	Cohen Leonard	Canadian
49	Conrad Joseph	Polish-British
50	Corman Leela	American
51	Corneille Pierre	French
52	Curwood James Oliver	American
53	Czechowicz Józef	Polish
54	Czubaj Mariusz	Polish
55	Däniken Erich von	Swiss
56	Danielewski Mark Z.	American
57	Defoe Daniel	British
58	Demick Barbara	American
59	Dickens Charles	British
60	Dostoevsky Fyodor Mikhailovich	Russian
61	Dukaj Jacek	Polish
62	Dumas Alexandre	French
63	Dzido Marta	Polish
64	Edgar Allan Poe	American
65	Eilat Koren	Israeli
66	Elsberg Marc	Austrian
67	Erikson Thomas	Swedish
68	Evaristo Bernardine	British
69	Falcones Ildefonso	Spanish
70	Faulkner William	American
71	Feldman Deborah	American
72	Ferrante Elena	Italian

No.	Author	Cultural affiliation
73	Filipowicz Kornel	Polish
74	Fish Stanley	American
75	Flanagan John	Australian
76	Flores Suzana E.	American
77	Follett Ken	British
78	Foster Alan Dean	American
79	Francis John	American
80	Gaarder Jostein	Norwegian
81	Gabaldon Diana	American
82	Gałczyński Konstanty Ildefons	Polish
83	Gargaś Gabriela	Polish
84	Gauden Grzegorz	Polish
85	Gessler Magda	Polish
86	Ginzburg Yevgenia Solomonovna	Russian
87	Gitkiewicz Olga	Polish
88	Glukhovsky Dmitry Alekseyevich	Russian
89	Głowińska Anita	Polish
90	Goethe Johann Wolfgang von	German
91	Gombrowicz Witold	Polish
92	Gorki Maxim	Russian
93	Gorzka Mirosław	Polish
94	Goscinny René	French
95	Grimm Brothers	German
96	Grochola Katarzyna	Polish
97	Grochowiak Stanisław	Polish
98	Grodzieńska Stefania	Polish
99	Grogan John	American
100	Grzędowicz Jarosław	Polish
101	Grzywaczewski Tomasz	Polish
102	Hannah Kristin	American
103	Harari Yuval Noah	Israeli
104	Harris Robert	British
105	Harris William Thomas	American
106	Hemingway Ernest	American
107	Herbert Frank	American
108	Herbert Zbigniew	Polish
109	Herron Mick	British

No.	Author	Cultural affiliation
110	Hesse Hermann	German
111	Hitler Adolf	Austrian
112	Hłasko Marek	Polish
113	Houellebecq Michel	French
114	Howard Robert Eric	American
115	Hrabal Bohumil	Czech
116	Hugo-Bader Jacek	Polish
117	Ishiguro Kazuo	British-Japanese
118	Iturbe Antonio González	Spanish
119	Iwaszkiewicz Jarosław	Polish
120	James E. L.	British
121	Jergovic Miljenko	Bosnian
122	Jezernik Božidar	Slovenian
123	Johnson Mendal W.	American
124	Joyce James	Irish
125	Kafka Franz	German
126	Kalwas Piotr	Polish
127	Kamiński Aleksander	Polish
128	Kapuściński Ryszard	Polish
129	Kavafis Konstantinos Petrou	Greek
130	King Stephen	American
131	Knausgård Karl Ove	Norwegian
132	Knight Eric	American
133	Kochanowski Jan	Polish
134	Kowalewska Hanna	Polish
135	Kownacka Gabriela	Polish
136	Koziołek Krzysztof	Polish
137	Krajewski Marek	Polish
138	Krall Hanna	Polish
139	Kret Jarosław	Polish
140	Krynicki Ryszard	Polish
141	Kundera Milan	Czech-French
142	Kurzweil Ray	American
143	Läckberg Camilla	Swedish
144	Lagercrantz David	Swedish
145	Larsson Stieg	Swedish
146	Le Guin Ursula	American

No.	Author	Cultural affiliation
147	Lebda Małgorzata	Polish
148	Lechoń Jan	Polish
149	Lem Stanisław	Polish
150	Leśmian Bolesław	Polish
151	Lewis C. S.	British
152	Lindgren Astrid	Swedish
153	Lipińska Blanka	Polish
154	Llosa Mario Vargas	Peruvian
155	Lodge David	British
156	Lovecraft H. P.	American
157	Lowry Malcolm	British
158	Ludlum Robert	American
159	Łazarewicz Cezary	Polish
160	Machen Artur	Polish
161	Mackiewicz Józef	Polish
162	Majewska Beata	Polish
163	Małecki Jakub	Polish
164	Mankell Henning	Swedish
165	Mann Klaus	German
166	Mann Thomas	German
167	Marlon James	Jamaican
168	Márquez García Gabriel	Colombian
169	Martin George R. R.	American
170	Martorell Joanot	Catalan/Valencian
171	Masłowska Dorota	Polish
172	Masterton Graham	British
173	May Karol	German
174	Mayakovsky Vladimir Vladimirovich	Russian
175	Michaelides Alex	British-Cypriot
176	Mickiewicz Adam	Polish
177	Milka Mikołaj	Polish
178	Miller Henry	American
179	Miłosz Czesław	Polish
180	Miłoszewski Zygmunt	Polish
181	Miszczuk Berenika	Polish
182	Mitchell David	British
183	Mitchell Margaret	American

No.	Author	Cultural affiliation
184	Montefiore Santa	British
185	Montgomery Lucy Maud	Canadian
186	Moro Simone	Italian
187	Morris Heather	New Zealandian
188	Mrożek Sławomir	Polish
189	Mróz Remigiusz	Polish
190	Munro Alice	Canadian
191	Musierowicz Małgorzata	Polish
192	Myśliwski Wiesław	Polish
193	Navarro Julia	Spanish
194	Nealon Louise	Irish
195	Negev Yehud	Israeli
196	Nesbo Jø	Norwegian
197	Nienacki Zbigniew	Polish
198	Nietzsche Friedrich	German
199	Niziurski Edmund	Polish
200	Nosowska Katarzyna	Polish
201	Obama Michelle	American
202	Orwell George	British
203	Orzeszkowa Eliza	Polish
204	Osiecka Agnieszka	Polish
205	Owens Delia	American
206	Pajączkowska Agnieszka	Polish
207	Pakuła Mateusz	Polish
208	Parsons Talcott	American
209	Pasek Jan Chryzostom	Polish
210	Pavel Ota	Czech
211	Pawlikowska Beata	Polish
212	Pawlukiewicz Piotr	Polish
213	Pazzi Roberto	Italian
214	Peiper Tadeusz	Polish
215	Pérez-Reverte Arturo	Spanish
216	Pernoud Régine	French
217	Pilch Jerzy	Polish
218	Pilipiuk Andrzej	Polish
219	Pinker Steven	Canadian-American
220	Piotrowski Przemysław	Polish

No.	Author	Cultural affiliation
221	Pisarski Roman	Polish
222	Pizgacz Herytiera	Polish
223	Platon	Greek
224	Pollak Martin	Austrian
225	Posteguilllo Santiago	Spanish
226	Pratchett Terry	British
227	Proust Marcel	French
228	Prus Bolesław	Polish
229	Przechrzta Adam	Polish
230	Przerwa-Tetmajer Kazimierz	Polish
231	Przybora Jeremi	Polish
232	Przyboś Julian	Polish
233	Puzo Mario	Italian-American
234	Rak Radosław	Polish
235	Randi James	Canadian-American
236	Reymont Władysław	Polish
237	Reznikoff Charles	American
238	Rilke Rainer Maria	Austrian
239	Riordan Rick	American
240	Robiński Adam	Polish
241	Rooney Sally	Irish
242	Rowling J. K.	British
243	Różewicz Tadeusz	Polish
244	Sade Marquis de	French
245	Saint-Exupéry Antoine de	French
246	Sánchez Piñol Albert	Catalan
247	Sapkowski Andrzej	Polish
248	Saramago José	Portuguese
249	Sartre Jean-Paul	French
250	Schnajderman Monika	Polish
251	Schulz Bruno	Polish
252	Schuyler James	American
253	Sebald W. G.	German
254	Seierstad Åsne	Norwegian
255	Severski Vincent V.	Polish
256	Shagan Steve	American
257	Shakespeare William	British

No.	Author	Cultural affiliation
258	Shelley Mary	British
259	Shukri Laila	Polish
260	Sienkiewicz Henryk	Polish
261	Simenon Georges	Belgian
262	Simons Paullina	American
263	Škvorecký Josef	Czech
264	Słowacki Juliusz	Polish
265	Sokrates	Greek
266	Solomon Andrew	American
267	Sowa Aleksander	Polish
268	Spiegleman Art.	American
269	Springer Filip	Polish
270	Stachura Edward	Polish
271	Steinbeck John	American
272	Stendhal	French
273	Stępowski Jerzy	Polish
274	Stoker Bram	Irish
275	Stryjkowski Julian	Polish
276	Surosz Mariusz	Polish
277	Szczerek Ziemowit	Polish
278	Szczygielski Marcin	Polish
279	Szczygieł Mariusz	Polish
280	Szejnert Małgorzata	Polish
281	Szklarski Alfred	Polish
282	Sznajderman Monika	Polish
283	Szpila Agnieszka	Polish
284	Szwaja Monika	Polish
285	Szymborska Wisława	Polish
286	Świetlicki Marcin	Polish
287	Thompson Hunter S.	American
288	Tochman Wojciecj	Polish
289	Tokarczuk Olga	Polish
290	Tolkien J. R. R.	British
291	Tolstoy Leo	Russian
292	Tranströmer Tomas	Swedish
293	Turgenev Ivan	Russian
294	Tuszyńska Agata	Polish

Appendix

No.	Author	Cultural affiliation
295	Tuwim Julian	Polish
296	Twardoch Szczepan	Polish
297	Tyrmand Leopold	Polish
298	Uderzo Albert	French
299	Updike John	American
300	Urbanik-Kopeć Alicja	Polish
301	Uzdański Grzegorz	Polish
302	Verne Jules	French
303	Vian Boris	French
304	Virgil/Vergil	ancient Roman
305	Vonnegut Kurt	American
306	Wańkowicz Melchior	Polish
307	Wegner Robert M.	Polish
308	Wells George	British
309	Wharton William	American
310	Wicha Marcin	Polish
311	Wierzyński Kazimierz	Polish
312	Wilber Ken	American
313	Winnicka Ewa	Polish
314	Witkiewicz Stanisław Ignacy	Polish
315	Witkowski Michał	Polish
316	Witoszek Nina	Polish
317	Wittlin Józef	Polish
318	Woolf Virginia	British
319	Wynne Clive D. L.	British-Australian
320	Yerofeyev Viktor Vladimirovich	Russian
321	Zabuzhko Oksana	Ukrainian
322	Žamboch Miroslav	Czech
323	Zaremba-Bielawski Maciej	Polish
324	Ziemiański Andrzej	Polish

Table 4. Books mentioned in interviews with readers

No.	Author	Title in Polish	Title in English
1	Amelina Wiktoria	*Dom dla doma*	
2	Applebaum Anne	*Czerwony głód*	*Red famine*
3	Austen Jane	*Duma i uprzedzenie*	*Pride and Prejudice*
4	Bahdaj Adam	*Do przerwy 0:1*	
5	Bahdaj Adam	*Wakacje z duchami*	
6	Bainter Thomas N.		*Shit*
7	Barbaro Natalia de	*Czuła przewodniczka*	
8	Barnes Julian	*Arthur i George*	*Arthur & George*
9	Barnes Julian	*Wymiary życia*	*Levels of life*
10	Beckett Samuel	*Czekając na Godota*	*Waiting for Godot*
11	Boček Evžen	*Ostatnia arystokratka*	
12	Bradbury Ray	*451 stopni Fahrenheita*	*Fahrenheit 451*
13	Broch Hermann	*Śmierć Wergiliusza*	*The Death of Virgil*
14	Brontë Emily Jane	*Wichrowe wzgórza*	*Wuthering Heights*
15	Brown Dan	*Kod Leonarda da Vinci*	*The da Vinci Code*
16	Bulgakov Mikhail	*Mistrz i Małgorzata*	*The Master and Margarita*
17	Cabré Jaume	*Głosy Pamano*	
18	Cabré Jaume	*Wyznaję*	*Confessions*
19	Camus Albert	*Obcy*	*The Stranger*
20	Canetti Elias	*Auto da fé*	*Auto-Da-Fé*
21	Caroll Lewis	*Alicja w Krainie Czarów*	*Alice's Adventures in Wonderland*
22	Centkiewicz Czesław	*Anaruk, chłopiec z Grenlandii*	*Anaruk, a boy from Greenland*
23	Cervantes Miguel de	*Don Kichot*	*Don Quixote*
24	Corman Leela	*Unterzakhn*	*Unterzakhn*
25	Corneille Pierre	*Cyd*	*Le Cid*
26	von Däniken Erich	*"Danikeny"*	
27	Defoe Daniel	*Robinson Crusoe*	
28	Dostoevsky Fyodor	*Idiota*	*The Idiot*
29	Dostoevsky Fyodor	*Bracia Karamazow*	*The Brothers Karamazov*
30	Dostoevsky Fyodor	*Zbrodnia i kara*	*Crime and Punishment*
31	Dukaj Jacek	*Po piśmie*	
32	Dzido Marta	*Małż*	
33	Elsberg Marc	*Blackout*	*Blackout*

Appendix

No.	Author	Title in Polish	Title in English
34	Erikson Thomas	Otoczeni przez psychopatów. Jak rozpoznać tych, którzy tobą manipulują	Surrounded by Idiots
35	Falcones Ildefonso	Dziedzice Ziemi	Those That Inherit the Earth
36	Falcones Ildefonso	Katedra w Barcelonie	Cathedral of the Sea
37	Falcones Ildefonso	Ręka Fatimy	Hand of Fatima
38	Feldman Deborah	Unortodox	Unorthodox: The Scandalous Rejection of My Hasidic Roots
39	Flanagan John	Zwiadowcy	Ranger's Apprentice
40	Flores Suzana E.	Sfejsowani	Facehooked
41	Follett Ken	Filary Ziemi	The Pillars of the Earth
42	Follett Ken	Słupy ognia	A Column of Fire
43	Francis John	Bimble i przyjaciele	Bimble & Friends
44	Gaarder Jostein	Świat Zofii	Sophie's World
45	García Márquez Gabriel	Opowieść rozbitka	The Story of a Shipwrecked Sailor
46	Gargaś Gabriela	Pośród żółtych płatków róż	
47	Ginzburg Eugenia	Stroma ściana	Within the Whirlwind
48	Głowińska Anita	Kicia Kocia	
49	Goethe Johann Wolfgang	Cierpienia młodego Wertera	The Sorrows of Young Werther
50	Goscinny René, Uderzo Alberto	Asteriks	Asterix
51	Grimm Brothers	Baśnie braci Grimm	Grimms' Fairy Tales
52	Grogan John	Mój przyjaciel Marley	Marley & me. Life and love with the world's worst dog
53	Grzędowicz Jarosław	Pan Lodowego Ogrodu	The Lord of the Ice Garden
54	Grzywaczewski Tomasz	Wymazana granica. Śladami II Rzeczypospolitej	
55	Hannah Kristin	Słowik	The Nightingale
56	Hannah Kristin	Wielka samotność	The Great Alone
57	Harari Yuval Noah	Homo Deus	Homo Deus: A Brief History of Tomorrow
58	Harris Robert	Konklave	Conclave
59	Harris William Thomas	Milczenie owiec	The Silence of the Lambs
60	Hemingway Ernest	Pożegnanie z bronią	A Farewell to Arms
61	Herbert Frank	Diuna	Diuna
62	Herron Mick	Kulawe konie	Slow Horses

Appendix

No.	Author	Title in Polish	Title in English
63	Hitler Adolf	*Mein Kampf*	*Mein Kampf*
64	Howard Robert E.	*Conan*	*Conan the Barbarian*
65	Iturbe Antonio González	*Bibliotekarka z Auschwitz*	*The Librarian of Auschwitz*
66	James E. L.	*Pięćdziesiąt twarzy Greya*	*Fifty Shades of Grey*
67	Johnson Mendal W.	*Zabawmy się u Adamsów*	*Let's Go Play at the Adams'*
68	Joyce James	*Finneaganów Tren*	*Finnegans Wake*
69	Joyce James	*Ulysses*	*Ulysses*
70	Kamiński Aleksander	*Kamienie na Szaniec*	*Stones on the Barricade*
71	Kapuściński Ryszard	*Gdyby cała Afryka*	*If All Africa…*
72	Kieniewicz Jan	*Historia Indii*	
73	King Stephen	*Zielona Mila*	*The Green Mile*
74	Knight Eric	*Lessie wróć*	*Lessie Come-Home*
75	Koren Eilat Negev Yehud	*Kukiełki doktora Mengele*	*Giants: The Dwarfs of Auschwitz*
76	Kownacka Gabriela	*Plastusiowy pamiętnik*	
77	Krall Hanna	*Synapsy Marii H.*	
78	Kret Jarosław	*Moje Indie*	
79	Kurzweil Ray	*Nadchodzi osobliwość*	*The Singularity Is Near: When Humans Transcend Biology*
80	Larsson Stieg	saga *Millenium*	*Millenium* (series)
81	Lem Stanisław	*Niezwyciężony*	*The Invincible*
82	Lem Stanisław	*Solaris*	*Solaris*
83	Lem Stanisław	*Szpital przemienienia*	*Hospital of the Transfiguration*
84	Lewis C. S.	*Opowieści z Narnii*	*The Chronicles of Narnia*
85	Lindgren Astrid	*Dzieci z Bullerbyn*	*Children of Noisy Village*
86	Lindgren Astrid	*Pipi Pończoszanka*	*Pippi Longstocking*
87	Lovecraft H. P.	*Elektryczny kat*	*The Electric Executioner*
88	Lowry Malcolm	*Pod wulkanem*	*Under the Volcano*
89	Majewska Beata	*Trylogia owocowa*	
90	Mann Thomas	*Czarodziejska góra*	*The Magic Mountain*
91	Mann Thomas	*Doktor Faustus*	*Doctor Faustus*
92	Márquez Gabriel García	*100 lat samotności*	*One Hundred Years of Solitude*
93	Márquez Gabriel García	*Miłość w czasach zarazy*	*Love in the Time of Cholera*
94	Martin George R. R.	*Gra o Tron*	*A Game of Thrones*

Appendix

No.	Author	Title in Polish	Title in English
95	Martorell Joanot	*Tirant biały*	*Tirant the White*
96	Maud Montgomery Lucy	*Ania z Zielonego Wzgórza*	*Anne of Green Gables*
97	May Karl	*Winnetou*	*Winnetou*
98	Michaelides Alex	*Pacjentka*	*The Salient Patient*
99	Mickiewicz Adam	*Pan Tadeusz*	*Sir Thaddeus*
100	Miłosz Czesław	*Zdobycie władzy*	*The Seizure of Power*
101	Mitchell David	*Atlas chmur*	*Cloud Atlas*
102	Mitchell Margaret	*Przeminęło z wiatrem*	*Gone with the wind*
103	Montefiore Santa	*Spotkajmy się pod drzewem Ombu*	*Meet Me Under the Ombu Tree*
104	Moro Simone	*Widziałem otchłań*	
105	Morris Heather	*Tatuażysta z Auschwitz*	*The Tattooist of Auschwitz*
106	Myśliwski Wiesław	*Nagi sad*	
107	Myśliwski Wiesław	*Traktat o łuskaniu fasoli*	*A Treatise on Shelling Beans*
108	Nienacki Zbigniew	*Pan Samochodzik*	*Pan Samochodzik Series*
109	Niziurski Edmund	*Przygody Marka Piegusa*	
110	Orwell George	*Folwark zwierzęcy*	*Animal Farm*
111	Orwell George	*Rok 1984*	*Nineteen Eighty-Four*
112	Orzeszkowa Eliza	*Nad Niemnem*	
113	Osiecka Agnieszka, Przybora Jeremi	*Agnieszki Osieckiej i Jeremiego Przybory listy na wyczerpanym papierze*	
114	Owens Delia	*Gdzie śpiewają raki*	*Where the Crawdads Sing*
115	Pakuła Mateusz	*Jak nie zabiłem swojego ojca*	
116	Pasek Jan Chryzostom	*Pamiętniki Paska*	
117	Pérez-Reverte Arturo	*Klub Dumas*	*The Club Dumas*
118	Pernoud Régine	*Opowieść Leonor z Akwitanii*	*Eleanor of Aquitaine*
119	Pisarski Roman	*O psie, który jeździł koleją*	
120	Posteguillo Santiago	*Afrikanus*	*Africanus: Son of the Consul*
121	Posteguillo Santiago	*Roma soy yo*	
122	Prus Bolesław	*Lalka*	*The Doll*
123	Przechrzta Adam	*Demony czasu pokoju*	
124	Przechrzta Adam	*Demony Stalingradu*	
125	Przechrzta Adam	*Demony wojny*	
126	Puzo Mario	*Ojciec chrzestny*	*The Godfather*

No.	Author	Title in Polish	Title in English
127	Rak Radosław	Agla.Alef	
128	Rak Radosław	Baśń o wężowym sercu	
129	Reymont Stanisław	Chłopi	The Peasants
130	Riordan Rick	Percy Jackson	Percy Jackson & the Olympians
131	Rodziński Witold	Historia Chin	
132	Rooney Sally	Gdzie jesteś piękny świecie	Beautiful World, Where Are You
133	Rooney Sally	Normalni ludzie	Normal People
134	Rowling J. K.	Fantastyczne zwierzęta	Fantastic Beasts and Where to Find Them
135	Rowling J. K.	Harry Potter	Harry Potter Series
136	Rowling J. K.	Zakon Feniksa	The Order of the Phoenix
137	de Saint-Exupéry Antoine	Mały książę	Le Petit Prince
138	Sánchez Piñol Albert	Pandora w Kongo	Pandora in the Congo
139	Sánchez Piñol Albert	Victus. Upadek Barcelony 1714	Victus, the Fall of Barcelona
140	Sapkowski Andrzej	Narrentum	The Tower of Fools
141	Sapkowski Andrzej	Trylogia husycka	Hussite Trilogy
142	Sapkowski Andrzej	Wiedźmin	The Witcher
143	Scott Card Orson	Gra Endera	Ender's Game
144	Shakespeare William	Makbet	The Tragedie of Macbeth
145	Shakespeare William	Otello	Othello
146	Shelley Mary	Frankenstein	Frankenstein or The Modern Prometheus
147	Shukri Laila	Byłam żoną szejka/mordercy	
148	Sienkiewicz Henryk	Krzyżacy	The Knights of the Cross
149	Sienkiewicz Henryk	Ogniem i mieczem	With Fire and Sword
150	Sienkiewicz Henryk	Pan Wołodyjowski	Sir Michael
151	Sienkiewicz Henryk	Potop	The Deluge
152	Sienkiewicz Henryk	W pustyni i w puszczy	In Desert and Wilderness
153	Simons Paullina	Miedziany jeździec	The Bronze Horseman
154	Spiegelman Art.	Maus	Maus: A Survivor's Tale
155	Springer Filip	Miedzianka	
156	Stoker Bram	Dracula	Dracula
157	Stryjkowski Julian	Austeria	
158	Szczerek Ziemowit	Przyjdzie Mordor i nas zje, czyli Tajna historia Słowian	

No.	Author	Title in Polish	Title in English
159	Szczygielski Marcin	*Berek*	
160	Szczygielski Marcin	*Bierki*	
161	Szczygielski Marcin	*Bingo*	
162	Szczygielski Marcin	*Poczet królowych polskich*	
163	Szczygieł Mariusz	*Gottland*	
164	Szejnert Małgorzata	*Wyspa Klucz*	
165	Szklarski Alfred	*Tomek w krainie Yeti*	
166	Sznajderman Monika	*Fałszerze pieprzu. Historia rodzinna*	
167	Szpila Agnieszka	*Bardo*	
168	Tokarczuk Olga	*Bieguni*	*Flights*
169	Tokarczuk Olga	*Empuzjon*	*Empusium*
170	Tokarczuk Olga	*Księgi Jakubowe*	*The Books of Jacob*
171	Tokarczuk Olga	*Prawiek i inne czasy*	*Primeval and other times*
172	Tokarczuk Olga	*Prowadząc pług przez kości umarłych*	*Drive your plow over the bones of the dead*
173	Tolkien J. R. R.	*Hobbit*	*Hobbit*
174	Tolkien J. R. R.	*Silmarilion*	*The Silmarillion*
175	Tolkien J. R. R.	*Władca Pierścieni*	*The Lord of The Rings*
176	Tolstoy Leo	*Anna Karenina*	*Anna Karenina*
177	Tuszyńska Agata	*Ćwiczenia z utraty*	
178	Updike John	*Uciekaj króliczku*	*Rabbit, Run*
179	Vargas Llosa Mario	*Rozmowa w katedrze*	*Conversation in The Cathedral*
180	Vargas Llosa Mario	*Święto Kozła*	*The Feast of the Goat*
181	Vian Boris	*Piana złudzeń*	*Foam of the Days*
182	Wańkowicz Melchior	*Monte Cassino*	
183	Wells George	*Wehikuł czasu*	*The Time Machine*
184	Wharton William	*Ptasiek*	*Birdy*
185	Wicha Marcin	*Jak przestałem kochać design*	*How I Stopped Loving Design*
186	Wicha Marcin	*Kierunek zwiedzania*	
187	Wicha Marcin	*Rzeczy, których nie wyrzuciłem*	*Things I Didn't Throw Out*
188	Wilber Ken	*Śmiertelni nieśmiertelni*	*Grace and Grit*
189	Witkowski Michał	*Lubiewo*	*Lovetown*
190	Wynne Clive D. L.	*Pies jest miłością. Dlaczego i jak Twój pies Cię kocha*	*Dog Is Love: Why and How Your Dog Loves You*
191	Yerofeyev Venedikt	*Moskwa Pietuszki*	*Moscow-Petushki*

No.	Author	Title in Polish	Title in English
192	Zabużko Oksana	*Planeta Piołun*	
193	Žamboch Miroslav	*Łowcy*	
194	Zanielewski Mark Z.	*Dom z liści*	*House of Leaves*
195	Ziemiański Andrzej	*Achaja (seria)*	
196	Ziemiański Andrzej	*Twierdza Breslau*	
197	Ziemiański Andrzej	*Virion (seria)*	
198		*Epos o Gilgameszu*	*Epic of Gilgamesh*
199		*Ewangelia Judasza*	*The Gospel of Judas*
200		*Gwiezdne wojny*	*Star Wars*
201		*Historia narodów (Ossolineum)*	
202		*Mahabharata*	*The Mahābhārata*
203		*Pierścień Nibelungów*	*The Song of the Nibelungs*
204		*Pieśń o Rolandzie*	*The Song of Roland*
205		*Ramajana*	*The Ramayana*

Index

absorption 14, 16, 49–50, 57, 80
Aghajanian George K. 44
Altick Richard 5
Andersen Marc Malmdorf 73
Andersen Tine Riis 5–6, 15–16, 29, 38, 80
anger 69, 72, 78, 94
annoyance 69, 77
anticipation 15, 25, 56, 73
anxiety 12, 43, 45, 73, 75, 78, 89, 94
appraisal theory 4, 6, 75, 84–85, 87–88
attachment 14, 63, 77
attention 1, 2, 6, 10–11, 13–15, 21, 32, 41, 43–46, 66, 95, 98–99
audiobook 10, 39–41, 43, 96
Aue Tatjana 14, 54
Augustyn Kamila 43
autonomy 25, 28–29, 97–98
aversion 5, 34, 85
avoidance 5, 85
Baker Linda 16
Bal P. Matthijs 14
Bálint Katalin 12, 14–15, 58, 64–66
Bandura Albert 12
Baron Naomi 13, 40–42,
Baron-Cohen Simon 16
Barrett Lisa Feldman 1
Bartlett Frederic C. 15
Bartsch Anne 12, 14, 44, 49, 67, 89, 99
Batson Daniel 13
Baumeister Roy 21–22
Benwell Bethan 12
Berglund Karl 3
Bermejo-Berros Jesús 60, 86
Bernardo Allan B.I. 12
Berry Erica 73
Bilandzic Helena 14, 16, 45, 49, 51–52, 62,
Black Sirius 69
Bläsi Christoph 3, 12, 16
Bloom Harold 26, 90
Boddice Rob 5
Bond James 68

book studies 2–3, 12, 16–17
Bortolussi Marisa 1–2, 5, 12, 51, 55, 70
Brewer William F. 13, 51
Brinberg David 59, 81, 86
Brock Timothy C. 12, 14, 16, 35, 48–49, 83
Brouwer Anne Marie 85
Bruinsma Max 39
Bryant Jennings 14, 84
Burman Jeremy T. 22
Busselle Rick W. 16, 51, 62
Cannon-Bard theory 83
Cantor Joanne 14, 58, 64, 84
Carpenter Patricia A. 13
Carver Charles 16
Carver Raymond 1
Castano Emanuele 14, 61, 99
catharsis 14, 73, 89
Charmaz Kathy 2, 6, 9, 17, 21–22, 29, 34, 64, 72, 83, 88–89
Chelsea D. 14
Christiansen Charlotte 5, 13, 15, 63, 67, 100
Clark Andy 87
cognitive science 2, 12, 16–17
Colombetti Giovanna 69–70, 87
comprehension 13, 19, 27, 40, 85, 89
Conde Gisela 14
consumption/consuming 3, 25, 42–43, 80, 87, 89–92, 94–95, 99, 101
Coplan Amy 14
Csabai David 85
Csíkszentmihályi Mihály 6, 10, 12, 14–15, 20, 43–44, 75, 92, 95
Culler Jonathan 12
Cupchik Gerald C. 12, 15, 61, 99
Curwood James Oliver 47
Da Silva Sergio 87–88
Dalsgård Anne Line 5, 13, 15, 63, 67, 100
Damasio Antonio 12, 53, 62, 73, 78, 89, 92–93
Davis Mark. H. 14, 16
de Mulder Hanna 16,

de Vignemont Frederique 53, 63
Decety Jean 13
Delgado Pablo 13, 40
deprivation 45, 55
digital technologies 6, 10, 42
disappointment 72, 78, 90, 94, 98
disease 36–37
disgust 69, 71, 78, 85, 87, 94
Dixon Peter 1, 2, 5, 12, 51, 55, 70
Djikic Maja 12, 14–16, 73, 77
Donahue John 16
Dostoevsky Fyodor 81
Dror Otniel E. 84
Dufrenne Mikel 50
Duman Ronald S. 44
Dvash Jonathan 13–14, 69
e-books 10, 24, 39, 96, 102
emotion 1–2, 4, 6–7, 10–12, 14–16, 19, 26, 50, 52–53, 60–62, 65, 69, 73, 75, 77–78, 80–81, 83–88, 90–92, 94, 98–99, 101
emotional memories 1, 3–6, 9, 11, 15, 44, 52, 60, 65–66, 70, 74, 77, 84, 86, 88, 99
emotional processes 2, 5, 7, 15, 53, 61, 73–74, 84, 87, 89, 92–94, 99
emotional response/reaction 1–2, 5, 14, 26, 49, 61, 78, 83–85
emotional state 3, 6–7, 15, 22, 58, 60–61, 87
empathy 5, 14, 16, 51, 54, 60, 65, 69–70, 78, 81, 84–85, 87
enjoyment 14, 32, 66, 73, 94, 97
episodic memories 1, 5–6, 66, 70, 77, 86
Esrock Ellen 49
Esses Vitoria M. 16
Etkin Amit 44
eudaimonia 16, 29, 66, 72, 88, 92–94, 98–99
experience-taking 44, 55, 57, 59, 62, 64
exploration 27, 29–30, 34, 92, 97–98
fear 28, 52, 61, 64, 68, 73–75, 77–78, 83–84, 99
feelings 1, 3, 4, 6–7, 9, 11, 15–16, 21, 32, 36, 50, 55, 60–61, 65–67, 73, 80, 82, 87, 89, 91, 99
Fenigstein Allan 16
Fernandez-Blanco Victor 14
Festinger Leon 67
Fischer Stephen Roger 12–13
Fish Stanley 22

flow 7, 16, 20, 42–46, 85, 94, 101
Folkman Susan 75, 84, 87
fresh emotions 15, 40, 60, 99
Fuller Danielle 6, 12–13, 28, 64, 92
Gallese Vittorio 14, 48, 58, 60–63
Garnefski Nadia 84
Gerčar Jaka 15, 102
Gerrig Richard J. 12, 14, 34, 51–52, 54–55, 62–64, 80, 83
Gibbs Raymond W. Jr 65
Gigerenzer Gerd 87
Giner-Sorolla Roger 87
Glaser Barney 2
Goldman Alvin I. 62
Goldman S. R. 13
Góralska Małgorzata 3, 12–13, 43
Gottschall Jonathan 3, 4, 11–12, 22, 48–49, 55, 58, 81–82
Gottwald Stephanie 40, 42, 48, 64, 95
Green Melanie C. 12, 14, 16, 35, 48–49, 83
grounded theory 2, 4, 11, 17, 100
Guthrie John T. 14
Hakemulder Frank 5–6, 12–16, 29, 38, 55, 80
Hamby Anne 59, 81, 86
Hanich Julian 64, 72, 78, 82, 92
Hartley Jenny 13
Hartung Franziska 14, 49, 55
Hayles Katherine 43
Hogan Patrick C. 4, 5, 9, 12, 21, 26, 28–29, 44, 53–54, 61, 70, 73, 77, 86, 88, 100
Holland Norman 11–12, 45, 64, 99–100
Hornby Nick 29
Howie Linsey 13, 15, 17, 100
Hsu Chu-Ting 13, 74
Hunt Russell A. 15
hyperattention 43, 95
hyper-reading 40, 42
ideal self 67, 88, 92, 94, 99
identification 11, 14, 53, 55, 60, 63, 65–66, 81
Illouz Eva 7
imagining 11, 14, 19, 48, 61, 64–65, 96
Imbir Kamil 85–86, 93
Ingarden Roman 50, 52, 64
inner critic 44, 55, 102
interpassivity 61
Inzlicht Michael 22
Iser Wolfgang 12

Iyer Pico 91
Jacovina Matthew E. 12, 14, 54, 63
James William 10
James-Lange theory 83
Jarymowicz Maria 85–86, 93
Johnson Dan R. 14
Jørgensen Helene 17
Joseph Vijayakumari 14
Just Marcel A. 13, 37, 53
Kang Hyo Jung 85
Karamazov Alosha 81
Karamazov Dmitri 81
Karamazov Ivan 81
Kardash Carol Anne 16
Kaufman Geoff 14, 44, 55, 57, 59, 62, 64
Keen Suzanne 12, 14, 56, 70, 73
Kendeou Panayiota 13
Kentle R. L. 16
Keplinger Caterina 12, 14, 74
Kidd David Comer 14, 61, 99
Kintsch Walter 13
Kirby Leslie D. 4, 35, 69, 76, 84, 87
Kirsch Irwin S. 14
Klimecki Olga M. 14, 73
Klopf Donald 6
Kneepkens E. W. E. M. 13
Knobloch-Westerwick Silvia 12, 14, 50, 74, 89
Koelsch Stefan 73
Koenigs Michael 85
Koopman Emy 12, 14–16, 55, 64–67, 72, 89, 91
Koryś Izabela 13
Kovač Miha 12, 13, 40, 102
Kretz Valerie Ellen 67
Kristeva Julia 100
Kristjánsson Kristján 21
Kruger Daniel J. 70
Kruglanski Arie W. 34, 87
Kuijpers Moniek 3, 12, 14–16, 47, 50
Kuiken Don 12, 14–16, 50–52, 65–67, 88, 91
Kuppens Peter 69
Lacan Jacques 61
Läckberg Camilla 74
Lamb Lessa 73
Lamm Claus 69
Larsson Stieg 70
Lauer Gerhard 102

Lazarus Richard S. 6, 75, 84, 87
Le Doux Joseph 85
Le Guin Ursula 23
Lecter Hannibal 67
Leder Andrzej 61, 63
Lehne Moritz 73
Libby Lisa K. 14, 44, 55, 57, 59, 62, 64
literary studies 2, 12, 14
Loi Cristina 13, 56, 67, 99
Long Elizabeth 75
Łukaszewicz Barbara 6
Luong Kate T. 89
Maio Gregory R. 16
Mangen Anne 12, 13, 19, 40
Manguel Alberto 10, 45, 63, 92, 98
Mann Thomas 25, 26
Mar Raymond A. 14, 20, 34, 49, 58, 61, 66, 73, 89, 99
Martin George R. R. 70–71
Martínez María-Ángele 34, 64, 67, 88
Mason Lucia 85
Mathiesen Signe Lund 13–14
McKoon Gail 52
McLuhan Marshall 39
McQuillan Jeff 14
Mega Laura F. 87, 93
mentalising 11, 60–61, 70, 93, 99
Miall David 12, 14–16, 51, 65–67, 88, 91
Michalak Dominika 13
Michalik-Jeżowska Magdalena 99
Mickiewicz Adam 66
Miron Dorina 14, 84
Młynarczyk Marcin 21
monitoring 13, 22
mood management theory 89, 92
Murray Simone 3, 6, 11–13, 22
Myshkin Prince 81
Myśliwski Wiesław 37
narrative emotions 65–66
non-fiction 14–15, 25, 30, 36, 60
Norrick-Rühl Corinna 12–13
Nowak Andrzej 12
Nussbaum Martha 7
Oatley Keith 6, 9, 12, 14–15, 45, 51, 58, 61–64, 67, 70, 72–74, 76–77, 82–83, 87, 89, 91, 99
observer 15, 55, 62–63, 65

Oliver Mary Beth 12, 14, 16, 47, 49, 67, 70, 72, 89, 99
Otis Laura 49, 83–84
ought-other self 28, 88, 92, 99
ought-own self 21, 88, 92, 94, 99
pain 60, 69–70, 73, 78
Pander Maat Hendrik Ludwig Walther 12, 51
paper book 13, 39
Pawley Christine 4, 6, 11–13
Pennington Martha C. 40, 42, 91
Perfetti Charles 13
perspective-taking 14, 16, 62, 64, 70, 88
Phillips Nathalie 55
pleasure 5, 19–20, 26, 32, 35, 38, 42, 63, 70, 78–79, 84, 88–92, 94, 98
Poulet Georges 55
predicting 5, 11, 13–14, 46, 49, 51–52, 61, 64, 73, 77–78, 88, 96
Price Leah 2, 12–13, 42
Procter James 12
Proust Marcel 66
Prus Bolesław 33
psychology of fiction 2, 12, 16–17
psychonarratology 2, 12
Purchase Eric 20, 63, 92
Rambo John 68
Raney Arthur A. 64, 89, 92
Ratcliff Roger 52
reading habits 3, 21, 25, 29, 39, 95
reading practices 5, 11, 13, 19, 22, 24, 42, 95–96
Rehberg Sedo DeNel 6, 12–13, 28, 64, 92
Reinke Owena 3, 12, 16
rereading 10, 14, 32, 76, 78, 81, 98
Retelsdorf Jan 14
Riečanský Igor 69
Riese Katrin 73
Riggs Elizabeth E. 14, 50, 79
Rosaldo Michelle Z. 7
Rose Jonathan 5, 11–13, 27
Rosenblatt Louise 11–12
Roth Philip 1, 100
Ruby Perrine 13
Russell James A. 1
Ryan Marie-Laure 29, 52, 72, 88, 90
Sabo John S. 59
sadness 14, 69, 71–72, 78, 81, 86, 94

Salgaro Massimo 60
Sapkowski Andrzej 23, 52
Scapin Giulia 15–16
Schachter-Singer two-factor theory of emotion 84
Scheff Thomas 73, 99
Scheier Michael F. 16
Scher Deborah 1, 6, 16
Scherer Klaus R. 1, 6
Schindler Ines 14–16, 82
Schmidt Fabian T. C. 14
Schwabe Annika 12
self 5, 7, 21–22, 26, 29, 38, 54–55, 62, 65, 67, 73–75, 82, 87–88, 90, 92, 94, 97, 99, 100
self-concept 4, 14, 21, 28, 44, 56, 88, 98–99
self-efficacy 44, 49, 88
self-esteem 14, 28, 44, 73, 82, 90, 92, 94–95, 97
self-expansion 29, 68, 88, 92, 94
self-regulation 22, 94, 99
self-understanding 65–66, 73, 92, 94, 99
Shamay-Tsoory Simone G. 13–14, 53, 69
shame 25, 27, 47, 73, 75–76, 78, 81, 88, 90, 94, 98
Shklovsky Victor 15
Sikora Shelley 64–65
Šileris Arunas 29
Silvestri Julia A. 17
Simenon Georges 49–50
Simons Paullina 68–69
simulation 61–62, 67, 69–70, 74, 83, 99
Singer Jerome E. 69, 84
Singer Tania 13–14, 53, 63, 73, 85
Sinykin Dan 21
Skinner Ellen A. 87
Škvorecký Josef 66
Smith Craig 4, 35, 69, 76, 84, 87
Smith M. Cecil 14
Smith Mark 5
Soederberg Miller Lisa M. 14
Sosnoski James 13, 42
Stafura Joe 13
Stanisławski Krzysztof 84, 87
Stanovich Keith 16, 44
Stine-Morrow Elizabeth 14
Stockwell Peter 12, 34
Strauss Anselm 2

sympathy 60, 65, 70, 87
Tan Ed 12, 14–16, 58, 64–65, 67
Thissen Birte A. K. 14, 16, 49, 85
Thompson Jacqueline 49
Tokarczuk Olga 75
Tolkien J. R. R. 23, 81
Tosi Giorgia 61, 73
Towey Cathleen A. 14
transportation 1, 14–16, 31, 34–36, 42–43,
    47–51, 53, 55, 62, 83, 85
Treyens James C. 13
Turczyn Anna 61
Turvey Sarah 13
Tuszyńska Agata 37
Updike John 60
van de Ven Inge 12–13, 42–43
van der Weel Adriaan 12–13, 15, 19
van Dijk Teun A. 13
van Laer Tom 12, 14, 36, 48–49, 51, 58
van Peer Willie Willie 12, 15
Varma Sashank 13
Veltkamp Martijn 14
Verplanken Bas 14
video game 40, 43, 63
Vipond Douglas 15
Vohs Kathleen D. 22
Vonnegut Kurt 53
Vorderer Peter 12, 86, 92
Wang Ye 17

Waters Sandra J. 21, 28
Watson David 16
Waxler Robert P. 40–42, 91
Webster Donna M. 34
wellbeing 5, 73, 78
Wellborn James G. 87
West Richard 12, 14, 16, 26, 50, 74, 79
Wheelwright Sally 16
Wick John 68
Wierzbicka Anna 6–7
Williams DeWayne P. 85
Williamson Pamela 13
Wills Thomas A. 67
Wimmer Lena Franziska 66
Wirth Werner 12, 16, 60, 68, 90
Wojciechowski Jacek 12, 19, 97
Wojciehowski Hannah 14, 48, 58, 60–63
Wolf Maryanne 13, 40, 42–43, 48, 51, 53,
    55, 60, 64, 73, 76, 82, 90
Wood Phillip Karl 16
Woolley Gary 13
Yalom Irvine 37
Young Liane 86
Zasacka Zofia 12
Zebarjadi Niloufar 70
Zhang Huiwen 15
Zillmann Dolf 14, 58, 64, 84
Žižek Slavoj 61
Zwann Rolf A. 13, 80